The Political Thought of
Elizabeth Cady Stanton

The Political
Thought of
Elizabeth
Cady Stanton

*Women's Rights and the American
Political Traditions*

Sue Davis

NEW YORK UNIVERSITY PRESS
New York and London

NEW YORK UNIVERSITY PRESS
New York and London
www.nyupress.org

Library of Congress Cataloging-in-Publication Data
Davis, Sue, 1948–
The political thought of Elizabeth Cady Stanton : women's rights
and the American political traditions / Sue Davis.
p. cm.
Includes bibliographical references and index.
ISBN-13: 978-0-8147-1998-5 (cl : alk. paper)
ISBN-10: 0-8147-1998-8 (cl : alk. paper)
1. Stanton, Elizabeth Cady, 1815–1902. 2. Suffrage—United
States—History—19th century. 3. Women's rights—United
States—History—19th century. 4. Feminist theory—United
States—History—19th century. I. Title.
HQ1413.S67D39 2007
305.42092—dc22   2007043896

New York University Press books are printed on acid-free paper,
and their binding materials are chosen for strength and durability.

Manufactured in the United States of America

10 9 8 7 6 5 4 3 2 1

*For my very good friends
whose lives and work reflect the best of feminism,
Miriam Willis
and
Lily Davidson*

Contents

Acknowledgments

Writing a book like this requires many solitary hours of research, writing, and revising, yet the finished product can never be said to be the work of only one person. Indeed, all scholarly work requires the input and support of a number of people. The idea for this book began when I first learned of Rogers M. Smith's Multiple-Traditions Thesis and immediately became convinced that it provided the key to understanding the contradictions that run through the history of American political ideas and practice. Smith's unsurpassed scholarship and his kindness have provided me with a model that I have tried to emulate in both my research and my teaching from nearly the beginning of my career. Any errors in the way I have used Smith's framework in my study of Elizabeth Cady Stanton's thought are entirely mine.

I would also like to thank the many friends and colleagues who provided support and suggestions in the early stages of the development of this book, including Virginia Lewis, Judith A. Baer, Eileen M. McDonagh, Susan Burgess, Suzanne M. Marilley, and Howard Gillman. Also, Kimberly Segal, who worked as my research assistant in the summer of 2000, spent long hours in the library searching the microfilm collections of Cady Stanton's work.

There are also a number of scholars whom I have never met but whose work was essential to my study of Elizabeth Cady Stanton. Without Patricia G. Holland's and Ann D. Gordon's microfilm collection *The Papers of Elizabeth Cady Stanton and Susan B. Anthony* and Ann D. Gordon's four-volume *The Selected Papers of Elizabeth Cady Stanton and Susan B. Anthony*, this book would not have been possible. In addition, over the years I have read and reread the work of a number of scholars, including Nancy F. Cott, Zillah R. Eisenstein, Eric Foner, Linda K. Kerber, Aileen S. Kraditor, Ellen Carol DuBois, Mary Beth Norton, Karen Offen, Carroll Smith-Rosenberg, and Carole Pateman. I have found a variety of perspectives in their work that have provided me with valuable insights, as well as inspiration. I can only hope that some portion of what I have learned from them is reflected in this book.

I would also like to thank the two anonymous reviewers who read my manuscript for New York University Press and one anonymous reviewer for Yale University Press. Their comments provided guidance at a crucial juncture in the development of this work. Thank you also to Ilene Kalish, executive editor at New York University Press, and to Salwa C. Jabado, editorial assistant, who saw the project through the review process with great patience and charm.

Finally, my friends in Newark, Delaware, have maintained an interest in the progress of this book over the years that indicates the depth of their friendship. Miriam's pool ladies have never forgotten to ask when they can expect to receive a copy. Sue Cherrin, Alice Ba, Fredy Rodriguez, and Henry Reynolds were excellent listeners during a difficult time. My partner, Jeff Davidson, has read and reread every draft of every chapter with infinite patience. For their friendship and support, I will always be grateful.

1

Elizabeth Cady Stanton and the Multiple Traditions

Introduction

The meeting that began on July 19, 1848, in the Wesleyan chapel in Seneca Falls, New York, launched the first organized movement for women's rights in the United States. The Seneca Falls Convention also marked the beginning of the long career of its chief organizer, thirty-three-year-old Elizabeth Cady Stanton. Not only was Cady Stanton[1] one of the most important leaders of the woman's rights movement for nearly half a century, but she was also the movement's principal philosopher. Her ideas challenged the conventions of the nineteenth century that constrained women's lives and excluded women from public life. Although it may seem paradoxical at first glance, Cady Stanton's ideas also grew out of the very traditions that she seemed to reject so thoroughly.

Because this book is a study of Cady Stanton's political thought, it differs fundamentally from the several excellent biographies that have examined her life in rich detail and have provided insights into her character.[2] It also differs from the considerable body of literature published since the late 1970s that analyzes the nineteenth- and early twentieth-century woman's movement.[3] The idea for the book began with my conviction that Cady Stanton deserves recognition as a central figure in the political thought of the United States in the nineteenth century. Her work represents a contribution of enormous importance to the woman's rights movement and to an understanding of the sources of and solutions to the subordination of women. Her ideas also had a major influence on the development of feminist theory in the twentieth century.

Elizabeth Cady Stanton's thought reflects the rich tapestry of American political culture in the second half of the nineteenth century. My purpose in analyzing her work is to demonstrate how this is so and why it is important. She drew on a wide spectrum of traditions of political thought to support her demands for women's rights, utilizing ideas that were available to her, adapting them, and often subverting them to further her goals. From the beginning of her career as a leader of the woman's rights movement, she relied on liberal-egalitarian arguments, asserting that the principles of natural rights and equality applied to women, as well as to men. She also drew on the republican tradition that moved away from an emphasis on natural rights and equality of individuals to focus on the importance to a successful political community of a body of virtuous citizens who transcend self-interest to participate in public affairs in order to promote the common good. She subverted the tradition of republicanism that so thoroughly excluded women from participation in public life by emphasizing the special qualities of women—the "mothers of the race"—that they would bring to the political life of the nation.

Cady Stanton also utilized inegalitarian, undemocratic arguments to argue that educated, white, native-born women were far better suited to participate in the political life of the nation than were males who were uneducated, nonwhite, and foreign born. Such arguments reinforced racist and nativist justifications for exclusion and intolerance that were popular during the last two decades of the nineteenth century. But, in Cady Stanton's rendering, inegalitarian arguments served to demonstrate the need for women's full participation in public life. She thereby subverted the tradition that held women to be morally and intellectually inferior to men and thus incapable of functioning successfully beyond the realm of home and family by emphasizing their superiority over certain groups of men.

In addition, she drew from a radical tradition to develop her argument that fundamental change in social, political, and cultural arrangements of the United States would be essential for women to achieve equality. For example, the positions that Cady Stanton took regarding marriage reveal her conviction that radical change not only in the institution of marriage itself but also in widespread attitudes about women would be necessary for women and men to become equal partners in marriage. Moreover, her critique of organized religion pointed to deeply imbedded cultural sources of women's subordination that could not be eliminated without a major transformation of institutions and values.

Thus, she was fully aware that legal and political reform alone would never be sufficient to eliminate women's subordinate status that was so thoroughly embedded in the culture of the nineteenth century.

Arguments that reflect those four very different and contradictory traditions run through Cady Stanton's work. She often combined different strains of thought in the same speech or employed contrasting approaches in different speeches concerning the same topic. Moreover, she relied on the different traditions to a greater or lesser extent at different times. Indeed, the extent to which she relied on inegalitarian, antidemocratic arguments increased over the years and assumed a prominent role in her work during the last twenty years of the nineteenth century.

The basis of her arguments shifted over time in a way that coincided with the changing political culture of the United States in the second half of the nineteenth century. She began to rely on inegalitarian arguments, for example, at the same time that social Darwinism began to play a leading role in the American political culture. The way that Cady Stanton shifted the basis of her arguments over time clearly had a practical dimension. By the 1880s, not only had social Darwinism become a popular ideology that attempted to justify vast inequalities in wealth and power, but it also offered new possibilities for success in the campaign for women's rights after all the years during which liberal arguments met with only limited success.

There has been considerable disagreement among scholars as to the nature of Cady Stanton's political thought. Was she genuinely committed to a philosophy of individual rights and equality? Did she act out of a belief that those individual rights belong to women as well as men on the grounds that all men *and women* are created equal? Alternatively, did she consider women to be different from or morally superior to men because of their unique experiences as childbearers and mothers? Did she subscribe to inegalitarian arguments that humans are not naturally equal and that a hierarchically organized society is most consistent with the natural order of the world? Is it possible that she was less a political thinker than a rational political actor—a strategist—who simply gauged which type of argument would be most likely to further her goals in any given context?

I argue throughout this study that the ways in which Cady Stanton drew on the panoply of political traditions makes it impossible to label her work as belonging to only one system of thought. Indeed, the way she combined different and conflicting strands of political thought, emphasizing first one and then another depending on the time and circumstances, not only mirrors the development of American political thought in the second half of the nineteenth century but also is consistent with the way that other political thinkers have developed their arguments. For example, Thomas Jefferson, who wrote in the Declaration of Independence that "all men are created equal," also expressed a belief that black people were intellectually inferior to whites.[4] In addition, the fact that Cady Stanton's work had a strategic dimension should not detract from her status as a major political thinker, because strategy is invariably an ingredient in the making of political theory.

Another controversy among scholars that bears on attempts to understand the political thought of the nineteenth-century woman's rights movement or even, for that matter, feminism in the twentieth century revolves around the very nature of liberalism. Carole Pateman has argued that liberalism cannot be separated from its original narrative in which men entered into a social contract from which women—who were already subordinate to men—were excluded. Thus, while men were envisioned as the bearers of equal rights, women were either ignored or relegated to the subordinate role of wives, mothers, and daughters.[5] Cady Stanton, however, was able to make use of liberalism's emphasis on natural rights, subverting traditional patriarchal ideas about the natural inequality of women, by insisting that those rights belonged to women, as well as to men. She thereby used liberal principles to advance the cause of women's rights. But those principles were not by themselves sufficient to challenge the overwhelming structure of inequality and exclusion, nor were they the only ideas with which she was familiar. Thus, Cady Stanton relied on other traditions to support her demands for bringing an end to the subordination of women.

Over the years as I have worked to develop an understanding of the contradictions in American political thought and practice, I have found Rogers M. Smith's explanation of American political culture as a dynamic of contradictory traditions to be the most useful for explaining the conflict between egalitarian and inegalitarian currents and between democratic and antidemocratic trends that mark American history. Because Elizabeth Cady Stanton's work mirrors the complexity of the conflicting traditions, Smith's Multiple-Traditions Thesis provides an extremely useful framework for understanding her political thought.[6]

The Emergence of a Reformer and Political Thinker

Elizabeth Cady Stanton devoted her long life to the arduous task of redressing the enormous imbalance of power between men and women. Her role as a leader of the woman's rights movement began in 1848 with the Seneca Falls Convention and continued until the 1890s. Her life as a political thinker and her commitment to reform, however, began earlier and did not end until her death, in 1902. Born in Johnstown, New York, in 1815, into a large and prosperous family, Cady Stanton grew into a young woman with the education, skills, and social standing that made it possible for her to begin to organize for reform. Her mother, Margaret Livingstone Cady, the daughter of an officer in the American Revolution, was the descendant of early Dutch settlers and was well connected to the most prominent families in New York. Her father, Daniel Cady, was a lawyer who served several terms in the New York State Assembly and one term in the U.S. House of Representatives and who, in 1847, became a justice on the New York Supreme Court.

According to her autobiography, Cady Stanton learned as a child, by reading her father's law books and listening to his clients, that the law was unfair to women.[7] She related how, "supposing that [her] father and his library were the beginning and the end of the laws," she determined to eliminate the problem by using scissors to literally cut the unjust laws out of his books. According to the story, when he discovered his daughter's plan, Daniel Cady suggested that when Elizabeth was grown she "go down to Albany and talk to the legislators" to persuade them to change the laws.[8] While Cady Stanton's account of that conversation was most likely an invention, the anecdote suggests that her lifelong commitment to expanding women's rights began at an early age.[9]

The last years of Elizabeth Cady Stanton's life were distinguished by her thoroughgoing critique of religion as a major force in the creation and perpetuation of women's subordinate status. *The Woman's Bible*, which Cady Stanton wrote with several other women, was published in two volumes in 1895 and 1898, respectively, and represented the culmination of her analysis of the role of the church and the Bible in the oppression of women. The same theme was prominent in her autobiography, *Eighty Years and More*, published in 1898, where she explained how her earliest experiences with religion led to her determination to reject what she viewed as superstition and to embrace science and reason.[10] As Calvinist Presbyterians, her family believed in original sin and subscribed to the doctrine of predestination. Biographers have attributed the young Elizabeth Cady's recurring nightmares about death, her depression, and her fear of her surroundings to her parents' childrearing practices and their religion.[11] In 1831, when she was a student at the Troy Female Seminary, she attended a series of revivals conducted by the evangelist minister Charles Grandison Finney, the leader of the Second Great Awakening, whose efforts are said to have been responsible for the conversion of some 500,000 people. Finney's theology departed from the Calvinist doctrine of predestination and original sin to embrace the idea of free will and the possibility of human perfection. He also encouraged women to pray in public and later became an advocate of abolition, temperance, and women's rights.[12] Nevertheless, his emotional, demanding, even threatening methods of winning souls repelled Cady Stanton. She recalled in her autobiography that, as a result of her Calvinistic training, she was one of Finney's first victims. She found the notions of conversion and salvation "puzzling and harrowing to the young mind." After listening to Finney every day for six weeks, she tried to "repent and believe" as he implored, although she confessed that the more "sincerely I believe, the more unhappy I am." His preaching, she concluded, "worked incalculable harm to the very souls he sought to save." Her conversion, as she described it, had disturbing consequences: "Fear of the judgment seized my soul. Visions of the lost haunted my dreams. Mental anguish prostrated my health. Dethronement of my reason was apprehended by friends. . . . Returning home, I often at night roused my father from his slumbers to pray for me, lest I should be cast into the bottomless pit before morning."[13]

Cady Stanton related how she traveled with her father, sister, and brother-in-law to Niagara Falls, still feeling nervous and unsettled. But, as the group read and discussed books such as George Combe's *Constitution of Man* and *Moral Philosophy* and new research on phrenology, she "found [her] way out of the darkness into the clear sunlight of Truth [as] . . . religious superstitions gave place to rational ideas based on scientific facts."[14] She recalled that she grew happier as her new perspective restored her to a normal state of mind. Her juxtaposition of rational thought and scientific inquiry as sources of light and happiness on the one hand and religious superstition linked to darkness and despair on the other underlines a major theme in her life and work. In the mature Cady Stanton's own analysis, the outlines of that theme were firmly in place when she was only fifteen.

The prominent abolitionist Gerrit Smith was Elizabeth Cady's cousin, and it was through him that she was first exposed to the abolitionist movement. At his home in Peterboro, New York, in the late 1830s, she came into contact with escaped slaves, as well as other abolitionists, including Henry Brewster Stanton. As a theological student at Lane Seminary in Cincinnati, Henry Stanton had participated in the revival debates on slavery in 1834 that resulted in the conversion of an overwhelming number of the students to abolitionism. He led a walkout of fifty students when the trustees forbade further activity or discussion of the slavery issue and then became an agent of the American Anti-Slavery Society. Although he initially embraced William Lloyd Garrison's moral-suasion approach, by the time Stanton met Elizabeth Cady in 1839, he had broken with the Garrisonians and had joined the abolitionists who embraced political action.

In 1840, Elizabeth Cady married Henry Stanton, and the couple traveled to London to attend the World's Anti-Slavery Convention. At that meeting, the political abolitionists and the Garrisonians disagreed over whether to admit women to the convention. When the political abolitionists prevailed and the women delegates were excluded, Garrison himself chose to sit with the women in their curtained-off area in the gallery. Cady Stanton claimed later that the debate among the abolitionists over the role of women in the movement sharpened her awareness of women's condition and helped to spark her interest in women's rights. It was at that time as well that her ideas began to diverge markedly from those of her husband, who abandoned his support for women's participation in the abolitionist movement when he broke with the Garrisonians.

Some of the major elements of Cady Stanton's thought—primarily her commitment to legal reform and her opposition to organized religion—were forged out of her early experiences. Those ideas, however, provided only a basic outline of the structure of thought that she would develop over the next several decades. Her thought is a complex web composed of interconnected but often contradictory strands. I argue throughout this book that Cady Stanton's political thought cannot be understood apart from the traditions of American political culture that were familiar to her, as well as the changing political, social, and economic conditions of the nineteenth century. The remainder of this chapter is devoted to explaining the approach I use to take those ideological and historical factors into account.

American Political Culture: The Multiple-Traditions Thesis

The liberal-consensus view of American political thought became virtually all-pervasive in the years after World War II and was still widely accepted as late as the 1980s. Richard Hofstadter began to articulate the principles upon which the consensus theory was based when he published *The American Political Tradition*, in 1948, arguing that an unusually high level of consensus over the central tenets of liberal capitalism underlay the apparent conflicts that have run through the history of the United States. Thus, Hofstadter noted, "However much at odds on specific issues, the major political traditions have shared a belief in the rights of property, the philosophy of economic individualism, the value of competition; they have accepted the economic virtues of capitalism as necessary qualities of man."[15] Seven years later, Louis Hartz published the work that did the most to establish the consensus theory of American political thought. In *The Liberal Tradition in America*, Hartz claimed that American thought has invariably been dominated by a liberal ideology with a commitment not only to capitalism but also to democracy and to legal and political equality.[16] It was Lockean liberalism, in Hartz's view, that explained the major developments in American political ideas, institutions, and practice. Indeed, Hartz emphasized that conflicts in American history were circumscribed by liberal boundaries. Because the United States lacked a feudal past and a rigid class system, neither a socialist movement nor a serious traditionalist conservatism emerged to either challenge that class system or to preserve tradition. Americans thus never seriously considered any alternatives to the Lockeanism that they embraced with a devotion that was almost irrational. Hartz characterized the feudal, slaveholding South as "an alien child in a liberal family, tortured and confused, driven to a fantasy life which, instead of disproving the power of Locke in America, portrays more poignantly than anything else the tyranny he has had."[17] He thereby dismissed illiberal inegalitarian aspects of American thought, institutions, and practices as aberrations—somewhat bizarre departures from the liberal consensus.

Several scholars subsequently refined Hartz's thesis by arguing that liberalism is far more complex than his analysis suggested. J. David Greenstone, for example, contrasted "humanist liberalism" with "reform liberalism," arguing that "at its core American political culture is pervasively liberal—but not consensually so; that although American liberalism excludes nonliberal alternatives, it is nevertheless fundamentally divided, philosophically, as well as politically."[18] Humanist liberalism, in Greenstone's view, was primarily concerned with the satisfaction of the preferences of individuals and thus prescribed a passive role for government. In contrast, reform liberalism was more religiously based and emphasized ideas of human perfection and moral duties and a more active state. Humanist liberalism could be and was used to support slavery. Greenstone used the contrast between the humanist liberal ideas of Thomas Jefferson and the reform liberal perspective of John Adams to illustrate the differences between the two strands of liberalism. Jefferson's humanist liberalism included three claims that made his tolerance of slavery possible. First, "the human *will* was self-sufficient, because individuals were able to decide on legitimate goals for themselves."[19] That notion of self-sufficiency allowed for balancing various conflicting claims and interests, including those of the slaveholders. Second, because "human *rationality* was sufficient . . . and free individuals could generally be trusted to implement the goals they adopted . . . exchanges of either goods or ideas would produce beneficent outcomes."[20] On such a basis, it was possible to tolerate the institution of slavery. Third, "Human *cognition* was self-sufficient, because ordinary sense perceptions accurately conveyed reality, and therefore the phenomenal world of material objects was the real world."[21] Thus, to Jefferson, the differences he observed between the races were real.

In contrast, as Greenstone explained, John Adams's reform liberalism denied Jefferson's three claims and was consequently critical of slavery. The human will, Adams contended, could not be sufficient because individuals were not capable of determining their goals for themselves—"religious and ethical duty commanded [the] individual not only to cultivate his or her own moral, intellectual, and physical faculties, but to help others to do so as well."[22] Thus, the notion of balancing competing claims was out of the question. In addition, the emphasis that Adams placed on self-development led him to adopt a broader view of human rationality and thus precluded individuals pursuing their interests if they subverted the obligation to promote self-development. Finally, Adams, who rejected Jefferson's materialism and empiricism, conceived of human souls as immaterial objects possessed of moral equality.

Greenstone's analysis is useful here insofar as it reveals the multifaceted nature of the phenomenon that is commonly labeled liberalism. Nevertheless, in so doing, his analysis stretches the category of liberalism into the realm of republicanism and illiberal, inegalitiarian, racist doctrines. In addition, as Smith pointed out, insofar as Greenstone treated the Jacksonians' racism simply as an issue of value-neutral deference to preferences of the white majority, he failed to treat racism in American ideas and practice as a central part of American political culture.[23]

James P. Young, like Greenstone, argued that Hartz failed to deal with the complexity of liberalism and relegated the frequent conflicts in American history to the background. In Young's view, liberalism includes at least three major currents of thought. First, it comprises the Lockean "image of humans as equal, rights-bearing, interest-oriented individuals—individuals who are entitled to have those rights defended, particularly against government intrusion."[24] Second, there is the economic—free-market, laissez-faire—liberalism of Adam Smith. The reform liberalism of John Stuart Mill and John Dewey that allowed for a more active role for government in economic matters is the third iteration of liberalism. Young also maintained that American thought was not liberal from the beginning but "became so through the course of its frequently stormy history."[25] Indeed, he argued that until slavery was abolished, the United States could not be a liberal country: "The liberalism that Louis Hartz saw as dominant from the start of American history finally emerged triumphant with the destruction of the most fundamentally antiliberal institution and the emergence of full-scale industrial capitalism."[26] Young, like Greenstone, emphasized the elasticity of the concept of liberalism and even went so far as to include some aspects of pre-Revolutionary republicanism under the liberal label.[27]

Others have gone further than the refiners of Hartz's thesis to confront it head on with the argument that multiple strands of thought that lie outside the boundaries of liberalism have been central to the history of American ideas since the early colonial period.[28] Challenging the liberal paradigm of American thought, Rogers M. Smith developed an immensely valuable alternative framework for understanding the complex character of American political culture and used it to demonstrate not only that liberalism is more complex than the consensus school alleged but also that American political culture has not invariably revolved around liberal democratic principles. Moreover, American political development has not followed an unbroken course toward the full realization of liberal egalitarian ideals. Contrary to the Hartz thesis and to the arguments of its refiners, Smith argues that political conflicts have not been confined by liberal boundaries. Nor have illiberal and inegalitarian beliefs been relegated to the margins of American thought and practice. Indeed, according to Smith, such beliefs have played such a central role that it is impossible to understand the history of American ideas without taking such ideas into account.[29]

For Smith, the flaw in the story of a pervasively liberal American political tradition is its narrow focus on relationships among white men of property, who were predominantly of northern European ancestry. Relationships between the white male minority and subordinate groups were defined by very different sorts of ideas, he explained: "an array of other fixed, ascriptive systems of unequal status" according to which men were naturally suited to rule over women; white northern Europeans were superior to Africans and native Americans as well as to all other races and civilizations; and Protestants were chosen by God to be morally and politically superior to Catholics, Jews, Muslims, and others.[30] In short, coexisting with liberalism were "intellectual and political traditions conceiving of America in inegalitarian racial, patriarchal, and religious terms."[31]

With his alternative framework, which he termed the Multiple-Traditions Thesis, Smith posited that American political culture is best understood as a complicated interaction between the three contrasting traditions of liberalism, republicanism, and inegalitarian ascriptive forms of Americanism—"a complex pattern of apparently inconsistent combinations of the traditions, accompanied by recurring conflicts."[32] The three traditions have coexisted in American ideologies and practices—none has ever been strong enough to overcome the others, but they have had a restraining effect on each other.

Because the Multiple-Traditions Thesis provides the foundation for my analysis of Elizabeth Cady Stanton's political thought, in the rest of this section I elaborate on the three traditions to describe the most prominent features of each of those traditions and to highlight the major junctures at which they diverge. The liberalism that John Locke articulated in the late seventeenth century in opposition to royal prerogatives was distinguished by its commitment to securing the natural rights that it held to belong to every human being. The Declaration of Independence expounded the liberal claim that all men are created equal and endowed with the inalienable rights of life, liberty, and the pursuit of happiness. In the classical liberal view, the role of government, whose authority is derived from the consent of the people, was limited to protecting individual rights. As a result, although liberalism espoused equality, it actually left a great deal of room for conditions under which inequalities were virtually inevitable. Liberalism's principle of equal rights turned out to be a commitment to an abstract right for individuals to pursue goods without hindrance or help from government. Thus, the existence of major inequalities—economic, social, and even political —that were judged to be the result of free choices in the private sphere, an area that was off limits to government, was not considered to betray the principles of liberalism. In fact, within the framework of liberalism, the highly valued individual autonomy was seen as inconsistent with and took precedence over any form of substantive equality.

Republicanism shifted the concern from the pursuit of happiness by and for the individual to the achievement of collective self-governance for the pursuit of the common good for the community. Republican ideas thus emphasized the necessity of public-spirited citizens enthusiastically participating in public affairs. Smith pointed out that republicanism "offered a view of civic membership that conveyed a more concrete sense of shared virtuous endeavor and social solidarity than did liberal ideas. The cause of republicanism thereby provided a more obvious promise of meaningful, morally worthwhile, and closely knit political communities in America."[33] It is important to note, however, that republicanism's insistence that it was imperative for a republic to have a relatively small number of economically independent and homogeneous citizens led to the proposition that not all people could be citizens, thus justifying exclusion and discrimination.[34] Republicans made clear that economic independence and a shared life of civic virtue would be possible, as Smith noted, only if a

> body of subjects performed many of the most arduous, dangerous, or menial tasks. Since these subjects—conquered peoples, poor laborers, servants, slaves, and women—lacked the leisure, education, and economic freedom they made possible for others, they were unfit for the franchise or other aspects of full citizenship. They were properly subject to near-absolute rule, so that citizens could live in freedom.[35]

The third tradition, ascriptive forms of Americanism, includes a variety of doctrines that have emphasized "the unique and distinctive character of a gender, race, or ethnocultural group."[36] Ascribing particular moral, intellectual, and physical qualities to people on the basis of their sex, race, or nationality and maintaining that such qualities are natural and unchangeable, those doctrines have been used to justify rigid social, political, and economic hierarchies. Ascriptive forms of Americanism, Smith argued, have played a central role in American ideas and practice. Ideologies—including "scientific" racism and, subsequently, Anglo-Saxonism and social Darwinism—that were used to posit the inferiority of African Americans in order to defend slavery and, later, to defend segregation, discrimination, and restrictions on immigration all argued that inequality was natural and inevitable. Thus, hierarchical and exclusionary social, political, and economic arrangements were good for society insofar as they were crucial to maintaining order, protecting the weaker members of the community, and protecting the "better" sorts of people from those who were, for reasons of race, sex, or nationality, undesirable.

The notion that Protestant Americans were chosen by God to create a new society in the New World was the earliest version of ascriptive Americanism. A more developed version emerged with the argument that Americans had a distinct character and were uniquely suited for self-government because they were descended from Anglo-Saxons who developed democratic institutions. In the late nineteenth century, Anglo-Saxonism took on a more racial quality when it combined with social Darwinism to charge that the superior Anglo-Saxon race was naturally better suited to compete in the struggle for survival than people with strange customs and dark skin. Such doctrines served to justify policies ranging from immigration restriction to racial segregation and the disfranchisement of African Americans in the South.

Women's Status and the Multiple Traditions

All three traditions played a role in fashioning women's status in the middle of the nineteenth century, and these traditions provided the material with which Cady Stanton would work—expanding, adapting, subverting them to challenge women's subordinate status. The prevailing beliefs and values concerning women's proper role were predominantly ascriptive insofar as they revolved around the certainty that natural differences between the sexes mandated that their roles be separate and distinct. They also contained elements of republicanism insofar as they set forth prescriptions for how women could contribute to the

well-being of the political community without becoming fully participating citizens. The ascriptive view of women's natural differences from
men overlapped with republican notions of the qualities of a virtuous
citizen that excluded women from full citizenship. Good republicans
were self-reliant, given to simple needs and tastes, decisive, and committed to the public interest—all masculine qualities. In contrast, attrib-
utes that were purportedly feminine, such as attraction to luxury, self-
indulgence, timidity, dependence, and passion, were linked in republican
thought to corruption and viewed as a threat to the health of the community. In addition, the idea that ownership of land provided the basis
for an independent citizenry that was essential to republican government reinforced women's exclusion, as they were legally precluded from
owning property under most circumstances.[37]

Liberalism also served as a tool to justify and perpetuate women's
subordinate position. While liberal principles promoted the expansion
of suffrage to all white men during the Jacksonian era, democratization
did not include women. Indeed, despite its claims of natural rights,
equality, and government by consent, Lockean liberalism's contention
that society and government should be treated as though they are based
on a contract left out what Carole Pateman termed the "sexual contract" and thereby retained the patriarchal social order that made up
the reality of relations between husbands and wives—relations in which
the woman was invariably subordinate.[38] In other words, when men left
Locke's hypothetical state of nature and entered the social contract, they
did so as free agents, whereas women had already "been conquered by
men and are now their subjects (servants)."[39] Thus, when women entered society, they were not free and equal to men but were already
bound by the marriage contract. Liberalism's division of the world into
the spheres of public and private and its focus only on the public, as
well as its insistence that everyone be treated as though they were equal,
left women in a subordinate position in the neglected private sphere. Indeed, liberalism envisioned men as the bearers of equal rights, either ignoring women altogether or justifying their exclusion by casting them in
the subordinate role of wives, mothers, and daughters.

As Linda K. Kerber pointed out, in the Revolutionary period, men
who challenged "inherited understandings of the relationship between
kings and men, fathers and sons, nevertheless refused to revise inherited
understandings of the relationship between men and women, husbands
and wives, mothers and children. They continued to assert patriarchal

privilege as heads of households and as civic actors."[40] Moreover, that tradition, fundamentally part of liberalism, yet with clearly ascriptive implications and results, has continued into the present. As Kerber explained,

> [T]he substitution of married women's obligations to their husbands and families for their obligations to the state has been a central element in the way Americans have thought about the relation of all women, including unmarried women, to state power. One by one, most of these substitutions have come to seem inappropriate and have been abandoned, but in each case only after a long and complicated struggle.[41]

The emphasis on the Lockean argument that the right to property promoted the independence that provided the foundation for political equality went a long way toward justifying the exclusion of women. Given their lack of property rights, women could not hope to achieve the requisite individual autonomy. Although women's dependent status was guaranteed by the common law rules pertaining to property and by patriarchal customs regarding the family, their lack of autonomy was most often assumed to be natural, which made it possible to argue that although women had natural rights, they did not extend to political rights. When it came to women, liberal equality did not include political, legal, or social equality but encompassed only a general notion of roughly equal moral worth. The failure of the law to protect women's property rights and women's consequent lack of the autonomy that was requisite for political rights was inextricably linked to the problem of liberalism that both Pateman and Kerber pointed out: in liberal theory, women were not rights-bearing autonomous individuals. They were, instead, the wives, daughters, and mothers of such individuals, and their rights were defined accordingly.[42]

In short, all three traditions functioned to justify and perpetuate women's subordinate status. Whereas ascriptivism's insistence that women were by nature different and inferior to men most obviously supported women's subordinate position, the republican ideal of a body of virtuous property-owning citizens protecting the public good also justified the exclusion of women from public life. Also, liberalism, with its emphasis on individual autonomy and property rights as well as equality for men, reinforced the unequal position of women. The eighteenth-century hierarchical worldview that posited that women, lacking the capacity for reason with which men were endowed, were inferior and suited only for household tasks, child rearing, and diversionary activities such as singing and needlework garnered support from all three traditions. That view did not disappear in the first half of the nineteenth century but was modified in some important ways.

After the Revolution, a set of beliefs and prescriptions that historians have termed the ideology of republican motherhood assigned to women the role of bearing and raising sons to be virtuous citizens. By fulfilling their responsibilities as wives and mothers, they would play a crucial role in ensuring the success of the Republic.[43] The republican mother had a special role—for which she was uniquely suited—to provide moral guidance to her sons and her husband. She was responsible for imparting the values and discipline that would make her sons virtuous citizens. Thus, although republican motherhood did not question woman's confinement to the domestic sphere, it elevated her traditional role within that sphere. The republican mother was responsible for the future of the new nation; nevertheless, her ability to make a contribution depended upon limiting her activities to the private realm of home and family. If she were to venture out to participate in public life, she would lose the special qualities that enabled her to provide her husband and sons with moral guidance. Political equality for women, therefore, would be dangerous to the future of the Republic.

Republican motherhood was both ascriptive and republican. Woman's special nature dictated her subordinate status and political exclusion, but women had an important—albeit indirect—role to play in the political life of the nation. Republican motherhood was also decidedly elitist. While republican mothers stayed at home shaping future citizens, an elite body of economically independent, virtuous male citizens could carry on the work of governing. Furthermore, its focus on white, middle-class, relatively educated women excluded those who were less well off and whose sons and husbands were generally not considered capable of becoming virtuous citizens.

Historians have examined extensively the pervasive nineteenth-century doctrine of separate spheres and its impact on women's lives.[44] The ideology of republican motherhood evidences the elevation of woman's role within the home after the Revolution and is therefore generally considered to represent an improvement in the status of women. A number of developments in the early nineteenth century, however, converged to define the activities and roles that were appropriate for women in narrower and more rigid terms, thus guaranteeing the continuation of—perhaps even intensifying—the subordinate status of women.[45] The changes that accompanied industrialization, including the demise of the agrarian economy, the development of a commercial economy, and a shift to town and city life, resulted in a more distinct separation of the sexes. As the home ceased to be a center of production, men's work lives were increasingly located away from home. Woman's work within the home became physically easier, as she was no longer responsible for producing necessities such as food and clothing and could turn more attention to child rearing—an important activity but very different from men's income-producing work. Because of the new focus on production outside the home, the work that women continued to do at home was marginalized as the sexual division of labor became more clearly defined. Accompanying the increased physical separation of men and women were cultural norms that placed much more emphasis on the importance of separate and distinct roles for men and women.

By the beginning of the 1830s, republican motherhood had evolved into an ideology that became known as the cult of domesticity.[46] As Gerda Lerner explained,

> [V]alues and beliefs that clustered around the assertion "Woman's place is in the home" changed from being descriptive of an existing reality to becoming an ideology . . . [that] extolled woman's predominance in the domestic sphere, while it tried to justify women's exclusion from the public domain, from equal education and from participation in the political process by claims to tradition, universality, and a history dating back to antiquity, or at least to the Mayflower. In a century of modernization and industrialization women alone were to remain unchanging, embodying in their behavior and attitudes the longing of men and women caught in rapid social change for a mythical archaic past of agrarian family self-sufficiency.[47]

The cult of domesticity portrayed women as the opposite of men. Men were alleged to be strong and intelligent, while women were perceived as delicate and emotional. Nevertheless, a number of positive qualities were attributed to women. They were selfless, sympathetic, affectionate, trusting, cooperative, modest, virtuous, benevolent, intuitive, peaceful, and serene. Men, in contrast, were self-interested, competitive, ambitious, and acquisitive. Those were the natural qualities that rendered men fit for the world of business and commerce, government and politics, while women's sex determined their domestic vocation.

Although it was thoroughly ascriptive, the cult of domesticity did not purport to portray women as inferior to men. Indeed, women were commonly depicted as morally superior to members of "the grosser sex."[48] Woman was "God's appointed agent of morality."[49] The cult of domesticity set forth a sentimentalized, idealized image of the true woman as a saintly, pious, pure, and submissive wife and mother. In the *Ladies Magazine,* in 1830, Sarah Josepha Hale explained the importance and advantages of women's role:

> [W]omen may, if they exert their talents and the opportunities nature
> has furnished, obtain an influence in society that will be paramount
> with authority. They may enjoy the luxuries of wealth, without endur-
> ing the labors to acquire it; and the honors of office, without feeling its
> cares, and glory of victory, without suffering the dangers of battle.[50]

Untouched by the heartless, competitive world, the "true woman" could comfort her husband when he returned home from work, provide him with moral guidance, and protect him from the insecurities of the rapidly changing society. As Mary Beth Norton noted, "women became the keepers of the nation's conscience, the only citizens specifically charged with maintaining the traditional republican commitment to the good of the entire community."[51] Because virtuous, selfless wives and mothers protected republican values in their domestic domain, their husbands and sons were able to engage more extensively in the individual pursuit of self-interest in the public sphere. Thus, the cult of domesticity had important connections to both republicanism and liberalism.

The republican strains of the cult of domesticity grew more pronounced as women, following the popular view that true Christians must work to improve the world, began to form associations—Bible and tract, missionary, and charitable societies and Sunday school associations. By 1830, there was a firmly established tradition of female association that extended to a variety of benevolent activities. Women worked for moral reform and prison reform and engaged in charitable work for poor women, children, orphans, and elderly women. Benevolent groups instituted employment services and trained women for work as seamstresses and housekeepers. By participating in such endeavors in all-female organizations, a woman could make a contribution to her community without crossing the forbidden boundary of the domestic sphere. Women also gained valuable experience by drawing up constitutions, voting, running for office, and working out platforms within their organizations.[52] Just as the republican mother earlier had indirectly improved the political life of the community, the "true woman" of the 1830s could work for benevolent causes in her unique feminine way without dirtying her hands in politics. With its republican and ascriptive elements, the cult of domesticity portrayed women as either morally superior to men or different from but not inferior to them, with an important but clearly distinct function to perform in the world.

At the same time that liberalism, republicanism, and ascriptive forms of Americanism functioned to support women's subordinate status, each set of ideas contained the potential for generating change. In other words, there was a tension in each tradition between its normative and its subversive dimensions. In spite of historic uses to the contrary, liberal principles of natural rights and equality could be presented in universal terms and reinterpreted to apply to women.[53] Cady Stanton's earliest work did just that by proclaiming and then repeatedly reiterating that women were equal to and thus entitled to the same rights as men.

The ascriptive and republican traditions also provided opportunities for women to expand the limits of the female sphere and to challenge the structure of customs and laws that limited their ability to move out of that sphere. The republican mother needed education in order to acquire the knowledge she would need if she were to provide her sons with moral guidance. Thus, educational reformers commonly justified expanding educational opportunities for women on the grounds that more educated women would be better equipped to shape future citizens of the Republic. Similarly, educational reform was perceived as consistent with the cult of domesticity as educational opportunities for women improved between 1820 and 1860. One educator argued, in 1830, that knowledge would make women "better daughters, wives, and sisters. Better qualified for usefulness in every path within the sphere of female exertions."[54] Teaching was seen as an appropriate occupation for women—the classroom could serve as an extension of the home as a place where women would shape the character of future citizens. Female teachers could also train other women to perform that task—always with much lower pay than male teachers would earn. Thus, female seminaries spread, and college education became available to a small number of women on a limited basis in the 1830s. Oberlin became the first coeducational college when it offered a special ladies' course in 1833 to prepare women for homemaking or teaching. In the 1840s, Catharine Beecher launched a campaign to establish teaching as a profession for women, raising funds to recruit and train teachers and to establish schools for training teachers.

Women's alleged unique moral virtues and talents that purportedly made them so good at shaping future citizens also bestowed on them a duty to work to raise the moral quality of America by working in female benevolent societies. Whether working, studying, or simply living in their separate sphere, women began to develop an awareness of their identity as women. That awareness, which developed in the context of a separate women's culture that grew out of women's confinement to the domestic sphere, has often been viewed as a necessary precursor to the organized campaign for women's rights.[55] As we will see, Cady Stanton seized on the republican tradition, turning it into an affirmation that women, with the special abilities that they acquired as wives and mothers, would be excellent citizens who would bring major improvements to the political life of the nation.

Women's rights reformers could respond to ascriptivist arguments that posited the inferiority of women by rejecting them and relying instead on liberal principles of equality or republican conceptions of the important contributions women could make to the political life of the community. Alternatively, reformers could adopt a subversive version of ascriptivism by asserting that women were superior to men and were endowed with distinct moral qualities that rendered them particularly well suited to participate in public life. According to that argument, with their special superior qualities, voting women would be a tremendous benefit to the nation—they would destroy the power of big business and the corrupt political machines and restore the power of the people. A nation in which women voted would also, it was alleged, be far less likely to go to war.[56]

As we will see, ascriptive forms of Americanism constituted a significantly more complex category than either liberalism or republicanism, particularly as such doctrines operated in Cady Stanton's thought. During the nineteenth century, there were a number of ascriptive statuses in addition to sex, including race, national origin, class, and religion.

Thus, ascriptive arguments operated in different ways, depending on the "natural" status that was at issue. Cady Stanton used ascriptive arguments in different ways to subvert the status quo regarding women's position, but, at the same time, she employed ascriptivism to reinforce other existing inequalities—including inequalities among women—in order to promote her goal of improving the status not of all women but of those whom she considered worthy. Although her use of ascriptivism thereby appears to be inconsistent, it is part of the complex web of ideas that drew from the multiple traditions to make up Cady Stanton's political thought.

As noted, liberalism and republicanism are political theories, with principles that Cady Stanton readily adapted to promote the cause of women's rights. In contrast, although ascriptive forms of Americanism are also grounded in major political theories, when Cady Stanton began to use ascriptivist arguments, she asserted the superiority or inferiority of particular groups of people without referring to any particular political theory or elevating it to the level of a principle. By the late nineteenth century, however, she was incorporating Positivism and social Darwinism into her ascriptivist arguments.

A Historical Institutional Approach

The traditions of liberalism, republicanism, and ascriptive forms of Americanism supplied the materials for Elizabeth Cady Stanton to fashion her challenge to women's subordinate status. Many of her arguments revolved around liberal principles of natural rights and equality. The Declaration of Sentiments, with which she launched the organized woman's rights movement in 1848, is a well-known example. She modeled that document on the Declaration of Independence, modifying the original language to include women by asserting the equality of all men and women. She was willing, however, to depart from liberalism to draw upon the classical republican vision of rule by an elite group of wise, public-spirited citizens. At times, she presented contrasting approaches in the same speech. For example, she would begin with a reminder that the American Revolution was fought to secure natural rights and equality, and she would assert that women possessed the same capacities as men and were endowed with the same rights. She would then turn to more republican and ascriptive themes by pointing out that women's moral superiority rendered them particularly valuable voting citizens. She would frequently go further to draw on the range of ascriptive statuses by arguing that women were superior to many of the men who had been given the vote—"ignorant Irishmen in the ditch," "drunkards, idiots, horse-racing, rumselling rowdies, ignorant foreigners, and silly boys."[57] Moreover, after the Civil War, when the Republican Party abandoned the cause of woman suffrage in order to pursue equal rights for black men, Cady Stanton often relied on racially ascriptivist rhetoric that was in sharp contrast to her liberal equal rights arguments.

The Multiple-Traditions Thesis provides an extremely useful framework for examining Cady Stanton's thought. Nevertheless, as I sifted through her speeches and writings, it became increasingly clear that although her departure from the liberal tradition was readily apparent in many of her arguments, what was not so clear was how those arguments fit into the traditions of either republicanism or ascriptivism. Where, for example, did her arguments regarding marriage fit? What about her critique of organized religion? She also developed a conception of women as members of a group who had obligations to one another that resembles but does not quite fit the tradition of republicanism. Something else that did not fit comfortably in any of the traditions was the breadth of her reform vision and her thoroughgoing belief that legal and political reform alone could never eliminate the subordinate status of women that was so imbedded in the culture of the nineteenth century. Consequently, I include a fourth category, radicalism, in the analysis.

I use the term "radicalism" to refer to sets of ideas and political agendas that call for fundamental change in social, political, and cultural arrangements. Cady Stanton's reform agenda included the transformation of marriage from an arrangement in which men had virtually absolute power over their wives into an equal partnership. Her vision of marriage so transformed included but went far beyond changes in the law regarding marriage to the most private area of intimate relations between husbands and wives. Thus, her ideas concerning marriage were radical in that they transcended the liberal boundary between public and private. Likewise, her critique of religion challenged a deeply ingrained facet of American culture that she understood to be thoroughly intertwined with women's subordination. The elimination of the religious sources of that subordination would involve a radical transformation of American society. Radicalism, as I use the term, also encompasses ideas and strategies that do not rely on the liberal tradition of individualism and rights or on republican notions of civic virtue or on ascriptivist assertions of the superiority of certain groups but instead draw from different theoretical paradigms. For example, in her later work, Cady Stanton offered a conception of women that departed from the individualism that is central to liberalism and from the ascriptive rhetoric of women's superiority to embrace the notion of women as a class with the potential to develop consciousness of itself as such and to organize for major social change.[58]

A shifting combination of the contrasting traditions runs through Cady Stanton's political thought. Liberalism, for example, dominated her earliest work, receded in later years, but never entirely disappeared. The different traditions shifted in their prominence in her work depending on the time and the particular situation. Much of this book is devoted to revealing the extent to which Cady Stanton's thought manifests the complexities and contradictions of multiple traditions and therefore cannot be located in one tradition to the exclusion of the others. But I also have a more ambitious goal—to shed light on the reasons why she enlisted such contradictory approaches by exploring the interaction between her ideas and the context in which they developed.

My study of Cady Stanton's ideas follows a historical institutional approach. When she embarked on a campaign to improve the status of women, she confronted a formidable structure of laws, customs, and beliefs regarding woman's nature, her proper function, and her relationship to man that was deeply rooted in American political culture. I explore the way she fashioned arguments out of the material available to her to challenge that structure, focusing on the connections among the following: the preexisting structure that shaped women's status, the shifting combinations of the multiple traditions in her arguments, and the changing political and social conditions and climate of ideas from the 1840s until the end of the nineteenth century. My major concern throughout the book is with the way that the various traditions interacted with one another and played different roles in her arguments, depending on the political context.

The interplay between Cady Stanton's arguments and the changing conditions in the nineteenth century plays a major role in my analysis. During the years between the Seneca Falls Convention in 1848 and Cady Stanton's death, in 1902, the United States underwent a major transformation. The Civil War not only brought an end to the institution of slavery but also altered the nature of the relationship between the states and the federal government. Rapid industrialization, economic growth, corporate organization in business, urbanization, and the new status of the United States as a world power at the end of the nineteenth century profoundly transformed American life. Such changes provide an important part of the backdrop against which Cady Stanton formulated, refined, and modified her arguments.

Further, her ideas took shape against a number of more specific political developments—the isolation of the woman's rights activists following the Civil War, for example, when the abolitionists formed an alliance with the radical Republicans and refused to include woman suffrage in the campaign for the vote for African American men. In the later years of the nineteenth century, Cady Stanton developed an attack on religion that was framed in the context of European intellectual critiques of religion, as well as the revival and proliferation of various denominations of Protestantism in the United States.[59] The changes that occurred within the woman's rights movement itself were also connected to the development of Cady Stanton's ideas. While her arguments undoubtedly had a major effect on the movement, developments within the movement—the split in 1869 and the shift in strategy after 1890, for example—also had an impact on the way she framed her arguments. Finally, her arguments helped to perpetuate the multiple traditions in the woman's rights movement and subsequently in the development of feminist thought in the twentieth century. At the most general level, Cady Stanton's political thought, with its shifting combinations of liberalism, republicanism, ascriptivism, and radicalism, reflects the extent to which no single tradition has been able to completely dominate American political culture.

I also explore the connections between the development of Cady Stanton's arguments and the changing climate of ideas in the second half of the nineteenth century. The emergence of Positivism and Darwinism, for example, had an important impact on her arguments. The resurgence of support for ascriptive Americanisms in the context of race and national origin in addition to sex during that time had a major influence on the development of her ideas. Anglo-Saxonism and social Darwinism, with its racial variant, posited differences in intelligence and the capacity for self-government based on race, ethnicity, sex, and national origin. These ideologies, presented as they were as scientific facts, became more popular than liberal notions of equality and natural rights. Smith noted that Anglo-Saxonism and Darwinism came to be so convincing that "More and more, evolution made old notions of un-changing individual natural rights seem like reassuring fairy tales. The hard truth seemed to be that all individuals and groups were engaged in a bitter struggle to survive amid an unfriendly nature."[60] Cady Stanton's work during the last twenty years of the nineteenth century reflects that sentiment; at the same time, her speeches and writings served to rein-force that view.

A number of scholars have recognized that the growth of ascriptive ideas influenced the arguments that the suffragists used to advance their cause.[61] There was a discernible move away from liberal egalitarian doctrine to ascriptive claims of the superiority of women—particularly those who were native born, white, and educated. Moreover, a number of women's rights advocates worked squarely within the framework of evolutionary theory to challenge Darwinian claims of male superior-ity.[62] Illiberal themes grew more pronounced in Cady Stanton's work at the same time that ascriptive ideologies gained increasing support in American political culture. Thus, ascriptive arguments combined with elements of republicanism grew more pronounced in her later work. For example, republican values are discernible in the argument she advanced in the 1890s for educational qualifications for suffrage. She contended that a literacy test and a requirement that voters under-stand English would make Americans more homogeneous; moreover, by the time foreigners fulfilled the requirement, she reasoned, they would know something about American institutions. But when she made a list of reasons for an educational qualification, limiting the foreign vote was at the top.[63] Moreover, Anglo-Saxonism and the extreme individualism of social Darwinism are readily apparent in many of the statements she made during the last twenty years of her life.

Political Thought and Strategy

Ideas are invariably connected to the circumstances in which they are constructed. It is beyond doubt that Cady Stanton's goals played a cen-tral role in the development of her political thought. She was not only a political philosopher but also a political actor—a leader of a major re-form movement. As such, she had to pay attention to the utility of her ideas to the cause of women's rights. She had to consider the impact that her arguments had upon her audience—both within and outside the movement. Her task of challenging the all-pervasive structure that relegated women to subordinate status required her to convince powerful men that change was warranted. Furthermore, if the movement was to gain momentum, it would need to attract women in significant numbers and it would need allies. Thus, her arguments would have to appeal to political leaders, large numbers of women, and other organized groups. Consequently, she could try a particular argument, gauge the response of her audience, and modify her approach in an effort to develop the most effective means to achieving her ends.

It is possible to treat the shifting combinations of the multiple traditions in Cady Stanton's arguments simply as a result of the rational behavior of a political actor seeking to maximize her chances for success. All three traditions operated to justify and perpetuate women's subordinate status, just as all three had a subversive use insofar as they provided tools for reform. In addition, the relative popularity of the different traditions varied with time and circumstance. Consequently, arguments drawn solely from any single tradition could never have been sufficient to overcome the obstacles to reform. Thus, when her initial approach, which relied heavily on liberal principles, was repeatedly ridiculed, ignored, or refuted, she shifted ground to construct a line of argument that was more likely to be effective. Liberal claims for women's political equality based on natural rights and shared humanity did not overcome arguments raised against women's rights that maintained that nature intended women to remain in the private sphere. Thus, Cady Stanton began to place more emphasis on women's alleged special nature in her arguments for women's suffrage. Aileen S. Kraditor identified a shift in the arguments employed by the woman suffrage movement after 1890 away from statements of universal natural rights and toward a focus on the ways that voting women would improve government and society.[64] The shift to arguments based on expediency, she argued, had the strategic advantage of turning the traditional view that women and men had different natures and were thus suited to different spheres and distinct functions into an argument for enfranchising women. Moreover, popular Darwinian and Anglo-Saxon doctrines lent credibility to ascriptive arguments for women's rights and appealed to popular prejudices.

I explore the strategic aspects of Cady Stanton's ideas—the ways that she adjusted her arguments in light of the way they were received both within the movement and elsewhere at different times and under different circumstances. Its importance notwithstanding, strategy was only one of a number of elements that constituted Cady Stanton's political thought. In keeping with the historical institutional approach, I do not treat Cady Stanton purely as a political actor, rationally maneuvering through a thicket of opposition in pursuit of her goals.[65] In my analysis, her behavior was shaped not entirely by exogenous forces but also by her own normative assessments that evolved in connection with the political conditions in which she operated during the course of her career. Thus, she adopted ascriptive Americanist doctrines for strategic purposes when she found that they were more effective tools for achieving her goals than liberal claims. Nevertheless, she had normative theoretical commitments that shaped the direction of her arguments. On the one hand, the fact that liberal claims of natural rights and equality never entirely disappeared from her arguments even as they continually failed to achieve results and as she turned increasingly to ascriptive claims may suggest that Cady Stanton's underlying commitment to liberal values persisted throughout her life regardless of the external conditions that pushed her in other directions. On the other hand, the presence of illiberal strains in Cady Stanton's earliest work suggests that her own predisposition may have been toward elitist republican and ascriptive principles. Ellen Carol DuBois took such a position, noting that although the leaders of the women's movement in the post–Civil War years were victims of the Republicans' policy of dividing them,

> The swiftness and energy with which Stanton and Anthony turned from their own abolitionist traditions to Train's racism remains remarkable. At this point, their racism was opportunist and superficial, an artifact of their anti-Republicanism and their alienation from abolitionists. However, it drew on and strengthened a much deeper strain within their feminism, a tendency to envision women's emancipation in exclusively white terms.[66]

Regardless of whether Cady Stanton had a philosophical commitment to liberalism or whether racism, nativism, and class snobbery were more important in shaping her ideas, the development of her political thought encompasses considerably more than strategy.

Woman's Rights and Feminism

The issues that have divided feminism in the twentieth century and continue to do so in the twenty-first lurked at the edges but were not paramount to nineteenth-century women's rights reformers. There were conflicts, nevertheless. Disagreement during the 1850s over whether easier divorce was an appropriate solution to women's unequal position in marriage and whether divorce reform was an appropriate issue for the woman's rights movement culminated at the woman's rights convention in 1860. Reconstruction politics that gave priority to the enfranchisement of black men and abandoned woman suffrage was central to the division of the woman's rights movement into two organizations in 1869. The American Woman Suffrage Association (AWSA), led by Lucy Stone and Henry Blackwell, supported the Fifteenth Amendment, which prohibited the states from denying the right to vote on the basis of race, on the grounds that it represented a step toward the enfranchisement of women. The AWSA aimed its campaign to secure the vote for women at the states and focused its efforts entirely on suffrage, vowing not to be distracted by other issues. Cady Stanton and Susan B. Anthony, who refused to support either the Fourteenth or Fifteenth Amendments, organized the National Woman Suffrage Association (NWSA), which sought not only a constitutional amendment to enfranchise women but additional reforms that would secure women's rights in work, education, and marriage.

Tensions in the movement persisted after the two organizations were reunited in 1890. Women's rights reformers disagreed over a variety of issues, including religion, moral reform, marriage, divorce, and sex, as well as the emphasis that should be placed on suffrage.[67] The positions that Cady Stanton adopted in regard to such issues reveal the outlines of her ideas about women's nature, their relationship to one another and to men, the sources of their oppression, and the appropriate agenda for change—in twenty-first-century terms, her feminist thought. The term "feminism" was not used during Cady Stanton's lifetime. It did not come into use in the United States until after 1910.[68] In the nineteenth century, Americans spoke of the advancement of woman or the cause of woman, woman's rights, and woman suffrage. According to historian Nancy F. Cott, the use of the singular "woman," which sounds awkward today, symbolized the unity of the female sex.[69] But, beginning about 1910, diversity in the woman suffrage movement increased as blacks, new immigrants, and political radicals joined the movement. The heightened diversity began to reveal the paradoxes that were rooted in women's situation: women's equality to and difference from men, the need for sex solidarity to pursue individual freedoms, unity and diversity among women, and the need for gender consciousness, as well as the elimination of prescribed gender roles. Those paradoxes provided the source of the divisions in the woman's rights movement once the Nineteenth Amendment was ratified.[70]

Feminism in the early twenty-first century is not singular but plural. We are confronted with a confusing array of overlapping but distinguishable feminisms—with a variety of labels including but not limited to liberal, assimilationist, radical, socialist, Marxist, dominance, difference, relational, cultural, postmodern, postegalitarian, and "third wave" feminism—each of which claims to have the solution to the problem of gender hierarchy. The multiplicity of labels underlines the discord that dominates contemporary feminism. Liberal feminists charge that the alleged differences between the sexes claimed by difference and relational feminists are not only unproved but can be used against women,[71] while radical, socialist, and dominance feminists argue that feminism grounded in the principles of liberal individualism perpetuates the status quo.[72] Others castigate liberal feminism for its failure to take the needs of men and women and children as members of families and communities into account.[73] Radical and dominance feminists have pointed out the limits of the formal legal equality that remains a central goal of liberal feminists,[74] while postegalitarian feminists have explicitly repudiated formal equality as the central objective of feminism.[75]

The divisions among the varieties of feminist theory are most usefully organized around three sets of issues. First, the identity-difference debate revolves around the questions of whether the similarities between women and men mandate equal treatment without regard to sex, whether the distinctive qualities and activities of women warrant special consideration, or whether it is more useful to shift the focus to women's subordination. Liberal feminists have focused on legal prohibitions on sex discrimination in education and employment, arguing that an individual's sex is irrelevant to his or her qualifications. Others, including difference, relational, and cultural feminists, have focused on women's differences from men, arguing that women's unique way of experiencing the world and approaching moral problems needs to be fully recognized and valued. Feminists of the difference persuasion also argue that, given women's roles as childbearers as well as the disproportionate responsibility they bear for child care, sex-blind policies typically leave them at a disadvantage. Dominance feminists contend that a policy of sex neutrality cannot begin to overcome the forces that perpetuate male privilege in all realms of society.

The second issue, individualism-group or social consciousness, involves alternative conceptions of women in terms of their position in society and their relations to each other as well as to men. Contemporary liberal feminism maintains a primary concern with the rights of women as autonomous individuals and places a premium on equal rights as a means to individual self-fulfillment. Other feminist theories have moved away from individualism to focus on group consciousness, conceptualizing women as a sex-class distinguished by its lack of power or emphasizing that women tend to define themselves in relation to others. Some versions of feminism also focus on how women as a group can contribute to the well-being of society rather than how individuals might further their own interests.

The third issue concerns the viability of the distinction between public and private. Since the 1960s, liberal feminists have defended the public-private distinction against the challenge that the "personal is political" and have continued to focus on discrimination in the public realm of education and employment. In contrast, radical and, subsequently, dominance feminists have located the source of women's oppression in the patriarchal family, denying that changes in public policies can cure the problems that women face at home, which invariably disadvantage them in the workplace. Thus, they argue that feminists should focus their efforts on eliminating the sex-based hierarchy within the family as well as throughout society.

A number of scholars have emphasized the limits of trying to use contemporary varieties of feminism to analyze arguments for women's rights in the nineteenth century. In an article published in 1988, Karen Offen remarked that categories of contemporary feminism do not "serve the analytical needs of historians who want to understand feminism prior to the twentieth century."[76] Scholars have frequently noted that nineteenth-century activists did not perceive women's rights in terms of the dichotomies that characterize the thinking of contemporary feminisms. Indeed, reformers often expressed contrasting perspectives without any awareness that they were doing so.[77] Cott observed that "In its genesis Feminism was full of double aims, joining the concept of women's equality with men to the concept of women's sexual difference, joining the aim of antinomian individual release with concerted social action, endorsing the 'human sex' while deploying political solidarity among women."[78] Carole Pateman pointed out that "Most suffragists . . . argued that womanhood suffrage was required as a matter of justice and to make government by consent a reality, and also that the distinctive contribution that they could make to political life as women was a major reason why they should be enfranchised."[79] Offen made the same point when she noted that prior to the twentieth century, feminists often combined the individualist and the relational modes of argument: "evidence of both these modes can often be located in the utterances of a single individual, or among members of a particular group."[80]

It is essential not to lose sight of either the historical context of Cady Stanton's thought or the differences between the nineteenth-century movement and contemporary feminisms. Still, there are parallels between the two periods that render the three sets of contemporary dividing issues useful for examining Cady Stanton's ideas. Like other women's rights activists in the nineteenth century, she did not perceive the issues that came to divide feminism in the second half of the twentieth century in dichotomous terms. Instead, she combined what we now consider to be contradictory approaches, just as she blended the different traditions in American political culture. She frequently supported her demands for access to education, business, and the professions and the right to vote with the claim that women and men possessed the same natural abilities. Yet, she also often claimed that women's distinct characteristics and activities rendered them particularly well suited for political life and that women's participation in public life was essential to the health and progress of society. She joined claims based on both individual rights and social consciousness, while a conception of woman both as a unified group and women as diverse individuals informed her arguments. Cady Stanton not only fought to obtain political and legal rights for women and access to business and the professions but also identified religion as a source of women's oppression and condemned "man-made marriage." She argued that women ought to be able to control their own sexual lives and denounced the male domination that pervaded not only public life but also the most intimate relationships. Thus, while she sought access for women to the public sphere via suffrage, educational opportunities, and access to the professions, she also emphasized that political and legal rights would improve women's position within the family. Moreover, she was convinced that the full realization of women's rights would require more than legal and political change—much more fundamental change in customs, habits, and values throughout society would be necessary. In short, for Cady Stanton, public and private were never really separable. The risks inherent in employing twentieth-century categories of feminism to analyze nineteenth-century ideas are enormous. Nevertheless, I remain convinced that it is helpful to be aware of the ways that Cady Stanton dealt with issues of women's nature and identity and to consider parallels between her arguments and those of contemporary feminisms.

I do not attempt to force Cady Stanton's ideas into the mold of any variety of twentieth- or twenty-first century feminism. On the contrary, I contend that, given the extent to which the defining characteristics of the various feminisms are thoroughly intertwined in her attempts to resolve the questions about women in the nineteenth century, it is neither useful nor accurate to cast her as a particular type of feminist in twenty-first-century terms. As late-twentieth-century feminists of different persuasions began to revive Cady Stanton's work, they often claimed her as one of their own, contending that the feminism that she embraced was akin to the variety of feminism they favored. In so doing, scholars tended to ignore the interplay between contrasting approaches, emphasizing one aspect of Cady Stanton's ideas at the expense of others. For example, Lois W. Banner, one of Cady Stanton's biographers, argued that she was committed to feminist individualism and believed that women and men had similar natures. Banner minimized the significance of Cady Stanton's assertions of women's moral superiority, noting that she (Cady Stanton) had difficulty with the argument, she could not really accept it, and her "theorizing about woman's superiority was generally encompassed within the larger context of what she saw as the complementary nature of the sexes."[81]

Valerie Bryson explored the ways that Cady Stanton combined liberal feminism with radical feminist arguments and concluded that her arguments for equal rights ultimately rested on the claim that women and men were equally rational. Moreover, Bryson argued, Cady Stanton's conception of women as individuals dominated her thought: "despite her analysis of sex, class and the multi-faceted nature of women's oppression, these rights were in the last analysis the rights of each woman *as an individual.*"[82] In contrast, Josephine Donovan emphasized Cady Stanton's later work—particularly *The Woman's Bible*—and concluded that she went beyond liberal feminism when she introduced "an important new vein in feminist theory: the idea that women, and in particular mothers, have special experiences and capabilities that lead them to express a life-affirming, pacifist, creative world view."[83] Zillah Eisenstein, in *The Radical Future of Liberal Feminism,* located Cady Stanton's work within the framework of liberal feminism and criticized her for not developing a more radical approach with greater potential for bringing about major change. Eisenstein applauded the way that Cady Stanton's analysis of women's oppression in marriage and the power of men over women in patriarchal society moved beyond liberal feminism insofar as it recognized women's collective existence as a sex class. Nevertheless, she argued that Cady Stanton failed to depart sufficiently from the liberal feminism that protected patriarchy.[84]

An exchange between two distinguished historians suggests the ways in which the conflicts between twentieth-century varieties of feminism can influence interpretations of nineteenth-century ideas. In an article published in 1988, Karen Offen argued that relational feminism has had a longer and stronger tradition than its individualist variant and claimed that relational arguments dominate Cady Stanton's thought.[85] Ellen Carol DuBois responded by characterizing Offen's piece as a brief for relational feminism and accusing her of trying to appropriate Cady Stanton's feminism by downplaying her belief in the fundamental identity of the sexes and of distorting Cady Stanton's views about women's condition.[86] She then pointed to a number of Cady Stanton's statements that reflect an individualist orientation. In her rejoinder, Offen accused DuBois of discounting the historical importance of relational feminist arguments because of her own distaste for such an approach.[87] Offen then pointed to the relational themes that run through a number of Cady Stanton's statements. Although both Offen and DuBois conceded that Cady Stanton's work to some extent reflects both perspectives, they apparently found it necessary to identify one dominant approach. The approach each historian identified as dominant coincided with the version of twentieth-century feminism that she believed to be most likely to lead to genuine progress for women.

An awareness of the ways in which Cady Stanton combined arguments that are now considered to distinguish different—indeed, incompatible—varieties of feminism helps to understand her political thought and, more specifically, what today we would call her feminism. Still, the normative aspect of my analysis does not include any attempt to promote one type of feminism over another. Neither do I seek to demonstrate that one variety of feminism—in terms of contemporary categories—ultimately prevailed in Cady Stanton's thought. Instead, my primary concern is to explore the relationships among the different strands of her ideas against the background of the political culture of the United States in the second half of the nineteenth century. It is in this particular context that the Multiple-Traditions Thesis is most useful, as it allows us to examine the richness of Cady Stanton's thought without attempting to identify her ideas with one particular tradition or one particular type of feminism.

Elizabeth Cady Stanton in Nineteenth-Century Political Thought

Historical institutionalism and the Multiple-Traditions Thesis are particularly useful for studying Cady Stanton's political thought. First, they facilitate a focus on the interplay between the development of her ideas and a variety of contextual factors, including the changing political conditions and the shifting climate of ideas in the nineteenth century. They also make it easier to explore the connections between the strategic components of her arguments and her normative commitments.

Second, although the approach reveals apparent contradictions in Cady Stanton's thought, the Multiple-Traditions Thesis teaches us to expect to find inconsistencies in the ideas of political thinkers and encourages us to see apparent contradictions in her arguments in a new light. The fact that the role that each tradition played in her arguments varied with the circumstances does not imply that Cady Stanton should be studied only as a political actor. She was both a political actor and a political thinker whose behavior was shaped by a combination of normative considerations and strategic concerns. Consistency should not be a requisite for political thinkers. Indeed, the Multiple-Traditions Thesis acknowledges the inevitability of inconsistency in the ideas of individuals who have operated within the multiple—and inconsistent—traditions of American political culture. Thus, the way Cady Stanton drew from the different traditions suggests that her thought was profoundly influenced by the multiple strands of thought in American political culture and that she in turn promoted the continued interaction among those traditions. The presence of liberalism, republicanism, ascriptivism, and radicalism in Cady Stanton's ideas supports the Multiple-Traditions Thesis, while the multifaceted combination of different strands of thought also suggests the importance of the fourth category of radicalism in American political thought.

The following chapters proceed chronologically, beginning with Cady Stanton's work in the abolitionist movement and concluding with her death, in 1902. In each chapter, I consider the ways in which she drew from the four traditions of liberalism, republicanism, ascriptive forms of Americanism, and radicalism to formulate her arguments against the background of various political developments and the shifting climate of ideas. I focus throughout on the ways in which the various traditions played different roles in her arguments depending on the subject, the time, and the circumstances. As we will see, Cady Stanton adapted the traditions, using them in a subversive way to serve her goal of improving women's position. Her use of the tradition of ascriptive forms of Americanism is particularly intriguing because she utilized it in a variety of ways—both subversive and normative—applying it not only to challenge the ascribed characteristics of women but also to reinforce ideas of the superiority-inferiority of people on the basis of their race, class, nationality, and religion. Ascriptivism clearly emerges in Cady Stanton's omission of black women in her category of "woman"—something that may have been a result of racial animosity or her own elitist proclivities. In either case, other white activists shared Cady Stanton's attitude. As Rosalyn Terborg-Penn pointed out, throughout the nineteenth century, white activists in the woman's rights movement either openly discriminated against black women or subtly communicated their wish to exclude them and, in so doing, erected major barriers to their participation.[88]

Chapter 2 covers the beginning of the woman's rights movement, when Cady Stanton composed the Declaration of Sentiments for the Seneca Falls Convention and addressed women's rights conventions. Themes that dominated the climate of reform in the 1840s, notably universal human rights and equality and the spiritual development of the individual to improve society, were rooted in liberal individualism and republicanism. Cady Stanton's arguments in the late 1840s reflect the same themes. She appealed to the unfulfilled promise of the American Revolution to secure the inalienable rights of all individuals and to the important obligations of citizenship, including voting. She drew from liberal themes of natural rights and equality to challenge the cult of domesticity by arguing that women were clearly equal to—essentially the same as—men. She supplemented her arguments, nevertheless, with republican assertions of women's duty to participate in public affairs and ascriptive claims of women's moral superiority.

Chapter 3 turns to Cady Stanton's work in the 1850s, when she led the campaign for married women's property rights in New York and argued for divorce reform. She typically relied on liberal principles to support her arguments. Nevertheless, with her analysis of marriage and her avowal of the need for divorce reform, she introduced a radical dimension to her thought. Her attempt to incorporate the women of the temperance movement into the struggle for women's rights illuminates her understanding of the interaction among women's political, legal, and economic disabilities.

In chapter 4, I examine the reactions to the woman's rights movement in the antebellum period and Cady Stanton's responses. Those responses are important because they shed light on the way she challenged the cultural traditions that constrained women's lives—namely the cult of domesticity and the doctrine of separate spheres—while at the same time she relied on those traditions to justify expanding women's rights. In chapter 5, I explore Cady Stanton's work during the Civil War, when she set aside women's rights in order to join the cause of emancipation and Union victory. During the war, her arguments emphasizing women's obligation to participate actively in those causes reflected republican themes. Most important, however, those arguments served to undermine the doctrine of separate spheres, with major implications for the future of the woman's rights movement.

In chapter 6, I move to the period from the conclusion of the Civil War through the 1870s, when Cady Stanton and Anthony took the lead in reviving the woman's rights movement. During this period, Reconstruction politics severed the connection between abolition and women's rights, resulting in the development of an independent movement for women's rights but one that increasingly emphasized suffrage over other issues. As the woman's rights movement began to focus more narrowly on suffrage and attempted to gain respectability by disassociating itself from ideas or movements that were tainted by radicalism, Cady Stanton first disputed that strategy and then began to distance herself from the organized movement for women's rights. Her arguments during this period reflect a more explicitly ascriptive and antidemocratic approach than was evident during the earlier years. The way that she contrasted the virtue, honor, and dignity of women with the ignorance and corruption of black men and male immigrants in her demands for woman suffrage combined elements of republicanism and ascriptivism—indeed, often, outright racism. Still, liberal themes continued to run through her arguments. In chapter 6, I also examine the Positivism of Auguste Comte in order to shed light on the intellectual context in which Cady Stanton was developing her arguments and strategies.

Chapter 7 underlines the radical dimensions of Cady Stanton's work by examining her alliance with labor and her determination to enlighten women about their subordinate position in marriage. Her attempt to work with labor reform suggests her conception of women as a class whose members needed to develop an awareness of themselves as such so that they could unite to work for change. Her analysis of marriage and her prescriptions for change illustrate her conviction that changes in the laws would never be sufficient to eradicate the subordination of women—much more fundamental change would be necessary.

Chapter 8 examines a portion of Cady Stanton's work during the final period of her life, from 1880 until her death in 1902. During this period, she wrote her autobiography and, with Anthony, compiled the first three volumes of *The History of Woman Suffrage*; in addition, in collaboration with several other women, Cady Stanton wrote *The Woman's Bible*. During this final period, she also grew isolated from the increasingly narrowly focused and conservative woman suffrage movement, particularly after the leaders condemned *The Woman's Bible*. Chapter 9 explores the impact of the popular ideas of social Darwinism and Anglo-Saxonism on Cady's Stanton's work during the last twenty years of the nineteenth century.

Cady Stanton's work during the last two decades of her life continued to reflect an interaction among liberal, republican, ascriptive Americanist, and radical arguments. Illiberal, inegalitarian ascriptive strains nevertheless grew more pronounced. Much of her work combined ascriptive elements with what might be viewed as republicanism—particularly her continuing advocacy of an educational qualification for suffrage. Ascriptivism clearly took the leading role, however, as her arguments came to reflect the prejudices of Anglo-Saxonism and the extreme individualism of social Darwinism.

Finally, chapter 10 offers comments on the links between Cady Stanton's ideas and the varieties of feminism in the late twentieth century. The final chapter also pulls together all the strands of Cady Stanton's work and summarizes the argument about the importance of her work to American political thought.

2

Seneca Falls and Beyond

Attacking the Cult of Domesticity with Equality and Inalienable Rights

Introduction

Elizabeth Cady Stanton was the driving force behind the Seneca Falls Convention—the meeting that launched the woman's rights movement in 1848. That gathering marked the beginning of her long career as a leader of the movement, and it was there that she first articulated a set of systematic arguments on behalf of women's rights. During the next dozen years, she prepared addresses for woman's rights conventions, lobbied for married women's property rights in New York State, organized a Conversation Club in Seneca Falls that lasted for several years,[1] was a regular contributor to the temperance journal the *Lily* and to the women's journal the *Una*, wrote articles for newspapers,[2] organized with Susan B. Anthony the Woman's State Temperance Society, and campaigned with Anthony for coeducation.

Cady Stanton's interaction with abolitionists in Peterboro, New York, in the late 1830s, in the British Isles in 1840, and subsequently with the Garrisonians in Boston during the early 1840s played a major role in her early activities and the development of her ideas. So too did her contact with Quaker women, most notably Lucretia Mott, and her exposure to the intellectual life of Boston, including her relationship with the transcendentalists Ralph Waldo Emerson and Theodore Parker. She described Boston as "a kind of moral museum," and reading Parker, she wrote to a friend, "feasts my soul—he speaks to me or rather God (through him) to me."[3] At the same time that she was listening to the ideas of transcendentalism, she was also exposed to the romanticism of Margaret Fuller's ideas as Cady Stanton attended her Conversations in late 1842 and early 1843 on religion, education, and the position of women and subsequently had access to "The Great Lawsuit" when it was published, in 1845.[4]

The all-pervasive cult of domesticity shaped the contours of her early married life. Although she took an avid interest in her husband's political activities, she and Henry Stanton led separate lives—as he first practiced law in Boston while she remained in her parents' home and later when he was frequently away from home for politics or business.[5] She had sole responsibility for running the household and raising their seven children. Her close friendship with Susan B. Anthony, whom she met in the spring of 1851, alleviated Cady Stanton's isolation; Anthony encouraged Cady Stanton to write speeches for the woman's rights conventions, to campaign for married women's property rights, and to attend conventions. Anthony's skills as a strategist and an effective public speaker supplemented her collaborator's more theoretical talents. Later, Cady Stanton described how they complemented each other, despite the disagreements that would mar their friendship in later years:

> In writing we did better work together than either could alone. While she is slow and analytical in composition, I am rapid and synthetic. I am the better writer, she the better critic. She supplied the facts and statistics, I the philosophy and rhetoric, and together we have made arguments that have stood unshaken by the storms of thirty long years.[6]

In this chapter I examine Cady Stanton's work in the early years of the woman's rights movement. I begin by exploring the links between her initial formulation of the arguments for women's rights and the ideas of Garrisonian abolitionism. I then proceed to consider the nature of the arguments she presented at the Seneca Falls Convention and in the address that she delivered later in 1848 to woman's rights conventions. Finally, I examine the position she took regarding the importance of suffrage in the campaign for women's rights. Throughout the chapter I pay particular attention to the way Cady Stanton drew from the available ideological materials, relying as she did on the traditions of liberalism, republicanism, and ascriptive forms of Americanism to challenge the formidable structure of laws, beliefs, and customs that defined women's subordinate status in the nineteenth century. In addition, even her earliest work suggests the radical dimension of her ideas, and I consider that briefly.

Scholars have noted the extent to which early advocates of women's rights, including Cady Stanton, relied on liberal ideas particularly during the early years of the movement.[7] My examination of Cady Stanton's early work underlines the way that she grounded her arguments in liberal claims of equality and natural rights while at the same time supplementing them—often in contradictory ways—with appeals to both republican and ascriptive inegalitarian ideas. The way she drew upon the multiple traditions in shifting combinations in response to a changing climate of ideas will become even more apparent in subsequent chapters. In the present chapter, however, it should become clear that Cady Stanton put the various traditions to her own use—at times reformulating them—with an eye toward convincing a diverse audience ranging from cautious supporters of limited change to improve women's position in the domestic sphere to hostile opponents of reform who ridiculed women's rights advocates.

Garrisonian Abolitionism and Cady Stanton's Early Work

It is well known that Garrisonian abolitionism was a major force in the emergence of the antebellum woman's rights movement.[8] William Lloyd Garrison encouraged women to join the antislavery crusade, initially calling upon them to "form charitable associations to relieve the degraded of their sex."[9] After men organized the American Anti-Slavery Society, in 1833, women began to establish their own female antislavery societies in New England and in the middle Atlantic regions, the largest of which were in Boston, Philadelphia, and New York. Women's initial work in separate female societies was consistent with their activities in female benevolent associations, particularly as many of the antislavery organizations opened schools for free blacks, worked to improve the conditions of poor blacks, and sought to teach them religious values. Women abolitionists also organized antislavery fairs—sales commonly held in conjunction with the men's antislavery meetings—to raise money. Those fairs became a major source of financial support for the abolitionist movement.

Activities such as recruiting other women to abolitionism, teaching, performing benevolent work, and making and selling items at fairs were perceived to be compatible with women's proper role because when women engaged in such activities they provided moral guidance without actually crossing into the forbidden public sphere. Antislavery women, however, soon embarked on activities that took them into the public sphere. Collecting signatures for petitions to send to Congress involved them in public affairs, where, according to the prevailing view, they had no business. Speaking before "promiscuous" audiences of men and women, which the American Anti-Slavery Society endorsed when it agreed to hire women as antislavery agents, was also clearly outside women's proper sphere. The controversy over the Grimké sisters' increasingly popular lectures, and more generally the question of the role that women should play in the antislavery movement, not only provoked outrage among the Congregational clergy in Massachusetts but also became a major issue within the movement. Indeed, the "woman question" split the abolitionist movement in 1840. When a majority of the delegates at the annual meeting of the American Anti-Slavery Society voted to allow women to participate fully in the organization, some three hundred members withdrew to form the American and Foreign Anti-Slavery Society.[10] The latter group, whose members were known as the political abolitionists, abjured Garrison's moral-suasion approach in favor of electoral politics.

Garrisonian abolitionism helped lay the foundation for the subsequent development of the organized movement for women's rights by allowing women who were discontent with the constraints on their lives to expand their sphere without initially appearing to cross forbidden boundaries. Abolitionism did not teach women that they were oppressed, for they were well aware of the extent of their exclusion from politics. What it did do was provide them with the means for organizing a movement around their shared problems and interests.[11] Abolitionism not only provided women with the idea that it was possible to organize for change but also, in the most practical way, gave them valuable experience in holding meetings, fundraising, conducting petition campaigns, and speaking in public.

While the young Elizabeth Cady's parents had no disagreement with temperance and religious benevolence, they regarded the abolitionists as fanatics. Judge Cady went so far as to forbid all discussion of abolition.[12] In contrast, Elizabeth's cousin Gerrit Smith had become a Garrisonian by 1835 and played an important role in the movement, serving as president of the New York chapter of the American Anti-Slavery Society from 1836 to 1839. He provided financial support for the movement, and his house was a station on the Underground Railroad. Although Smith later became a leader of the political abolitionists, he continued to share the Garrisonian criticism of organized religion's failure to condemn slavery and established a local nondenominational abolitionist church in 1843. Elizabeth Cady became acquainted with abolitionism as a frequent guest at Smith's family home in Peterboro in the late 1830s.

Scholars have frequently emphasized that Cady Stanton's activism on behalf of women's rights began with her involvement in the abolitionist movement.[13] Her actual participation in the abolitionist movement, however, was quite limited. She attended the World's Anti-Slavery Convention in 1840 with her husband, who was a delegate, on their honeymoon trip. Later, after Henry Stanton opened a law practice in Boston, she joined him there and during the early 1840s came into contact with a number of prominent abolitionists, including Frederick Douglass, Abby Kelley, Stephen Foster, Parker Pillsbury, and Lydia Maria Child. But even in Garrison's territory she did not assume a leadership role. Elisabeth Griffith, one of Cady Stanton's biographers, noted the absence of evidence that she joined in any reform society during the 1840s. Neither did she participate in Henry's Stanton's abolitionist efforts.[14] She did, however, attend antislavery conventions and fairs and collect signatures on antislavery petitions.[15]

A number of factors are likely to have limited her role. Her family did not approve of her marriage to Henry—not only was he an abolitionist but he had very little in the way of financial prospects. Nevertheless, Daniel Cady allowed Henry Stanton to study law with him and later gave the young couple a house in Boston. Between 1842 and 1845, Cady Stanton divided her time between her parents' home in Albany and the house in Boston. Thus, she may have hesitated to become involved in activities that she was well aware would have created conflict with her father. Also, her husband's work as a political abolitionist presented an obstacle to Cady Stanton. She could not collaborate with her husband because political abolitionism excluded women. She mentioned in 1841 that she had not attended recent business meetings with him "because I knew I would have no voice in those meetings."[16] Henry Stanton chose to practice law in Boston at least in part to challenge Garrison in his own territory. Consequently, although Cady Stanton maintained that she was sufficiently independent to attend the meetings of the Garrisonian American Anti-Slavery Society regardless of her husband's wishes,[17] if she had taken a more active role it would surely have been a source of conflict in her marriage. Moreover, Cady Stanton was preoccupied with domestic concerns during this time—she had three sons between 1842 and 1845.

Possibly the most important reason that Cady Stanton did not become more involved in abolitionism was that her primary concern was always women's rights. She described her reaction to the exclusion of women from the World's Anti-Slavery Convention as "fresh baptism into women's degradation."[18] Her conversations with Lucretia Mott in London and her interaction with the Grimké sisters by her own account heightened her awareness that other women shared her perception of women's position as unjust and encouraged her to begin to think about how she might work for change.[19] She wrote to a friend in 1841 that in England she "found many many women fully & painfully convinced of our present degradation as women."[20] Cady Stanton presents a clear contrast to prominent abolitionist women like Lucretia Mott, Sarah and Angelina Grimké, and Abby Kelley, who were prompted by deeply felt religious convictions to join the Garrisonian crusade to bring an end to the sin of slavery. Such women defended their right to speak out against slavery in the face of fierce opposition from both within the movement and outside it, emphasizing that women had both an obligation and a right to participate in the movement in order to defend the rights of the slaves. They were thus led to begin to argue more generally for women's emancipation from the limited sphere of home and family and to view the campaign for women's rights as part of abolitionism's broader struggle for human rights.

In contrast, Cady Stanton came to abolitionism through her cousin and then through her husband. The fight against slavery and the controversy over women's role in the movement served to enhance her already intense interest in women's rights and encouraged her to explore the possibilities for organizing women to seek change. Her differences from abolitionist women notwithstanding, Cady Stanton's connection to the abolitionist movement played a central role in the development of her arguments on behalf of women's rights. She relied heavily on Garrisonian ideas as she began to devise ways to challenge women's subordination. Anticlericalism, egalitarianism, and a theory of social change were theoretical aspects of Garrisonian abolitionism that were crucial to the emergence of the early woman's rights movement and were especially important to Cady Stanton.[21] Thus, they provide a useful starting point for considering the link between Cady Stanton's early work on behalf of women's rights and the ideas of the abolitionist movement.

First, Garrisonian abolitionism was fundamentally religious, and Garrison initially adopted the leadership style of a minister. Nevertheless, his natural-rights philosophy and his commitment to the doctrines of perfectionism and nonresistance prompted him to condemn the church as one of the corrupt institutions that allowed slavery to exist. He questioned clerical authority to govern congregations, repudiated the institution of the Sabbath, and criticized the Bible, declaring that not everything in it was divinely inspired. Cady Stanton found Garrison's anticlericalism consistent with her own feelings about organized religion, which were a result of her earlier experiences with revivalism. Although her anticlericalism would later become a more prominent facet of Cady Stanton's thought, in the early 1840s Garrison's attack on the churches encouraged her to challenge religious doctrines that supported women's subordinate status.

Second, for the Garrisonians, the equality of all human beings was one of the foremost principles of morality, and that principle provided women with a doctrine that they could use to challenge the ideology of separate spheres.[22] The Garrisonians developed their egalitarian doctrine from a number of sources, including the Bible, principles of natural law, and the Declaration of Independence. Drawing on the same sources, Cady Stanton used the Garrisonian notion of equality as a model for her own arguments, utilizing the abolitionist principle of human equality to develop a theory of women's equality. Initially drawn to Garrison for his behavior during the World's Anti-Slavery Convention when he sat with the women in their curtained-off area and remained silent as they were required to do, she praised him as an advocate of " 'Human Rights' not black man's merely."[23] She then went further to develop the legal claim that women deserved the equal protection of their individual rights out of the Garrisonian claim of moral equality. Such arguments, which drew predominantly on liberal political ideas revolving around the principles of natural rights and equality, ran through her work during these early years.

Cady Stanton, like other women's rights activists, made frequent use of the parallel between women and slaves that Garrisonian women initiated in the 1830s.[24] Her letter to the Ohio Women's Convention in 1850 captured the logic of the analogy.

A married woman has no legal existence; she has no more absolute rights than a slave on a Southern plantation. She takes the name of her master, holds nothing, owns nothing, can bring no action in her own name; and the principles on which she and the slave is educated is the same. The slave is taught what is considered best for him to know—which is nothing; the woman is taught what is best for her to know—which is little more than nothing; man being the umpire in both cases. A woman cannot follow out the impulses of her own immortal mind in her sphere, any further than the slave can in his sphere. Civilly, socially, and religiously, she is what man chooses her to be—nothing more or less—and such is the slave.[25]

Making use of that parallel again in 1856, she asserted that women commonly accepted their oppression because they could not conceive of any "way of escape. Her bondage, though it differs from that of the negro slave, frets and chafes her just the same. She too sighs and groans in her chains; and lives but in the hope of better things to come. She looks to heaven; whilst the more philosophical slave sets out for Canada."[26]

The parallel between woman and slave had a strategic as well as a theoretical dimension for Cady Stanton. It served as a rhetorical device to heighten women's awareness of their own oppression, to arouse their indignation, and to suggest that there was a remedy. In short, the woman-slave parallel would help bring women into the movement. Moreover, the parallel conveyed the idea that male opponents of slavery should also oppose the oppression of women, thus alluding to the prospect of garnering support for women's rights among antislavery men.

Her use of the parallel also illustrates how she adapted the Garrisonian concept of the equality of all humans, transforming it into an argument for legal rights for women. She pointed out that woman's degraded position, like the slave's, violated principles of natural rights and equality. It is important to note that Cady Stanton's rhetorical comparison between women and slaves explicitly referred to male slaves. The image of a white woman in the same degraded position as a black male seems to have been particularly repugnant to a white audience. Even more important, however, her failure to rely on the trope of abolitionist women's bond with female slaves was an early indication of the multifaceted way in which she would subsequently employ ascriptivism in her later arguments. Her failure to include female slaves in her condemnation of the position of women also suggests the extent to which Cady

Stanton would later construct arguments that would appeal primarily to white, educated, Protestant women.

The third aspect of Garrisonian abolitionism that served as an impetus for the woman's rights movement and that Cady Stanton found useful was a theory of social change positing that institutional and legal change could not occur until there had been a major change at the individual level. In Garrison's view, political and legal institutions were corrupt, and participation in the political process required morally unacceptable compromise. Thus, the Garrisonians demanded an immediate end to slavery as a moral necessity and set about achieving their goal by convincing individuals that slavery was wrong. Focusing entirely on moral suasion, they refused to participate in electoral politics and did not develop any plan for institutional or legal change. That Cady Stanton adopted the notion that a change in people's attitudes must precede institutional change is evidenced by her determination to focus public attention on women's oppression—she was the one who, more than any other women's rights reformer, developed the strategy of agitation.[27]

The power of the political parties in the United States government and the fact that neither party took a position against slavery reinforced the Garrisonian conviction that government and politics were corrupt. Consequently, Garrisonian women tended not to perceive the vote as particularly useful. It was on this matter that Cady Stanton most sharply disagreed with the Garrisonians. She applauded the Liberty Party and questioned the Garrisonian approach. In a letter to abolitionist Elizabeth J. Neall in 1841, she wrote:

> The question of no civil government is so great a one that I cannot decide upon it just now . . . taking it then for granted that civil government [is?] right—it is important that our good men should regulate this government, now our abolitionists are the best men in our country, & I should be unwilling that as a body they should exert no political influence. Slavery is a political question created & sustained by law, & must be put down by law. One great advantage of forming a party over that of scatteration is that in voting the abolitionists show their numbers, & make our corrupt politicians fear & tremble. There is great danger on the other hand of abolitionists themselves being corrupted, but it would take many years methinks to make them as a party so corrupt as either of our great national parties now are.[28]

She was more explicit about the need for abolitionists—"the best men" —to vote when she wrote in early 1842, "So long as we are to be governed by human laws, I should be unwilling to have the making & administering of those laws left entirely to the selfish & unprincipled part of the community, which would be the case should all our honest men, refuse to mingle in political affairs."[29]

Cady Stanton's path diverged sharply from the Garrisonian no-government approach when she demanded the franchise for women and lobbied for legal reform. It is possible to overlook the Garrisonian influence by focusing on the importance of the Declaration of Independence in Cady Stanton's assertion that the theory of natural rights and equality applies to women as well as men. But Garrisonian reform was so much a part of Cady Stanton's life during the late 1830s and throughout the 1840s—she wrote in her autobiography that in Boston all of her immediate friends were reformers[30]—that it seems surely to have been an important and direct force in the development of her ideas. What Cady Stanton took from Garrisonianism was singularly liberal, grounded as it was in the superiority of the moral individual over corrupt government and human-made law.

Her use of the comparison between male slaves and white women provided an early suggestion of one dimension of the ascriptivism that would become increasingly prominent in her work through the years. Cady Stanton also took the ascriptive notion that women were inferior to men and adapted it to develop the argument that white women were at least the equals of white men and superior to "other" women and men—that is to people of other races, nationalities, and classes.

She also introduced a republican element in her arguments when she demanded that women be allowed to become fully participating members in the political community, with the ability to fulfill their obligations as virtuous citizens. Suzanne Marilley pointed out an important connection between Garrisonian abolitionism and the ideology of republican motherhood: "As republican mothers—moral authorities who taught the values of equality and liberty to their children—women were well prepared to assist Garrison. His strategy and message applied the practice of republican motherhood to public antislavery reform; the only difference was that Garrison, a man, was its practitioner."[31] Those who practiced Garrisonian abolitionism were, in short, putting republican motherhood into practice. Like republican mothers who imparted the correct moral values to their sons but did not participate directly in politics, Garrisonian abolitionists were moral individuals who did not compromise their principles by involving themselves in politics. Garrison's no-government approach, like republican motherhood, would thus allow women to expand their sphere in limited ways—participating in antislavery reform, for example—but would not challenge the exclusion of women from the franchise. The Garrisonian refusal to participate in electoral politics would leave governing to men. Realizing that women could achieve their liberal goals of securing their natural rights and equality only if they had the ability to fulfill their republican obligations as virtuous citizens, Cady Stanton rejected the aspect of Garrisonianism that would have left intact the obstacles to women's entry into electoral politics.

Cady Stanton's departure from the Garrisonian rejection of politics was consistent with the turn that many moral reformers took toward elections and institutions in the late 1840s as they grew increasingly disillusioned with moral suasion.[32] Prominently displayed in the public statements she made in the 1850s along with the demand for the ballot were her efforts to convince legislators to give married women control of their property, to restrict the sale of liquor, and to permit wives to divorce intemperate husbands. Her keen interest in and awareness of the political developments of the 1850s—the collapse of the old party system of Whigs and Democrats, the realignment of the parties around the issue of slavery, the emergence of the Republican Party, the series of compromises enacted by Congress that did virtually nothing to resolve the heightening sectional conflict over slavery, and John Brown's raid on Harper's Ferry—surface in her letters. She wrote to Susan B. Anthony in 1852 criticizing Amelia Bloomer for not speaking against the Fugitive Slave Law.[33] In 1855, she wrote—again to Anthony—that she was attending "all the Republican meetings" and applauded the fact that her husband had joined the Republican movement.[34] She also commented on actions in Congress regarding the deepening sectional conflict.[35] In 1856, she expressed her view that the "staving off" policy should end and that she was "becoming more and more convinced that we shall be in the midst of violence, blood, and civil war before we look for it. Our fair republic must be the victim of the monster, slavery, unless we speedily rise in our might and boldly shout freedom."[36] In 1859, she lamented the hanging of John Brown, describing him as "grand and glorious."[37] In 1860, she wrote to Anthony of the "dreadful state of things at our national capital," asking, "Is there no way you and I can get an oar in there?"[38]

The Seneca Falls Convention: The Multiple Traditions and the Challenge to the Cult of Domesticity

The Stanton family moved from Boston to Seneca Falls, New York, in 1847 and it was there that Cady Stanton's and Lucretia Mott's plan to organize a woman's rights convention—conceived in 1840 or 1841— finally came to fruition.[39] Five women, including Cady Stanton and Mott, met in Waterloo, New York, in July 1848 and agreed to call a two-day convention.[40] Cady Stanton provided the crucial impetus for the effort, and she assumed primary responsibility for drafting the Declaration of Sentiments.

According to the *History of Woman Suffrage,* when Cady Stanton and the others embarked on the task of writing the Declaration of Sentiments, feeling as "hopeless as if they had been suddenly asked to construct a steam engine," they examined "various masculine productions." Finding the reports of antislavery, temperance, and peace conventions "too tame . . . for the inauguration of a rebellion such as the world had never before seen," they turned to the Declaration of Independence at Cady Stanton's suggestion.[41] They did, however, borrow the title of their founding document from William Lloyd Garrison's Declaration of Sentiments, which the American Anti-Slavery Society adopted in 1833.

Modeled closely on the Declaration of Independence, the Declaration of Sentiments began by announcing the necessity "for one portion of the family of man to assume among the people of the earth a position different from that which they have hitherto occupied, but one to which the laws of nature and of nature's God entitle them." It was a self-evident truth "that all men and women are created equal; that they are endowed by their Creator with certain inalienable rights; that among these are life, liberty, and the pursuit of happiness."[42] Following its model, the Declaration of Sentiments provided a list of grievances, with "Man" replacing the King as the tyrant who was responsible for the injustices. The grievances enumerated the "repeated injuries and usurpations on the part of man over woman, having in direct object the establishment of an absolute tyranny over her." They outlined the ways that men had deprived women of their natural rights and were followed by a set of resolutions reiterating the claim that everything the women were asking for was based on the natural right to pursue happiness and on women's natural equality to men and outlining the demands for redress of the wrongs that men had inflicted on them.

The value of Cady Stanton's choice of the Declaration of Independence as the model for the Declaration of Sentiments lay in the way it connected the woman's rights movement to the American Revolution, thereby lending the campaign for women's rights legitimacy and respectability. Moreover, the connection with the fight for independence from England emphasized the liberal nature of women's rights reform and minimized its most far-reaching implications insofar as it established that women were only seeking the rights for which men had fought. Because those rights had been withheld from women, the commitments of the Revolution remained unfulfilled. The remedy was simple: recognize that women are endowed with the same natural rights as men and reform the laws accordingly. Such reform would be entirely consistent with the goals of the American Revolution and the social order, as well as with American institutions and values. In short, the rhetoric of the American Revolution grounded woman's rights firmly in the liberal tradition of natural rights and equality—a tradition with which all Americans were familiar and with which it seemed to Cady Stanton and her colleagues there was little disagreement.

Every aspect of women's subordination that Cady Stanton detailed in the grievances and resolutions was fully supported by law and custom. As noted in chapter 1, the ideas of republican motherhood, which emerged after the Revolution, had by the 1840s become the cult of domesticity—an ideology that defined women's existence in rigid terms, drawing strict boundaries around their lives. According to the prevailing view, limiting women's lives to domestic pursuits was fully congruent with their natural capacities.

The cult of domesticity revolved around the idea that men and women were naturally so different that it was imperative for them to perform distinct functions. That thoroughgoing belief in natural differences provided a justification for the exclusion of women from politics and for the legal traditions that treated women essentially as the property of their husbands and fathers. The cult of domesticity fully supported women's exclusion from professions to which they had previously had some access. The professionalization of law and medicine, with the introduction of formal educational requirements, licensing, and professional societies, created an insurmountable barrier for nearly all women. Teaching was one career that was open to women because it was consistent with their alleged natural ability to care for children and to shape their character. Indeed, teaching opportunities for women were expanding in 1848. Women teachers, however, were invariably paid less than men were, and that too, was justified by the cult of domesticity. In order to support their arguments in favor of training women to be educators, reformers often pointed to the low cost of employing female teachers. When Catharine Beecher asked Congress for funding for women's training in the 1850s, assumptions about women's natural differences and their proper role ran through her argument. She also emphasized the financial advantages in that "women can afford to teach for one-half, or even less, the salary which men would ask, because the female teacher has only to sustain herself; she does not look forward to the duty of supporting a family, should she marry, nor has she the ambition to amass a fortune."[43] In addition, the increase in educational opportunities for women in female seminaries and at Oberlin College fit squarely within the framework of the separate spheres. Female education was justified as a means for improving women's ability to be good wives—the educational institutions required women to prepare themselves for the future by performing domestic chores—and guardians of the nation's youth. Organized religion's adamant opposition to allowing women a voice in the church was also consistent with the prevailing belief in natural differences between the sexes. In short, with the grievances and resolutions she presented in the Declaration of Sentiments, Cady Stanton directly confronted the ascriptive ideology of domesticity.

Historians have emphasized that the doctrine of separate spheres played an important role in the development of a women's culture that provided a basis for resistance to male dominance.[44] Although they differ on the nature of the relationship between women's culture and what eventually came to be called feminism, scholars generally agree that associations of women—whether in friendships, benevolent organizations, schools, or textile mills—were crucial to the development of a group consciousness among women. Limited as they were to their separate sphere, women began to claim a positive social role for themselves. An awareness of themselves as part of a group, a perception that they had a social role, and dissatisfaction with the limitations of their separate sphere eventually led women to organize for change. The cult of domesticity, in short, "contained within itself the preconditions for the organized woman's movement."[45]

Although they may not have been possible without the cult of domesticity that produced women's culture, the Seneca Falls Convention and the Declaration of Sentiments represented a repudiation of the idealized version of domesticity and of the notion that women could improve their position within a separate women's culture. With the Declaration of Sentiments, Cady Stanton revealed man's "absolute tyranny" over woman as the hidden reality behind the sentimentalized depiction of the selfless, serene "true woman" who found fulfillment in home and motherhood. Her goal in 1848 was to destroy the deeply embedded ascriptive belief in sexual differences and to replace it with the liberal principle of natural rights and equality. In other words, she rejected ascriptivist arguments and embraced the liberal vision of equality. Even so, her challenge to the ideology of domesticity did not constitute an attack on every aspect of the ideology of separate spheres. Neither did she reject every aspect of ascriptivism.

The grievances and resolutions of the Declaration of Sentiments covered the range of political, legal, and customary sources of women's subordination in all realms of life. The first four grievances and the ninth resolution addressed the exclusion of women from political life. Man had refused woman her inalienable right to vote, thereby depriving her of representation and requiring her to obey laws in the making of which she had no role. To her argument based on natural rights and equality Cady Stanton added an ascriptivist theme: man had withheld from woman "rights which are given to the most ignorant and degraded men—both natives and foreigners." She also introduced the republican theme of civic virtue, stating that man had deprived woman of "this first right as a citizen," thereby leaving her without representation. The ninth resolution also introduced the republican notion of civic virtue by linking the vote with citizenship, proclaiming that women had a duty to secure their "sacred right to the elective franchise."

Several of the resolutions emphasized women's natural equality and their right to happiness. Women's equal rights were intended "by the Creator," and any laws that did not protect those rights had no validity. According to the second resolution, for example, "all laws which prevent woman from occupying such a station in society as her conscience shall dictate, or which place her in a position inferior to that of man, are contrary to the great precept of nature, and therefore of no force or authority." Similarly, the tenth resolution proclaimed "that the equality of human rights results necessarily from the fact of the identity of the race in capabilities and responsibilities."

The fifth, sixth, and seventh grievances condemned the legal status of married women, challenging the common-law tradition that rendered a married woman, "in the eye of the law, civilly dead." She had no right to property, even her own wages; the law made a husband legally responsible for a crime his wife committed in his presence and rendered woman, "morally, an irresponsible being." Moreover, a wife's promise to obey allowed her husband to become her master, "the law giving him power to deprive her of her liberty, and to administer chastisement." The eighth grievance pointed out that divorce laws and rules concerning guardianship of children were framed by men, "going upon the false supposition of the supremacy of man, and giving all power into their hands." The ninth grievance turned to single women, who, although they could own property, were taxed without representation. All of these grievances focused on the laws that failed to respect women's equality and natural rights and were echoed in the several resolutions that proclaimed that women had the same right to happiness and the same capabilities and responsibilities as men.

The tenth and eleventh grievances turned to the absence of employment opportunities for women, charging that man had "monopolized nearly all the profitable employments" and "closed against [them] all the avenues of wealth and distinction." Moreover, when women were able to obtain employment, they were offered but "scanty remuneration." The twelfth grievance noted that women were denied an education, as colleges did not admit them.[46]

The thirteenth grievance targeted organized religion, charging that men had relegated women to a subordinate position within the church, excluding them from the ministry and from participation in church affairs. Identifying "the perverted application of the Scriptures" as a source of constraints on women, the eighth resolution charged that women should "move in the enlarged sphere which [their] great creator has assigned [them]." The fifth resolution, introduced the ascriptivist argument that, because of women's moral superiority, it was men's duty to encourage them to participate in all religious assemblies.

The fourteenth grievance pointed to the double standard in morality, condemning the rules "by which moral delinquencies which exclude women from society, are not only tolerated but deemed of little account in man." The sixth resolution reiterated the same theme, but with more emphasis on the natural equality between men and women: "That the same amount of virtue, delicacy, and refinement of behavior, that is required of woman in the social state, should also be required of man, and the same transgressions should be visited with equal severity on both man and woman." The seventh resolution also alluded to men's hypocrisy, charging that women should not be criticized for speaking in public by "those who encourage by their attendance, [their] appearance on the stage, in the concert, or in the feats of the circus."

The fifteenth and sixteenth grievances repudiated men's claim to the authority to control women's lives, "to assign for [them] a sphere of action" and to "destroy [their] confidence in [their] own powers, to lessen [their] self-respect, and to make [them] willing to lead a dependant [*sic*] and abject life." The final resolution made a sweeping statement emphasizing women's natural equality and introduced the republican theme of woman's duty to participate with men to

> promote every righteous cause, by every righteous means; and especially in regard to the great subjects of morals and religion, it is self-evidently her right to participate with her brother in teaching them, both in private and in public, by writing and by speaking, by any instrumentalities proper to be used, and in any assemblies proper to be held; and this being a self-evident truth, growing out of the divinely implanted principles of human nature, any custom or authority adverse to it, whether modern or wearing the hoary sanction of antiquity, is to be regarded as self-evident falsehood, and at war with the interests of mankind.

The prevailing view that women's unique nature rendered them incapable of functioning in the public sphere justified the laws and customs that kept women in a subordinate position. In the Declaration of Sentiments, Cady Stanton took the opportunity to challenge that view of women's nature, proclaiming repeatedly that women were endowed with the same natural rights as men. She argued that liberal principles of natural rights and equality and republican obligations of citizenship mandated that the artificial constraints on women's lives be removed and demanded an end to the male monopoly in the public sphere.

The rhetoric of the Declaration of Sentiments was overwhelmingly liberal, yet, as we have seen, Cady Stanton also included republican allusions to women's duty to participate in public life. Although there was very little that was ascriptive in that document, there was the one objection to women's being placed below degraded and ignorant men and the assertion of woman's moral superiority that rendered them particularly well suited for participating in the affairs of religion and morals.

Cady Stanton's willingness to delve deeply into the cultural norms that determined women's separate and subordinate status suggested that in 1848 she was already beginning to move outside the bounds of liberalism, republicanism, and ascriptivism to a radical strain of thought. Her criticism of the church and religion as a source of women's subordination, in particular, portended the radical critique of the church and the Bible that she was to develop in later years. Moreover, she issued a challenge in the fourth grievance, that women become enlightened about the laws under which they live "that they may no longer publish their degradation, by declaring themselves satisfied with their present position, nor their ignorance, by asserting that they have all the rights they want." That challenge represented the seed of a radical theme that she would develop much more fully a few years later in her responses to the opponents of women's rights when she would suggest that women constitute a class in need of developing an understanding of its degraded position.

Seneca Falls and the Sacred Right of the Elective Franchise

The demand for woman suffrage was the most controversial proposal at the Seneca Falls Convention. Lucretia Mott advised Cady Stanton not to include the resolution, and it was the only motion that did not receive the unanimous support of the convention.[47] With Cady Stanton's support and the endorsement of Frederick Douglass, the resolution passed by a small majority. The demand for the vote is often viewed as the most radical of all the claims advanced at the Seneca Falls Convention insofar as it challenged the assumption of male authority over women and "raised the prospect of female autonomy in a way that other claims to equal rights could not."[48] Woman suffrage had the potential to bring major change to the ideology that relegated women to the domestic sphere. With the vote, women would not only be able to participate in public affairs but also be able to work for passage of laws that would bring an end to women's exclusion from the professions and education and that would improve their position in marriage. Although suffrage had radical implications, Cady Stanton framed the call for the enfranchisement of women in predominately liberal terms—women had the same right to participate in politics as men. She also added the republican theme of women's duty to participate in public life and the ascriptivist claim that women's moral superiority would improve the political life of the nation.

The appeal for the ballot distinguished the Seneca Falls Convention and Cady Stanton's contribution from earlier arguments for women's rights. Advocates of women's rights who preceded Cady Stanton and with whose ideas she was familiar, including Mary Wollstonecraft, Frances Wright, the Grimké sisters, and Margaret Fuller, had stopped short of demanding the franchise for women.[49] In her *Vindication of the Rights of Woman*, published in 1792 in England, Wollstonecraft argued that improved education for women would allow them to develop their potential and to refute the prevailing view that they were naturally inferior to men. She presented her case within the framework of the separate spheres, however, emphasizing that educated women would make superior wives and mothers. As for the possibility of political equality, she conceded that she was likely "to excite laughter, by dropping an hint, which I mean to pursue, some future time, for I really think that women ought to have representatives, instead of being arbitrarily governed without having any direct share allowed them in the deliberations of government."[50]

Frances Wright was an educational and urban reformer, public lecturer, newspaper editor, and founder of Nashoba in Tennessee, a communal experiment in gradual emancipation that allowed slaves to earn their freedom through their own labor. Active in the 1820s, she contended "that the mind has no sex" and argued that women should have equal educational opportunities and equality under law. She also asserted that married women should have control over their own property and be the beneficiaries of easier divorce laws. Wright developed a utopian scheme for education the goal of which was "to wipe out inequality of class and sex and to regenerate society."[51] Involved in organizing workingmen, Wright was well aware of the importance of political organization but did not propose that women should have the right to vote.

The Grimkés, who so resolutely defended women's right to participate in the abolitionist movement, did not extend their claims about women's equal humanity, rights, and obligations to contribute to the crusade against slavery to women's right to the franchise. As noted earlier, Garrisonian women like the Grimké sisters and Abby Kelley, who were committed to moral suasion as a means to end slavery, did not place particular value on voting, as they, like Garrison, believed governmental institutions and processes to be inherently corrupt.

The transcendentalist Margaret Fuller, who conducted discussion sessions for women and published *Woman in the Nineteenth Century*, in 1845, condemned the traditions that confined women to the roles of wife and mother and rendered them dependent on men. She argued that the restrictions on women's lives obstructed their growth as human beings and precluded them from realizing their full potential. Arbitrary barriers needed to be thrown down, she proclaimed. Women needed to free themselves from domination by men; they needed equality in education and employment, and the institution of marriage needed to be reformed to make it a union of two independent and equal beings. As a transcendentalist, Fuller emphasized women's free and independent inner growth. Women needed to be free to develop in their own way—"as a nature to grow as an intellect to discern, as a soul to live freely, and unimpeded to unfold such powers as were given her when we left our common home."[52] Fuller envisioned a future in which men would have achieved their own self-reliance and would welcome independence in women. Fuller's romantic vision of the self-development of the individual genius of women was important to Cady Stanton, even though Fuller was concerned not with organizing for political or legal reform or participating in public affairs but rather with the spiritual development of the individual.[53]

Reiterating the Challenge: The 1848 Address on Women's Rights

Cady Stanton delivered her first address on women's rights in September 1848. She identified that address as one "delivered several times immediately after the first Woman's Rights Convention."[54] She took aim at the cult of domesticity in that address with the same determination as she had in the Declaration of Sentiments. Challenging the claim of male intellectual superiority, she pointed out that women had not had a fair trial and that only "When we shall have had our colleges, our professions, our trades, for a century a comparison may then be justly instituted."[55] She challenged the claim of male physical superiority on the same grounds: "Physically, as well as intellectually, it is use that produces growth and development."[56] She also observed the absence of a connection between the "power of mind" and the "size and strength of body."[57] The behavior of leaders of religious and governmental institutions, she noted, contradicted man's claim to moral superiority, and she ventured that man was "infinitely woman's inferior in every moral virtue" although only by a "false education."[58]

Confronting the idealized "true woman" whose purity would be lost if she were to participate in politics, Cady Stanton proclaimed, "The false ideas that prevail with regard to the purity necessary to constitute the perfect character in woman, and that requisite for man have done an infinite deal of mischief in the world. We would not have woman less pure, but we would have man more so. We would have the same code of morals for both."[59] To those who might object that the alleged differences between men and women did not amount to a claim of male superiority, Cady Stanton rejoined, "but you will find by following them up closely that they make this difference to be vastly in favour of man."[60]

Liberal claims of individual rights and natural equality were a major theme in Cady Stanton's challenge to the cult of domesticity in that address. She made clear that her primary concern was the exclusion of women from politics:

> But we did assemble to protest against a form of government, existing without the consent of the governed, to declare our right to be free as man is free—to be represented in the government which we are taxed to support—to have such disgraceful laws as give man the power to chastise and imprison his wife—to take the wages which she earns,—the property which she inherits, and, in case of separation the children of her love—laws which make her the mere dependent on his bounty—it was to protest against such unjust laws as these and to have them if possible forever erased from our statute books, deeming them a standing shame and disgrace to a professedly republican people in the nineteenth century.[61]

Although liberal arguments dominated Cady Stanton's attack on the system of customs, beliefs, and laws that guaranteed women's subordinate status, republican themes were also present. She advanced the republican notion that an excessive concentration of power leads to tyranny—in this case, men's monopoly on power has led to tyranny against women—that is inconsistent with the health of the community and destroys the liberty of its citizens. Specifically, she alluded to the interdependence of all members of the "human family," attributing the moral stagnation—"War, slavery, drunkenness, licentiousness and gluttony"—to the degradation of women:

> The voice of woman has been silenced. But man cannot fulfill his destiny alone—he cannot redeem his race unaided, there are deep and tender chords of sympathy and love in the breasts of the down fallen the crushed that woman can touch more skillfully than man. The earth has never yet seen a truly great and virtuous nation, for woman has never yet stood the equal with man. (As with nations so with families. It is the wise mother who has the wise son, and it requires but little thought to decide that as long as the women of this nation remain but half developed in mind and body, so long shall we have a succession of men decrepit in body and soul, so long as your women are mere slaves, you may throw your colleges and churches to the wind, there is no material to work upon, . . . the wife is degraded—made a mere creature of his caprice and now the foolish son is heaviness to his heart. . . . God in his wisdom has so linked together the whole human family that any violence done at one end of the chain is felt throughout its length.)[62]

An inegalitarian ascriptive theme also emerged in the way she lamented the fact that inferior, incapable men—"the most ignorant Irishman in the ditch"—possessed the rights that women were denied.[63] In the natural aristocracy of virtue and talents that Thomas Jefferson described, her comments implied, women would vote. The present system was more akin to the artificial aristocracy that Jefferson condemned as "a mischievous ingredient in government"[64] insofar as it elevated all men—including the least capable—without regard to their qualifications. Cady Stanton condemned the artificial aristocracy of sex where the rights of "ignorant Irishmen" and "drunkards, idiots, horse-racing, rum selling rowdies, ignorant foreigners, and silly boys" were fully recognized, while women were "thrust out from all that belong to citizens . . . [as] too grossly insulting to the dignity of woman to be longer quietly submitted to."[65]

That ascriptive language was consistent with the prejudices of the nineteenth century; it was also indicative of the elite composition of the antebellum woman's rights movement. Thus, Cady Stanton drew on the tradition of ascriptive Americanisms to challenge women's subordination by claiming that women (at least some women) were superior to certain men—those of different nationalities, customs, and classes. That language also served to draw attention to the hypocrisy of men who declared their commitment to republican principles at the same time that they betrayed those principles by maintaining their tyranny over women. She clarified her point in an address she composed several years later:

> Can it be that here, where we acknowledge no royal blood, no apostolic descent, that you, who have declared that all men were created equal— that governments derive their just powers from the consent of the governed, would willingly build up an aristocracy that places the ignorant and vulgar above the educated and refined—the alien and the ditch-digger above the authors and poets of the day—an aristocracy that would raise the sons above the mothers that bore them?[66]

Thus, for Cady Stanton, the liberal principles of natural rights and equality, as well as the republican concern with the destructive effects of an excessive concentration of power, required that women be included in the political life of the nation. At the same time, however, she drew on ascriptivism to draw attention to inequalities among men, arguing that such inequalities justified the exclusion of the undeserving and the incompetent. At any rate, Cady Stanton's willingness to combine republican and intolerant ascriptive elements with liberal claims of universal rights and equality to challenge women's subordinate status was already discernible in her first address on women's rights.

Beyond 1848: The Woman's Rights Movement in the 1850s

A second woman's rights convention convened in Rochester only two weeks after the Seneca Falls Convention, but the next gathering—in Salem, Ohio—did not take place for a year and a half. Then, from 1850 through 1860, national woman's rights conventions were held every year except 1857.[67] The organization of the antebellum woman's rights movement was marked by its informality.[68] Although there were several state societies and numerous local groups, there was no permanent national organization during the 1850s. A largely self-appointed, shifting group of women served on a coordinating or steering committee known as the Central Committee. An annually appointed president took responsibility for organizing the annual conventions.[69] In addition to those conventions, reformers organized petition and lobbying campaigns for legal reform, wrote for the periodicals that supported the movement—the abolitionist publications, and the *Lily,* the *Una,* the *Woman's Advocate,* and the *Sybil*—and spoke frequently on the lecture circuit, as well as at conventions. The movement was financially and promotionally dependent on the Garrisonian abolitionists. Indeed, the most reliable and visible support came from abolitionist women.[70]

The leaders deliberately elected not to have a formal organization. In fact, the National Woman's Rights Convention in 1852 rejected a proposal to create a national society. Angelina Grimké Weld sent a letter expressing her objections to artificial organizations that "do not protect the sacredness of the individual" and that would be a "burden, a clog, an incumbrance, rather than a help."[71] Lucy Stone said that they all dreaded permanent organizations, noting that she had "had enough of thumb-screws and soul screws ever to wish to be placed under them again."[72] A resolution that the convention did approve, however, encouraged women to organize yearly meetings in their states and counties.

A core of leaders linked by ties of personal friendship and common experience in other reform work included Lucretia Mott, Lucy Stone, Antoinette Brown,[73] Harriot Hunt, Paulina Wright Davis, Frances Dana Gage, Clarina Howard Nichols, and Ernestine Rose. Formerly involved in abolitionism and temperance, Susan B. Anthony became active in the woman's rights movement in 1852. According to Sylvia D. Hoffert, fourteen women and nine men who had the time, energy, money, and commitment to participate in at least three national conventions between 1848 and 1860 constituted the vanguard of the antebellum movement.[74] The antebellum woman's rights movement was made up of middle-class, relatively well-educated, white, and native-born women;[75] they were not, as Gerda Lerner pointed out, the most downtrodden but rather the most status-deprived group. They did not speak for the more exploited and oppressed factory workers or black women.[76]

The disputes that divided the post–Civil War woman's rights movement had not yet surfaced in the 1850s. Indeed, there was very little public disagreement among the leaders of the antebellum movement regarding goals and strategy. The conventions throughout the 1850s continued to present essentially the same resolutions that were formulated at Seneca Falls. According to Eleanor Flexner, the early movement was not as concerned with suffrage as it was with women's property rights, guardianship, divorce, educational and employment opportunities, women's unequal legal status, and the pervasive concept of female inferiority perpetuated by established religion.[77] Although some of the leaders downplayed suffrage as the defining goal of the movement in the mid-1850s, a resolution demanding the franchise for women was presented at every convention from 1848 through 1860. One of the resolutions adopted at the national convention in 1856, for example, proclaimed "that the main power of the woman's rights movement lies in this: that while always demanding for women better education, better employment, and better laws, it has kept steadily in view the one cardinal demand for the right of suffrage: in a democracy, the symbol and guarantee of all other rights."[78]

The Importance of Suffrage

As Cady Stanton developed her arguments for suffrage, she drew extensively from both republican and ascriptive traditions, blending them with liberal doctrine. The way she formulated her arguments not only illuminates the extent to which she relied on and combined the three traditions but also sheds light on the relationship between her ideas and those of other prominent leaders of the antebellum woman's rights movement.

Cady Stanton was severely constrained by domestic responsibilities during the 1850s. She added four children to her family between 1851 and 1859, and her husband was frequently away from home on legal or political business. She wrote to Susan B. Anthony in 1856 of pacing up and down her room like a caged lioness, "longing to bring nursing and housekeeping cares to a close."[79] Although she was unable to attend a woman's rights convention until 1860, all of the conventions in the 1850s opened with a letter that she had written for the occasion. In most of those letters, she highlighted the importance of the franchise, arguing that suffrage should be given the highest priority because it was a prerequisite to securing all other rights. Thus, she recommended to the Ohio convention in 1850 that women's rights reformers petition first for the right to vote:

> [N]othing short of this. The grant to you of this right will secure all others, and the granting of every other right, whilst this is denied, is a mockery. For instance: What is the right to property without the right to protect it? The enjoyment of that right to-day is no security that it will be continued to-morrow, so long as it is granted to us as a favor, and not claimed by us as a right.[80]

She went further to suggest that the franchise could bring more than legal rights to women; it could bring an end to women's subordination in all realms of life—along with the vote, she asserted, "comes equality in Church and State, in the family circle, and in all our social relations."[81]

Cady Stanton elaborated on her liberal, individual rights–oriented basis for women's suffrage when she contended that men's unwavering belief that women's nature differed from theirs rendered them incapable of either representing or legislating for them. Unable to see "that we think and feel exactly as he does, that we have the same sense of right and justice, the same love of freedom and independence," they enact laws that treat women differently from men, taking from women—she took the opportunity to reiterate—"the very rights which they fought, and bled, and died, to secure to themselves."[82] She also asserted, albeit inconsistently, that men legislated out of ignorance—they had no way to judge the interests of those people (women) who were so unlike them. She brought the two arguments together with a flourish: "If we are alike in our mental structure, then there is no reason why we should not have a voice in making the laws which govern us; but if we are not alike, most certainly we must make laws for ourselves; for who else can understand what we need and desire?"[83] Her argument was that if women were different from men, they needed representation so that they could protect their shared interests: to make it possible to "watch the passage of all bills affecting our own welfare or the good of our country."[84] Alternatively, if women were "free and equal" to men, they were entitled to a role in political life. Cady Stanton thus appropriated the assumption of natural differences and the doctrine of separate spheres, turning what seemed to be such an effective argument against including women in political life into a mandate for woman's suffrage.

Relying on liberal principles of individual entitlement to equal rights, Cady Stanton often reiterated her conviction that women would never be able to secure their rights until they obtained the ballot. She reasoned that woman's suffrage was not only justified but necessary for the protection of women's rights. She relied on republican principles as well, however, in her contention that women would not use the vote simply to advance their self-interest. Indeed, the special talents and concerns that women would bring to politics would vastly improve the life of the nation. To develop that argument, she drew upon the cult of domesticity's ascriptive insistence that there were immutable differences between the sexes. In her 1850 letter to the Ohio Convention—the same letter in which she placed such a strong emphasis on women's need to vote if they were to protect their rights—she asserted that if women had not been excluded from politics, the course of the nation would have been very different:

> [W]ould [it] have been stained with the guilt of aggressive warfare upon such weak defenceless nations as the Seminoles and Mexicans? Think you we should cherish and defend, in the heart of our nation, such a wholesale system of piracy, cruelty licentiousness and ignorance, as is our slavery? Think you that relic of barbarism, the gallows, by which the wretched murderer is sent with blood upon his soul, uncalled for, into the presence of his God, would be sustained by law? Verily no, or I mistake woman's heart, her instinctive love of justice and mercy, and truth.[85]

Cady Stanton's arguments embraced liberal principles of equal rights and autonomy and at the same time promoted a republican image of women as public-spirited citizens who would exercise the franchise to improve the life of the national community. Moreover, she included ascriptive themes by alluding to women's moral superiority, thereby transforming traditional ascriptive assertions of women's natural distinct qualities of women into a demonstration of the necessity of including women in the political life of the nation.

The small margin by which the participants at the Seneca Falls Convention agreed to include the elective franchise in the list of demands made clear to Cady Stanton that suffrage would be the most controversial goal of the woman's rights movement. As noted earlier, many

Garrisonian women had reservations about the value as well as the morality of participating in governmental institutions and processes. In addition, some women who were eager to advocate legal reform that would alleviate their subordinate position within the family were so thoroughly imbued with the notion that women's proper sphere was the private realm of domesticity that they were not yet ready to argue that women had a major role to play in the public business of governing. Cady Stanton also expressed her awareness of the obstacles that woman suffrage would encounter outside the movement when she referred to the vote as "the point to attack, the stronghold of the fortress—*the one* woman will find most difficult to take—*the one* man will most reluctantly give up." But, rather than turn more attention to goals that seemed more feasible in the short term, she consistently maintained that the vote must be the central focus of the movement, that the leaders should "spend all [their] time, strength and moral ammunition, year after year, with perseverance, courage and decision."[86]

In 1851, Cady Stanton recommended a series of practical steps that women could take to advance the cause. She urged them to engage in petition campaigns at every session of the legislature, to go to the polls with banners inscribed with the words of "our revolutionary fathers—such as, 'No Taxation without Representation,' 'No just Government can be formed without the consent of the Governed.'" She also recommended that women refuse to pay taxes "and, like the English dissenters, suffer our goods to be seized and sold, if need be."[87] Women could also make their way into the trades and professions and make themselves, "if not rich and famous, at least independent and respectable."[88] She reminded women that they were particularly suited for the pulpit because of their superiority to men "in the affections, high moral sentiments, and religious enthusiasm."[89] There was also important work to be done, she contended, in the education of young women who needed to be taught self-reliance and courage. In a passage that reflected the influence of Margaret Fuller, she admonished:

> Let the girl be thoroughly developed in body and soul, not modeled, like a piece of clay, after some artificial specimen of humanity, with a body like some plate in *Godey's* book of fashion, and a mind after some type of Father Gregory's pattern daughters, loaded down with the traditions, proprieties, and sentimentalities of generations of silly mothers and grandmothers, but left free to be, to feel, to think, to act.[90]

In 1852, in her letter to the third National Woman's Rights Convention, she again called upon women to refuse to pay taxes. Invoking the spirit of the Revolution, she implored, "shall we fear to suffer for the maintenance of the same glorious principle for which our forefathers fought, bled, and died? Shall we deny the faith of the old Revolutionary heroes, and purchase for ourselves a false power and ignoble ease, by declaring in action that taxation without representation is just?"[91] She underlined the need for women lawyers to interpret the laws in order to "discover the loopholes of retreat" to "see if there is no way by which we may shuffle off our shackles and assume our civil and political rights."[92] She called for coeducation and the admission of women to the best colleges to bring an end to the evils of the isolation of the sexes and to give women a place in the most profitable enterprises.

Making both liberal and republican claims in consecutive paragraphs, Cady Stanton averred that women have the same objects in life as men and that if the feminine element had been represented in government, the behavior of statesmen would certainly have been greatly improved. Finally, in her 1852 letter, she identified the clergy—"priestcraft"—as women's most violent enemies and opponents, who have provided women with a false understanding of God, the Bible, and her own nature, making "her bondage . . . more certain and lasting, her degradation more helpless and complete."[93] She urged women to withdraw their support for the churches and their benevolent societies and instead to devote their resources to the "education, elevation, and enfranchisement of their own sex."[94]

Cady Stanton's letters to the woman's rights conventions during the 1850s evidence her commitment to keeping suffrage at the center of the movement. That the resolutions adopted at the conventions gave such a prominent position to suffrage suggests that she was successful. At the 1851 convention, for example, the first resolution proclaimed, "That while we would not undervalue other methods, the Right of Suffrage for Women is, in our opinion, the corner-stone of this enterprise, since we do not seek to protect woman, but rather to place her in a position to protect herself."[95] Suffrage was not mentioned explicitly until the fourth resolution of those adopted at the convention in 1860, but the second and third resolutions implied the right to vote in their references to women's demand for the privileges of citizenship and the recognition of civil and political rights.[96] Reformers who spoke at those conventions did not always mention suffrage, often focusing instead on legal reform to protect the property rights of married women and to create more equitable inheritance laws. Nevertheless, they did not voice any objection to including suffrage as a primary goal. Moreover, when they discussed the issue of votes for women, they endorsed it with reasoning that was consistent with Cady Stanton's.[97]

Conclusion

Elizabeth Cady Stanton's earliest work reveals the ways in which she drew from and blended the multiple traditions to challenge the legal and cultural structure, including the cult of domesticity that sustained women's subordinate status. In her early years as a women's rights leader, she used liberal arguments to minimize the most far-reaching implications of her demands for reform by consistently reminding her audience that women were only asking for the rights that by nature belonged to every human being—the same rights for which men had fought the American Revolution. Granting equal legal and political rights to women, Cady Stanton often contended, would fulfill the promise of the Revolution. Withholding those rights would not only obstruct the progress of society but also confirm that America in the mid-nineteenth century had failed to live up to the principles on which the nation was founded. She presented women's degraded position as cruelly inconsistent with the liberal principles of natural rights and equality that ran through the Declaration of Independence. Her arguments also suggested that the male monopoly on power contradicted the republican mandate for balanced government that was institutionalized in the Constitution's system of checks and balances. Moreover, women's continued exclusion from political life after the democratic reforms of the Jacksonian era constituted an even more obvious travesty of both liberal and republican principles upon which the nation was based.

Cady Stanton interspersed her liberal claims of women's right to the same rights that men enjoyed with republican allusions to the evils of unchecked power and the need for women to participate in the political life of the community. She also made use of ascriptive claims that women's moral superiority would make them particularly good citizens —voting women would greatly improve the political life of the nation. The improvements would result not only from the redress of the imbalance of power created by the male monopoly—a republican claim—but also from the introduction of women's moral influence, which would combat men's self-seeking, corrupt approach to politics. That is, active women citizens could make up for men's natural shortcomings. Although Cady Stanton mounted a thoroughgoing challenge to the cult of domesticity, her ideas bear the unmistakable imprint of that all-pervasive nineteenth-century ideology, as evidenced by her emphasis on the need to protect women in the domestic realm.

The way that Cady Stanton combined traditions also had a strategic component. She attacked the cult of domesticity with the liberal claim that women were equal to men and endowed with the same inalienable rights. At the same time, however, she pointed to women's special qualifications because she knew that most people were not ready to relinquish their belief that there were natural differences between the sexes that made separate spheres necessary to the well-being of society. Thus, if women were similar to men in their capacity for rational decisions, they should have equal rights; if they were different—that is, morally superior—they should also have the right to participate in governing so that they could apply their special skills to cure the ills of male politics. Also, the way she used ascriptive arguments to assert women's superiority to some men buttressed her claims for women's rights, although it did not challenge—indeed, it served to reinforce—other established hierarchies of the United States in the nineteenth century.

The energy that Cady Stanton devoted to legal and political reform during the antebellum period and her efforts to downplay the extent of the changes that she sought by associating the woman's rights movement with the American Revolution tend to divert attention from the broader implications of her commitment to eradicating women's subordination. While she viewed suffrage as a means to secure women's legal rights—the only way, as she said, that women could protect their rights —she was aware that legal and political reform could not eradicate the culture of domesticity that perpetuated women's condition. As she said to Anthony in 1860, "Woman's degradation is in man's idea of his sexual rights. Our religion, laws, customs are all founded on the belief that woman was made for man."[98] Cady Stanton's belief in the need for fundamental social change became more pronounced later in her life, as we will see in subsequent chapters. Nevertheless, that conviction is discernible, if only slightly, in some of her earliest work.

3

The 1850s
Married Women's Property Rights, Divorce, and Temperance

Introduction

The legal disabilities of married women were of paramount importance to the antebellum woman's rights leaders, and especially to Elizabeth Cady Stanton. Indeed, the authors of the *History of Woman Suffrage* identified "discussion in several of the State Legislatures on the property rights of married women" as one of the "immediate causes that led to the demand for the equal political rights of women."[1] As we have seen, two of the grievances in the Declaration of Sentiments stated that "He has made her, if married, in the eye of the law, civilly dead. He has taken from her all right in property, even to the wages she earns." Another noted more generally that men had deprived married women of their rights.[2]

In this chapter, I examine the ways in which Cady Stanton's arguments for married women's property rights and divorce reform relied on the multiple traditions and how she introduced a radical theme with her analysis of marriage. In addition, I discuss the alliance that Cady Stanton formed with the temperance movement and the way her arguments demonstrated her understanding of the connections among the economic, legal, and political disabilities of women.

Married Women's Property Rights

According to the common law of England, which provided the basis of the American legal system, a woman's legal existence ended with her marriage. Blackstone's *Commentaries on the Laws of England*, published between 1765 and 1769 and reprinted in America in 1771, summed up the legal status of a married woman: "the very being or legal existence of the woman is suspended during the marriage, or at least is incorporated and consolidated into that of the husband; under whose wing, protection and cover, she performs every thing."[3] The doctrine of marital unity provided that when a man and woman married, they became one in the eyes of the law, with one will—the will of the husband. Under the concept of *coverture,* a married woman was a *feme covert,* covered by her husband. Thus, all property a woman brought to her marriage belonged to her husband. Although he could not sell her land or buildings without her consent, he could dispose of her other property —including her wages—as he saw fit. A married woman could not sue or be sued, nor could she enter into a contract. The dower right entitled a widow to use one-third of her husband's property, but she could not alter or dispose of it.[4] The law was sufficiently flexible to allow women more rights in special situations—an abandoned wife could petition the legislature to become a *feme sole* with the legal ability to conduct business.[5] A wealthy woman could keep her property separate from her husband through devices such as prenuptial contracts and trusts. A majority of women, however, had to live with the restrictions of coverture. Moreover, a woman who had the resources to attempt to attain some of the rights of a single woman was always considered to be a special case and remained dependent on others—if not her husband, then a male relative or the state.[6]

Legal reform to expand the property rights of married women began well before 1848. Beginning in the late 1830s, some state legislatures enacted laws to prohibit property that the wife brought to the marriage from being taken by creditors to pay the husband's debts.[7] More states adopted reforms—still very limited in scope—during the 1850s.[8] By 1865, twenty-nine states had enacted women's property acts in some form.[9]

The early advocates of reform in the marital property system included men who favored more lenient debtor laws amid the economic instability of antebellum America, advocates of codification, and women's rights reformers.[10] Women outside the woman's rights movement who opposed suffrage but celebrated women's moral influence within the framework of domesticity also commonly supported marital property reform. Sarah Hale, for example, considered such reform to be chivalrous, as men initiated them to confer benefits on women.[11] As Norma

Basch observed, although the drive for marital property reform "reflected the economic goals of the emergent bourgeoisie, both female and male, the ramifications of the drive were far broader. . . . In the context of the nineteenth century, the right of wives to own property entailed their right not to be property."[12]

Women's rights reformers viewed legal reform of property rights as inextricably connected to the demand for suffrage. They often reiterated the argument that women's legal disabilities evidenced men's inability to represent women and that only with the ballot would protection of their property rights become possible. Nevertheless, women who did not support suffrage also often favored married women's property rights. Thus, in the early 1850s, activists often circulated separate petitions—one for suffrage and one for property rights—to gather signatures to present to state legislatures. As Basch noted, the campaign for property rights provided the woman's rights movement with a "perfect bridge" between the more cautious supporters of women's property rights and the more daring advocates of suffrage. Those who were more cautious could work for married women's property rights with the goal of improving women's position in the domestic sphere, while others could seek legal reform as the first step in a logical sequence that allow women into the public sphere.[13] In addition, the more cautious could gradually move across the bridge to support suffrage once state legislatures began to enact married women's property acts.[14]

The New York Campaign: Property Rights for Married Women

Elizabeth Cady Stanton was campaigning for a married women's property act in New York during the years that she was writing letters to the national conventions urging her colleagues to keep the demand for suffrage at the center of the woman's rights movement. The debate over reform of the marital property system in New York began in 1836. Between 1841 and 1848, eight major bills for a married women's statute were introduced in the legislature, four in 1846 and 1847 alone, but none emerged from committee.[15] In addition, a women's property clause was proposed at the state constitutional convention in 1846 and approved by the delegates but was rescinded three days later. According to the authors of the *History of Woman Suffrage*, with the enactment of the married women's property statute in 1848, New York became the first state "to emancipate wives from the slavery of the old common law of England, and to secure to them equal property rights."[16]

Passage of the legislation in the spring of 1848, several months before the Seneca Falls Convention, was primarily a result of the convergence of overlapping interests in codification and in shielding men's property from creditors and opportunistic or incompetent sons-in-law and protecting the family finances in a time of economic instability.[17] Women's rights reformers nevertheless played an important role from the outset of the twelve-year campaign for marital property reform. Ernestine Rose and Paulina Wright Davis circulated petitions in 1836, though with little success, as only five women signed. Cady Stanton, staying in Albany in 1843, took the opportunity to discuss a proposed bill with lawyers and legislators.[18] Women from two counties petitioned the legislature in 1848, admonishing that "Our numerous and yearly petitions for this most desirable object having been disregarded, we now ask your *august* body . . . to abolish all laws which hold married women no more accountable for their acts than *infants, idiots*, and *lunatics*."[19]

The 1848 statute was quite limited. It insulated a married woman's property from her husband's debts and provided that the property "shall continue her sole and separate property, as if she were a single female." It also specified that property given to a married woman by any person other than her husband would be held "to her sole and separate use, as if she were a single female."[20] The law prohibited a husband from disposing of property that his wife brought to the marriage. But the husband was still assumed to be the manager of the property. Moreover, the statute did not give contractual rights to married women. An amendment to the law in 1849 allowed the wife "to convey and devise real and personal property...as if she were unmarried."[21] Other 1849 amendments provided that a married woman who was the beneficiary of a trust had to petition a court for personal control of her property. The court would review her capacity to manage and control her property and then could order the trustee to convey all or part of the trust to her.

Despite the praise they later inserted in the *History of Woman Suffrage*, the leaders of the woman's rights movement were well aware that the legislation of 1848 and 1849 was inadequate. Cady Stanton and Susan B. Anthony shared the conviction that reform in the marital property system was crucial to women's rights. Cady Stanton wrote to

Anthony in 1853 that "it is in vain to look for the elevation of woman, so long as she is dependent in marriage. . . . The right idea of marriage is at the foundation of all reforms."[22] Likewise, reflecting on the events of 1853, Anthony wrote that she understood that there "was no true freedom for woman without the possession of all her property rights and that those could be obtained through legislation only, and . . . the sooner the demand was made of the Legislature, the sooner would we be likely to obtain them."[23]

The woman's rights convention in Rochester in late 1853 adopted a resolution calling upon the legislature to appoint a joint committee "to examine and revise the statutes, and to propose remedies for the redress of all legal grievances from which women now suffer, and suitable measures for the full establishment of women's legal equality with men."[24] Two other resolutions asked for legislation making wives co-owners of income they earned jointly with their husbands and granting them equal rights in inheritance and in guardianship of children. Anthony launched a major petition campaign at the end of the convention, organizing sixty women for door-to-door petitioning. That winter, she and the other women collected six thousand signatures in support of legislation to expand the property rights of married women and four thousand in support of suffrage. She then organized a woman's rights convention in Albany in February 1854 to coincide with the next legislative session and used that occasion to deliver the petitions to the legislature.

Although Cady Stanton did not attend the meeting in Rochester, she was appointed to a committee to prepare an address to the legislature and to ask for a hearing to consider "the just and equal rights of women."[25] She prepared an address and delivered it to the convention in Albany, which agreed to adopt it as its address to the legislature.[26] The address began with an explanation of the women's demands for suffrage and representation on juries that relied on a combination of liberal, rights-based rhetoric,[27] republican notions of the destructive consequences of an excessive concentration of power and the need for "women's moral power" in politics, and the ascriptive argument that women were superior to many voting men: "moral, virtuous and intelligent, and in all respects quite equal to the proud white man himself, and yet by your laws we are classed with idiots, lunatics and negroes."[28] She thus made use of ascriptivism not only to make a claim to women's superiority but also to reinforce other inequalities by calling attention to the alleged inferiority of certain men. Ironically, she called for equality on liberal grounds but then charged that women deserved the vote because of their superiority on the basis of race and intelligence.

Asking the legislators what authority they had to "disfranchise one-half the people of this state," she turned to a respectable source for support. Elisha Powell Hurlbut, a retired judge on the Supreme Court of New York, had published a book in 1845 rejecting the common law and arguing that legislation should "be merely declaratory of natural rights and natural wrongs and that whatever is indifferent to the laws of nature shall be left unnoticed by human legislation."[29] In that volume he included a chapter, "The Rights of Woman," in which he condemned the rules that denied women the "dignity of a rational moral being" after marriage, reasoning that women had a right to live in the married state without surrendering any of their rights.[30]

Cady Stanton's address linked the campaign for women's property rights to the demand for the ballot, emphasizing that reform in the marital property system was only the beginning of her far-reaching agenda for change in women's status: "The right to property will, of necessity, compel us in due time to the exercise of our right to the elective franchise, and then naturally follows the right to hold office."[31] When she turned to the details of married women's property rights, the subject that constituted the greater part of her address, she retained a rights-based rationale, for example, admonishing the legislators,

> We ask no better laws than those you have made for yourselves. We need no other protection than that which your present laws secure to you . . . we *ask* for all that you have asked for yourselves in the progress of your development, since the *Mayflower* cast anchor beside Plymouth Rock; and simply on the ground that the rights of every human being are the same and identical.[32]

In spite of the way she pointed to women's equality and dignity, Cady Stanton's address focused primarily on portraying wives as victims of financially incompetent or dishonest husbands and as widows cruelly wrenched from their homes. A woman's position was often untenable, for example, "If she have a worthless husband, a confirmed drunkard, a villain or a vagrant, he has still all the rights of a man, husband and a father. Though the whole support of the family be thrown upon the wife, if the wages she earns be paid to her by her employer, the husband can receive them again." A woman who managed to provide her children with a home and security was nevertheless vulnerable to the husband, who had the legal right to "strip her of all her hard earnings, turn her and her little ones out in the cold northern blast, take the clothes from their backs, the bread from their mouths."[33]

She reproached the legislators: "your present laws . . . make the mother and her children the victims of vice and license."[34] Moreover, "cruel, vindictive fathers" have inflicted "untold sufferings" on children, and "a mother's love can be no protection to a child; she cannot appeal to you to save it from a father's cruelty. . . . Neither at home nor abroad can a mother protect her son."[35] Thus, without relinquishing the broader goal of obtaining the ballot, Cady Stanton drew the legislators' attention to the need to expand women's property rights so that mothers could provide a safe and secure environment for their children. Giving married women the right to control their own property, the right to make contracts, the right to sue and be sued, the right to equal inheritance, and the right to guardianship of children would protect women's position in the domestic sphere. If a woman did venture outside the home in pursuit of an income, it would be solely for the purpose of supporting her children in the all-too-common situation in which the husband failed to do so. Cady Stanton thus placed her demands firmly within the tradition of woman's separate sphere. At the same time, she exposed a great deal about the harsh reality behind the cult of domesticity's sentimentalized image of the "true woman," cared for and protected by her husband.

Disregarding the forceful arguments that Cady Stanton presented, the special joint committee that the legislature appointed to conduct hearings recommended that the "prayer of the petitioners be denied." The committee did make two suggestions, however. First, the consent of the mother should be required for any disposition made by the father regarding guardianship of their children. Second, when the husband neglected to support or educate his family, the wife should have the right to collect her earnings and those of her minor children and apply them to the family's support without interference from him.[36] That the committee made such recommendations suggests that the legislators, though not willing to endorse major changes in married women's property rights, were willing to expand wives' and mothers' ability to protect their children. In short, even as early as 1854, legislators were willing to consider changes in women's rights as a means of protecting women and children from abusive and neglectful husbands.

Susan B. Anthony devoted herself to the campaign for married women's property rights from 1854 until the Earnings Act became law, in 1860. She canvassed the state each year—and in one six-month period visited fifty-four of the sixty counties in the state. She organized state and county conventions and petitioning campaigns, gave lectures, knocked on doors, and delivered petitions to the legislature every year. Cady Stanton commented that donations in 1858 and 1859 made it easier "to send out agents and to commence anew our work which shall never end until in church and state, and at the fire-side, the equality of woman shall be fully recognized."[37]

In 1859, by a vote of 102 to 2, the New York State Assembly passed legislation protecting married women's earnings. The measure failed to come to a vote in the Senate, however.[38] On February 18, 1860, Cady Stanton addressed a joint session of the legislature, appealing once more for married women's property rights and suffrage. Her opening comments emphasized the natural rights of the individual—rights that are not transferable but "are a component part of himself, the laws which insure his growth and development . . . they live and die with him."[39] Withholding rights from women, she contended, does not benefit men: "No man can see, hear, or smell but just so far; and though hundreds are deprived of these senses, his are not the more acute" and "women's poverty does not add to man's wealth."[40] Conversely, if men were to allow women to exercise their rights, "her wealth could not bring poverty to him."[41] In short, rights were an unlimited resource—women's gain would not be men's loss; on the contrary, securing women's inalienable rights would benefit society.

Later in her address, however, Cady Stanton dropped her conciliatory tone and condemned white men for acting out of "shrewd selfishness" and comfortably ensconcing themselves while degrading women in the name of protection. She also returned to the notion that rights for women would unify rather than disrupt society, asking the legislators to "Undo what man did for us in the dark ages, and strike out all special legislation for us; strike the words 'white male' from all your constitutions, and then, with fair sailing, let us sink or swim, live or die, survive or perish together."[42]

When she turned to the legal status of married women, she drew the familiar comparison between the condition of the mothers, wives, and daughters of New York and slaves in the Carolinas. As she had before, she limited her comparison to male slaves. A wife, like a slave has no name—he is "Cuffy Douglas or Cuffy Brooks, just whose Cuffy he may chance to be. . . . She is Mrs. Richard Roe or Mrs. John Doe, just whose Mrs. she may chance to be." Neither had a right to their earnings, to buy, sell, or save. Nor did they have rights to their children. Finally, neither the wife nor the slave had any legal existence: "Mrs. Roe [like Cuffy] . . . has not the best right to her own person. The husband [like Cuffy's master] has the power to administer moderate chastisement."[43] Woman's position, she maintained was worse than that of the free negro: "the few social privileges which the man gives the woman, he makes up to the negro in civil rights."[44] The prejudice against sex, she contended, was more deeply rooted and more unreasonably maintained than that against color. A woman could sit at the same table and eat with a white man while a black man could not, but a free black man could hold property and vote and a woman could not. Moreover, she noted that a woman would sit in the same pew with a white man in church but could not preach in that church as a black man could.

With the support of members of the Senate Judiciary Committee, the Earnings Act passed in both the Assembly and the Senate. It became law on March 20, 1860. The new law covered female wage earners and businesswomen, providing that a wife's property would remain her own and that she would not be responsible for her husband's debts.[45] The Earnings Act also gave married women the right to buy and sell, contract, carry on any trade or business, and sue and be sued. It gave to the mother the right to be a joint guardian of her children with her husband and equalized intestate succession in real estate.

In November 1860, not satisfied with the advances in married women's property rights, Cady Stanton appealed to women in New York to sign petitions demanding the ballot, trial by a jury of their peers, and an equal right to the joint earnings of the marriage partnership. She compared the position of woman to that of the slave once more and alluded to the possibility of a rebellion: If the slaves rose "en masse, assert and demand their rights," they could secure their freedom.[46] Woman could do the same were it not for her "ignorance, her drapery, and her chains," which prevent her from realizing "that in advancing civilization, she too must soon be free, to counsel with her conscience and her God."[47] Cady Stanton's by then familiar comparison between the position of women and that of male slaves continued to distinguish her arguments from those of the antislavery women who drew attention to the plight of female slaves. In addition, the reference to a slave revolt pointed to her concern with the antislavery debate amid sharpening tensions on the eve of the Civil War.

In 1861, with the outbreak of the war, the campaign for improvements in married women's property rights ended. The following year, the New York legislature amended the Earnings Act of 1860 to remove a number of the rights it had granted to married women. The amendments returned legal guardianship to the father, giving the mother some veto power over his decisions, and removed the provisions of the 1860 law that gave women equal rights of inheritance. The legislators' action underlined the prescience of Cady Stanton's oft-repeated argument that the "granting of every other right . . . is a mockery" without the ballot; although property rights may be granted today, there can be no security that they will continue tomorrow, "so long as [they are] granted to us as a favor, and not claimed by us as a right."[48]

Divorce

Although marital property reform was a national issue, it elicited little controversy within the woman's rights movement. It was another national issue, divorce reform, that provoked serious disagreement among the leaders that culminated at the woman's rights convention in 1860. As we have seen, two of the grievances in the Declaration of Sentiments condemned the laws of marriage and divorce. In marriage, a woman was "compelled to promise obedience to her husband, he becoming, to all intents and purposes her master"; man had, "framed the laws of divorce, as to what shall be the proper causes, and in case of separation, to whom the guardianship of children shall be given."[49] The promise of obedience—which Cady Stanton and Henry Stanton eliminated from their marriage vows—included the husband's right to demand sex from his wife—his marital right to her body.

Although laws regarding divorce varied from state to state, divorces were generally available on three basic grounds in the 1850s: adultery, desertion, and cruelty. South Carolina did not recognize divorce at all.[50] Some states, however, began to enact laws that eased the route to divorce. Connecticut and Indiana, for example, included clauses that allowed judges to grant divorces on grounds other than those listed in the law if they thought they were justified. In 1852, Indiana enacted a lenient residency provision that required petitioners merely to submit an affidavit declaring that they resided in the county where they were filing for divorce. Indiana also allowed notification of divorce proceedings through publication in a local newspaper, which meant that the party seeking a divorce did not have to notify the defendant personally.[51] Such relatively lenient divorce laws engendered widespread public debate about divorce that revolved around alleged connections linking divorce, morality, and social organization. Timothy Dwight, the president of Yale, for example, condemned divorce, referring to its increase as "flaming proof . . . of the baleful influence of this corruption on a people, otherwise remarkably distinguished for their intelligence, morals, and religion!"[52] In contrast, there were utopian reformers who viewed marriage as a voluntary agreement that should be voidable at the request of the parties. Members of the free-love movement went even further to advocate the abolition of marriage on the grounds that it was inconsistent with the principle of individual sovereignty.[53] The woman's rights movement joined the debate in 1860 when some of the reformers—including Cady Stanton—argued that easy divorce would provide a partial solution to women's subordination in marriage. Although there was a consensus that marriage as it was then constituted made many women's lives unbearable and perpetuated their legal, social, even political disabilities, the leaders divided over the issue of divorce.

Cady Stanton on Marriage and Divorce: Toward a Radical Critique

Cady Stanton's views about divorce flowed logically from her conviction that marriage should be a contract freely accepted by two equal parties.[54] Forcing a woman to remain married to a man who "in a few short years . . . [became] a cowardly, mean tyrant, or a foul-mouthed, bloated drunkard" was in direct opposition to what she viewed as the sacred right of the individual to pursue happiness.[55] Marriage, moreover, affected women's lives far more than it did men's, she explained:

> Marriage is not all of life to man. His resources for amusement and occupation are boundless. He has the whole world for his home. His busi-

ness, his politics, his club, his friendships with either sex, can help to fill up the void made by an unfortunate union or separation. But to woman, marriage is all and everything; her sole object in life—that for which she is educated—the subject of all her sleeping and her waking dreams.[56]

Thus, not only were women entitled to equality in marriage on the basis of liberal principles of natural rights, but the conditions of their lives that grew out of the cult of domesticity made those equal rights even more crucial to their ability to pursue happiness.

Cady Stanton began to discuss divorce in 1850 in a contribution to the *Lily,* Amelia Bloomer's monthly women's temperance newspaper, which began publication in 1849. Cady Stanton expressed her support for pending legislation in New York that would make drunkenness a ground for divorce. If enacted, the bill would open "new doors through which unhappy prisoners may escape from the bonds of an ill-assorted marriage"[57] She concluded that, because "all can freely and *thoughtlessly* enter into the marriage state, they should be allowed to come as freely and *thoughtfully* out again."[58] Those statements confirm that her conception of divorce was based on her liberal vision of marriage as a dissoluble contract between two autonomous individuals. Nevertheless, other remarks that she made alluded to republican justifications for regulating people's behavior: "If legislators think they have the right to regulate marriage . . . [l]et them say who shall and who shall not be legally married. Instead of passing laws compelling a woman by law, to live with a Drunkard, they ought to pass laws forbidding Drunkards to marry."[59] Finally, in a statement that portended the Darwinian ascriptivism that would emerge more fully in her arguments later in the nineteenth century, Cady Stanton suggested that "Drunkard" fathers were responsible for passing mental deficiencies on to children and should therefore be prohibited from reproducing: "As the state has to provide homes for idiots, it certainly has a right to say how many there shall be. The Spartans had some good laws, in relation to marriage and children."[60] Her comments to the New York State Temperance Convention in April 1852 reflected the same sentiment.[61] She was even more forthright in a letter to Anthony in March of that year in which she contended that "nearly all" the inmates of "idiot asylums" are the offspring of "Drunkards." If legislators must regulate marriage, they might forbid a woman to marry until she is twenty-one and fine a woman for conceiving by a "Drunkard." Moreover, she was frank about the need to eliminate from marriage the wife's obligation to obey: "Man in his lust has regulated this whole question of sexual intercourse long enough; let the mother of mankind whose prerogative it is to set bounds to his indulgence, rouse up & give this whole question a thorough, fearless examination."[62] Cady Stanton's use of ascriptivism in her arguments about the need to control men's lust suggested that women's ability to control her sexual appetites entitled her to (at least) equal rights within marriage. Her claims about the fate of the offspring of "Drunkards" served to justify not only public policies that would protect women but also those that would control behavior by limiting the ability of certain undesirable people to reproduce. Such arguments suggested an alternative use of ascriptivism in which negative qualities were ascribed to individuals on the basis of characteristics other than sex but that were nevertheless perceived to be immutable. That variation on ascriptivism would play an increasingly important role in Cady Stanton's work after the Civil War.

Law professor Elizabeth Clark argued that Cady Stanton's view of marriage as a contract between two autonomous individuals exemplified her liberal individualism and served to promote the conception of family relations as private and beyond the reach of the law.[63] Such a statement fails to tell the whole story, however, for Cady Stanton's view of marriage constituted one element of what she would later develop into a radical critique of the institutions that perpetuated woman's subordinate status. In the 1850s, she issued a thoroughgoing challenge to the concept of marriage that was based on Christian doctrine as well as on the common-law tradition. Marriage, according to that tradition encompassed the union of two individuals, turning two people into one, the husband. The legal implications of marriage—women's inability to enter into contracts or control their own property, for example— were unacceptable to Cady Stanton. The political implications were just as unacceptable: women did not need to vote because their husbands would represent them. But what was radical about Cady Stanton's analysis was her determination to go further than the legal and political implications to the very cultural foundations of the institution of marriage. She would soon be arguing that women had to discover their identities and to seize control of their lives within their marriages. Women could not overcome their subordination until they did so, and their ability to do so would involve fundamental change in the structure of society and a major transformation in cultural norms that held man to be woman's master within the family.

When she pointed to the need to raise women's awareness of their "social wrongs" in her letter to the National Woman's Rights Convention in 1856, Cady Stanton again focused on marriage, charging that it was an institution that put women in a "false position" by ignoring their rights and dignity as individuals:

> Marriage is a divine institution, intended by God for the greater freedom and happiness of both parties—whatever therefore conflicts with woman's happiness is not legitimate to that relation. Woman has yet to learn that she has a right to be happy in and of herself; that she has a right to the free use, improvement, and development of all her faculties, for her own benefit and pleasure. The woman is greater than the wife or the mother; and in consenting to take upon herself these relations, she should never sacrifice one iota of her individuality to any senseless conventionalisms, or false codes of feminine delicacy and refinement.[64]

Adultery was the only ground for divorce in New York. Bills were introduced nearly every year from 1850 through 1860 that would have allowed divorce for cruel treatment and abandonment, but they consistently failed. In 1860, Horace Greeley, the editor of the *New York Tribune*, revived the debate that he had begun in his newspaper in 1852, when he reiterated his earlier biblical conception of marriage as an indissoluble union terminable only in cases of adultery and blamed Robert Dale Owen for making Indiana into a divorce mill.[65] Easy divorce was, to Greeley, emblematic of moral depravity and excessive selfishness. Owen responded that divorce law should evolve over time and that marriage should be an affectionate union.[66]

When Cady Stanton was finally able to attend a woman's rights convention, in May 1860, she delivered an address evidencing her determination to make divorce a central issue of the woman's rights movement. Her ten resolutions[67] emphasized her concept of marriage as a contract that like, "any constitution, compact or covenant between human beings that failed to produce or promote human happiness, could not . . . be of any force or authority; —and it would be not only a right, but a duty, to abolish it."[68] Marriage, moreover, was the most important of all human contracts both to the individual and to society. She condemned marriage as it was then constituted—"man marriage and nothing more"[69]—and urged the kind of marriage that had never been tried, "a contract made by equal parties to live an equal life, with equal restraints and privileges on either side."[70] Although she did not directly counter the biblical account of marriage upon which Greeley insisted in the exchange in the *Tribune,* Cady Stanton buttressed her argument by emphasizing the rights of individuals. All questions must be resolved, she asserted, by considering the highest good of the individual. It would be impossible for a law "that oppresses the individual" to "promote the highest good of society. The best interests of a community never can require the sacrifice of one innocent being—of one sacred right."[71] In addition, as she explained, the biblical view of marriage with severe restrictions on divorce had a particularly devastating effect on women, who often live in concealed misery or disgrace and isolation and for whom marriage is the center of life.

When Cady Stanton finished, Antoinette Brown Blackwell, who was an ordained Congregational minister, set forth a different concept of marriage.[72] She argued that marriage was a voluntary alliance that "from the nature of things, . . . must be as permanent and indissoluble as the relation of parent and child."[73] Blackwell maintained, nevertheless, that marriage was a union of equals and that every woman had a right, as well as a duty, to maintain her own independence and integrity of character. Underlying her argument was an idealized image of marriage. She stated, for example, that marriage was a "covenant to work together, to uphold each other in all excellence, and to mutually blend their lives and interests into a common harmony."[74] In short, if women fulfilled their obligation to work to improve themselves and their husbands, the result would be improved marriage. Ernestine Rose endorsed Cady Stanton's argument. Wendell Phillips then moved that the resolutions concerning divorce not appear in the journals of the convention. Divorce, he argued, affects men as much as women, admitting no statutory inequities between the sexes. Moreover, it was too complex, too open-ended, admitting of so many theories including "what is technically called 'free love.' "[75] Thus, he did not consider divorce to be a proper subject for the woman's rights movement. William Lloyd Garrison voiced his agreement with that view but argued that the resolutions, along with the speeches, should appear in the journal. Susan B. Anthony argued that marriage should be central to the woman's rights platform, as it "has ever been a one-sided matter. . . . By it, man gains all—woman loses all."[76]

Phillips's motion failed. Still, his argument, along with Blackwell's, made it clear that there was little support for Cady Stanton's position within the movement in 1860. Only Anthony and Rose supported her. The issue of divorce did not entirely disappear from the woman's rights agenda, however. In February 1861, at the New York State convention in Albany—the last convention before the Civil War—the speakers had a hearing on a slightly liberalized divorce bill that was before the legislature.[77]

As Norma Basch pointed out, leaders, like Blackwell, who opposed divorce and those who advocated it, like Cady Stanton, Anthony, and Rose, shared the view that the failings of marriage were the result of the lust of inadequately controlled men—a problem that was exacerbated by the legal and economic power of husbands over their wives.[78] The Cady Stanton group focused on reforming the law to make divorce easier and to expand the legal rights of divorcing women by providing alimony and custody rights, whereas the others concentrated on reforming men. Accordingly, whereas Blackwell maintained that the wife of an intemperate man should help her husband to overcome his weakness, Cady Stanton argued that drunkenness should be a ground for divorce.

Temperance and Women's Rights

Along with abolitionism, temperance was a central reform movement of the 1840s and 1850s.[79] Although the majority of participants in the early temperance movement were women, the leaders were men—mostly evangelical clergymen. The American Temperance Society, the leading temperance organization during this period, created an auxiliary organization for women, the Daughters of Temperance.[80] In 1851, the same year she met Elizabeth Cady Stanton, Susan B. Anthony was leading temperance meetings for the Daughters of Temperance in Rochester, New York. It was also in 1851 that Maine enacted a law prohibiting the manufacture and sale of liquor. The temperance crusaders of the 1850s used a variety of tactics to convey their message to legislators, including organizing mass demonstrations, lobbying state legislators, and pamphleteering. They lobbied for legislation enforcing prohibition, dry districts, Sunday closings, and married women's property rights. Like the abolitionists, temperance crusaders also made widespread use of petition campaigns. In New York, in 1851, temperance workers gathered more than 300,000 signatures for a petition urging passage of legislation similar to the Maine Law. The Daughters of Temperance gathered about 100,000 of those signatures and organized a meeting of women in Albany during the legislative session in January 1852.

At that meeting, Anthony read a letter from Cady Stanton in which the latter forged an important link between the excessive consumption of alcohol and the oppression of women—a link that would become a constant theme in her attempt to draw temperance women into the campaign for women's rights. She suggested two approaches that women might take to remove the cause of "existing evils." First, she recommended that they exercise their right to the elective franchise— "inasmuch as Intemperance is in part protected by law, we who are the innocent victims of the license system, should [have] a voice in pulling it down."[81] Second, the law regarding the obligations of wives needed to be changed, she declared: "We must raise a new standard of virtue, heroism, & true womanhood. Hitherto it has been declared the duty of woman, to love, honor, & obey her husband, no matter what his transformation might be from the lover to the tyrant, from the refined man, to the coarse licentious inebriate, or silly simpering fool."[82] Her second recommendation underlined her view that the socialization of woman, which demanded that she remain loyal to her husband regardless of his character, played a major role in perpetuating the misery of "drunkard's wives":

> Loud & long have been the praises bestowed on those wives who have faithfully loved & lived on in filth poverty & rags, the wretched companions of a drunkard's sorrows; & the more wretched mother of his ill starred children. It is pitiful to see how many excellent women are dragging out a weary existence in such relations; from mistaken ideas of duty; from a false sense of religious obligation.[83]

Her comments also reiterated her argument that intemperance should be grounds for divorce.

Cady Stanton's letters to the *Lily* in 1850, which she signed variously S.F. or Sun Flower, suggest that she began to formulate the link between temperance and women's rights even earlier. For example, in one letter that reflected her conviction that drunken fathers had a destructive impact on their children, she asserted that an enormous proportion of "idiots" were born of drunken parents and concluded, "the unspeakable misery of looking a laughing idiot in the face and calling him 'my son,' is known but to the mother's heart—the drunkard's wife."[84] In several pieces she constructed dialogues in which a mother and her son, Henry Neil, consider the effects of drinking and formulate possible solutions. In one, they consider the legislator, who is responsible for licensing drinking establishments, and the mother notes that the harms of drinking fall most heavily on women who find themselves married to drunkards: "First, the rumseller sanctioned by the State, robs her of husband and all she has of this world's goods. Then if she have the native energy, by hard labor to get for herself a new home, and gather round her something she can call her own, the State comes to collect its annual poor tax, and she must pay her proportion." The conversation continues, and mother and son agree that the lawmaker and the rumseller should pay the poor tax because a woman should not be taxed "when she has no voice in making the laws." When the mother outlines the obligations of various members of the community to work for temperance, she notes that it is women who have primary responsibility: "It is the mother who stamps her sons. Make the women of a nation wise and virtuous, and then men will be so too." Finally, the mother suggests that if women organized, they could "commence an united and systematic mode of attack, we could torment every rumseller in the land, out of . . . business in one year, and utterly ruin the . . . *speculators* for all coming time."[85]

By the early 1850s, Cady Stanton had already adopted the position that the Women's Christian Temperance Union would assume in 1881 when the organization endorsed woman suffrage: that women would use the ballot to secure restrictions on the sale of liquor.[86] Moreover, she had begun to develop the argument that drinking was a woman's rights issue because wives were so often the brutalized and impoverished victims of husbands who drank excessively. Indeed, she would repeatedly describe the hopeless situation of a financially dependent wife of a man who squandered all the money he earned on drink, leaving her and the children without food and perhaps without shelter, as a prime illustration of women's need to have access to the ballot and to legal protections.

Cady Stanton honed that argument, although it did not originate with her. Indeed, the position that a wife needed property rights to protect herself against the financial disasters created by her alcoholic husband was a prominent theme in temperance literature. Samuel Chipman, an agent for a New York temperance society, for example, visited jails, asylums, and poorhouses throughout the state and, after gathering evidence regarding the reasons for inmates' incarceration, concluded that drunken men abuse their families, especially their wives.[87]

Cady Stanton and Anthony helped to establish an organization, the New York State Woman's Temperance Society, in April 1852, as an alternative to the more conservative Daughters of Temperance. In her address to the new organization's first meeting, in Rochester, Cady Stanton further developed the link between the excessive drinking habits of husbands and the misery of their wives. She imagined a future in which women would establish their independence from men and assume moral leadership in temperance reform:

> hitherto the mere dependent of man, the passive recipient alike of truth and error, [woman] at length shakes off her lethargy, the shackles of a false education, customs and habits, and stands upright in the dignity of a moral being and not only proclaims her own freedom, but demands what she shall do to save man from the slavery of his own low appetites.[88]

She then turned to the issue of divorce, admonishing women to sever all connections with drunken husbands:

> Let no woman remain in the relation of wife with the confirmed drunkard. Let no drunkard be the father of her children. Let no woman form an alliance with any man who has been suspected even of the vice of intemperance; for the taste once acquired can never, never be eradicated. Be not misled by any pledges, resolves, promises, prayers, or tears. You can not rely on the word of a man who is, or has been, the victim of such an overpowering appetite.[89]

The laws must be changed, she declared, so that "the drunkard" would have no legal rights regarding either his wife or his children. The meeting endorsed a resolution that condemned women who stayed with "confirmed drunkard" husbands as "recreant to the cause of humanity, and to the dignity of a true womanhood."[90]

Cady Stanton was elected president of the new organization, and Anthony became secretary, as well as a traveling agent. Cady Stanton then issued an appeal to the women of New York in which she made a powerful plea for the thousands of wives

> with no hope on earth, [who] are raising their helpless hands to Heaven and pleading for mercy and for bread. Governments have no ears, corporations have no souls, and Man, claiming to be the natural protector of Woman, transformed into a demon by the vile drugs of the rumseller, becomes her most cruel oppressor and tyrant.[91]

She exhorted women to take their temperance principles into politics by demanding property rights, divorce reform, and suffrage. It would be another eight years before divorce reform would become a major factor in dividing the woman's rights movement. But, even in 1852, Cady Stanton's pronouncements regarding divorce provoked criticism from those who maintained that marriage was a "divine institution" and that Cady Stanton was "reviling Christianity."[92]

In January 1853, shortly after the birth of her fifth child, Cady Stanton was unable to leave home to deliver the address she prepared for the New York State Assembly, so Anthony read the address for her. She asked that women be allowed to vote on the issue of the regulation of alcohol or that the legislature enact the Maine Law and reiterated her demand that drunkenness be made grounds for divorce. Such a measure, she said, would "make a permanent reform in so regulating your laws on marriage that the pure and noble of our sex may be sustained by the power of government in dissolving all union with gross and vicious natures."[93] She asked also that women be given the right to keep joint earnings. For the "drunkard's wife," she asked that the legislators allow her to have "her property, without taxation, and her children, without fear of molestation."[94] If women were to remain in the home, they should be protected there: "if she is a sacred being, then make her so in her holiest relations."[95] In short, if women were not to have the legal right to protect themselves, legislators should represent women's interests by enacting measures that would protect them.

Cady Stanton's work with the temperance movement proved to be short-lived. In June 1852, the men's state temperance organization held a convention in Syracuse and invited delegates from other temperance organizations, including the New York State Woman's Temperance Society. Anthony and Amelia Bloomer accepted the invitation, only to be denied the right to speak.[96] At a meeting on the first anniversary of the Woman's Temperance Society, in June 1853, Cady Stanton stated, "We have been obliged to preach women's rights because many instead of listening to what we had to say on temperance, have questioned the right of a woman to speak on any subject.[97] At that meeting, the majority amended the organization's constitution to give voting privileges to men and to allow them to be officers in the society, to rename it the People's League, and to limit its activities to temperance reform. The majority then defeated Cady Stanton's bid for reelection to the presidency, and, although it allowed her to run for vice president, she refused, and both she and Anthony withdrew from the organization. To Anthony, Cady Stanton expressed no regret. She noted that "I accomplished at Rochester all I desired by having the divorce question brought up and so eloquently supported. . . . I do beg of you to let the past be past, and to waste no powder on the Woman's State Temperance Society. We have other and bigger fish to fry."[98] Both women then turned to lobbying for married women's property rights in New York, a reform that, as Cady Stanton had so effectively demonstrated, was inextricably connected to temperance.

To many women in the early 1850s, temperance was a more socially acceptable cause than women's rights partly because temperance women were asking for protection for women in the domestic sphere, rather than challenging their relegation to home and children. Moreover, in the 1840s, temperance women were still encouraging petitioning as a moral tool—they had not begun to urge women to venture into electoral politics, though this had changed by the 1850s.[99] Women who were fully committed to temperance seemed to see alcohol as the source of women's problem. Legal prohibitions on the sale and manufacture of alcohol would, in their view, provide a solution. In contrast, Cady Stanton perceived women's economic dependence on men, which was reinforced by their lack of legal or political rights, as the deeper cause of women's degradation at the hands of drunken husbands. But she also perceived and exploited a fundamental connection between temperance and women's rights. Drinking was a male problem that had profound consequences for women who, therefore, needed legal and political rights so that they could protect themselves. They needed to vote so that legislation would be enacted restricting the sale of liquor, wives needed to be able to divorce husbands who drank excessively, and they needed to have the right to keep their own earnings. In short, she used the temperance platform to raise women's consciousness and thereby draw more support for women's rights.

Although Cady Stanton failed in the short term to draw a majority of temperance women to what seemed to them a radical demand for suffrage and divorce reform, she succeeded in defining women's issues in a new way by underlining the intersection between temperance and women's rights. In so doing, she blended republican and liberal arguments—in her formulation, the equal right to own property and to vote was an essential prerequisite if women were to acquire the financial independence that would enable them to exercise a moral influence over their husbands and to protect their children from the corrupting effects of intemperate fathers.

Even though she ended her alliance with the temperance movement in 1853, Cady Stanton continued to emphasize the plight of "drunkard's wives." For example, in a letter to Gerrit Smith in 1855, she linked the dilemma of "the wife of a confirmed drunkard" to "human rights, the sacred right of a woman to her own person, to all her God-given powers of body and soul."[100] Again in 1859, in an appeal to the women of New York, she made a plea for suffrage and married women's property rights, pointing to the "40,000 drunkards' wives in this state—of the wives of men who are licentious—of gamblers—of the long line of those who do nothing; and is it no light matter that all these women who support themselves, their husbands, and families, too, shall have no right to the disposition of their own earnings?"[101]

Conclusion

Cady Stanton's work in the temperance movement, as well as her campaign for married women's property rights and divorce reform, illustrate how effectively she linked women's legal and political disabilities to the problems women encountered in the most intimate parts of their lives. If women could vote, they could convince legislators to protect the property rights of married women and to enact divorce laws that would make dissolution of marriage easier, give women custody of their children, and allow women to divorce husbands who drank excessively.

The arguments that Cady Stanton articulated in the 1850s were based predominantly on liberal claims that women were entitled to the same rights as men. She supplemented those arguments, however, with republican themes, as well as with ascriptive forms of Americanism. Moreover, she alluded to a radical theme in the way she intertwined women's legal and political disabilities with their inequality in marriage and the impact of alcoholism on their lives. In so doing, she began to suggest that more fundamental social and cultural change was needed to overcome the deeply embedded belief that "woman was made for man."[102]

4

Gatherings of Unsexed Women
Separate Spheres and Women's Rights

Introduction

This chapter revolves around one of Cady Stanton's responses to the cultural and political context of her life in the 1850s. The way she framed her answers to the opponents of women's rights underlines the way that she both relied on and rejected the ideology of the cult of domesticity, with its rigid division between the public and private spheres. I begin by examining the criticisms that came from legislators, reformers, and journalists and from women who maintained that they were satisfied with their status. Those criticisms underline the extent to which the cult of domesticity permeated American culture and shaped perceptions of the role and identity of women. Moreover, Cady Stanton's responses to the critics, to which I turn in the second section, demonstrate that although she explicitly rejected the cult of domesticity, it was so much a part of the fabric of her culture that she also relied on it, often adapting it to advance her argument. Her responses also reflect the way she drew from the multiple traditions and introduced a radical strain of thought, specifically in her critique of religion and in her conception of women as a group that had the potential to transform society.

Reactions to the Antebellum Woman's Rights Movement

From its inception, the campaign for women's rights aroused responses that ranged from shock to amusement to vicious ridicule. The rhetoric and the imagery of those responses reveal the overwhelming power of the predominant views of woman's nature and her proper role in the life of the nation. The cult of domesticity was so thoroughly ingrained in the culture of the United States that even the slightest departure from the role it prescribed for women was perceived as unnatural and as a dangerous threat to nearly every institution and every facet of American society.

Many of the most common objections to women's rights were expressed at the Woman's Rights Convention in New York City in September 1853. "[I]f the ladies have more intelligence, and more energy, and science than the male sex, they should rule," proclaimed Dr. H. K. Root, expressing his opposition to all the demands of the convention. He offered three reasons why women should not vote.[1] The Bible provided the foundation for his first reason: "there was an original command from God that man should rule." If men gave "up their rights to woman some great calamity might fall upon us," he reasoned, as with the original sin when man gave up his judgment to women.[2] The second reason that women should not vote, Root argued, was simply that man's physical strength was greater than woman's. Third, women should not vote "because if women enter the field of competition with men, it may lead not only to domestic unhappiness, but a great many other ill feelings."[3] In short, woman suffrage would be inconsistent with God's will, with the law of nature mandating that man should rule over woman, and with the natural moral and physical weakness of women.

Woman's rights leaders regularly invited reporters to their conventions in the 1850s, and the resulting coverage provided the movement with extensive public exposure. The three New York daily newspapers, the *New York Tribune*, the *New York Times*, and the *New York Herald*, were particularly important because newspapers in other parts of the country often picked up their stories and reprinted them. The press's treatment of women's rights activities in the 1850s typically ridiculed the campaign for women's rights and, in so doing, reflected the popular belief that the expansion of rights for women would pose a threat to the family and would be against nature. In the fall of 1853, for example, the *New York Herald* described the convention in New York as follows:

> We saw, in broad daylight, in a public hall in the city of New York, a gathering of unsexed women—unsexed in mind all of them, and many in habiliments—publicly propounding the doctrine that they should be allowed to step out of their appropriate sphere, and mingle in the busy walks of every-day life, to the neglect of those duties which both human and divine law have assigned to them. We do not stoop to argue against so ridiculous a set of ideas. We will only inquire who are to perform

those duties which we and our fathers before us have imagined belonged solely to women. Is the world to be depopulated? Are there to
be no more children?[4]

That article went on to describe the women's rights advocates as pa-
thetic, unattractive, and embittered females who were "entirely devoid
of personal attractions," "thin maiden ladies or women who perhaps
have been disappointed in their endeavors to appropriate the breeches
and the rights of their unlucky lords," women who "are now endeavor-
ing to revenge themselves upon the sex who have slighted them."[5]
Women's rights activists were also, according to the article, mentally un-
stable. In 1856, the *Herald* characterized the movement as "the greatest
absurdity in the world. Its conventions are the gatherings of an insane
asylum—the patients not yet . . . brought down by that physician, public opinion, to a low diet of common sense and a medical regimen of
ordinary insanity."[6]

Commentators commonly expressed the view that because female
women's rights activists were behaving in ways that were so glaringly
inappropriate for members of their sex, they had placed themselves
outside the boundaries of womanhood. Characterizing the reformers as
people who were supposed to be women but who clearly were not,
James Gordon Bennett, the editor of the *Herald,* observed that they had
"long shaggy beards" and a "general squareness of face, set off by singular determination and heaviness of the jaw." He went on to claim
that women's rights reformers were a kind of "hybrid," a third sex,
"mannish women like hens that crow." They were, moreover, "viragos"
and "Amazons" who were attempting to "reverse the law of nature."[7]
It was important too that men who supported reform were said to
possess feminine characteristics. They were "unmanned," "she-male,"
effeminate "husbands, mild and broken in spirit." The Syracuse *Star*
labeled all male supporters of women's rights "Aunt Nancy men."[8]

The theme that such comments reflect most clearly is that the wom-
en's rights reformers who demanded that women be given access to the
heretofore forbidden public sphere were infringing on territory reserved
exclusively for men and charged accordingly with transgressing the
bounds of womanhood. Indeed, they were asking for rights that belonged only to those who possessed male physical characteristics—
characteristics that rendered men deserving of the rights of citizens.
Thus, the reformers' behavior was condemned as unnatural because it

was masculine, and the women were charged with having masculine traits.

Opponents frequently reiterated that woman's nature rendered her unsuitable for public life; thus, it would be unnatural for women to venture out of the private sphere. In an editorial, Bennett asked his readers to consider how funny it would be if Lucy Stone, in the midst of arguing a case in court, were suddenly to be taken by the pangs of childbirth and give "birth to a fine bouncing boy in court."[9] How ridiculous it would be, such comments suggested, for females to attempt to function in the public space that was appropriate only for males.

Other critics of women's rights did not draw so directly on the framework of separate spheres, but their comments, nevertheless, were invariably related to the idea that women have a proper role from which they should not diverge. The editor of the *New York Times*, Henry Raymond, for example, opposed woman suffrage, arguing that no right to vote existed for anyone. Voting was a privilege that women had not earned. They were not fit to vote in their current condition, he argued, and reformers should work on giving them the basics of political training. Raymond also expressed concern that if women had the vote, the most respectable members of the female sex would not use it; thus, the less respectable would gain an undue influence in politics. Horace Greeley, the editor of the *New York Daily Tribune,* was more sympathetic—he supported woman suffrage and endorsed the idea that women should have equal rights before the law and access to better jobs and equal pay. Greeley, however, opposed Cady Stanton's position on divorce. In 1858, the *Tribune* complained that the woman's rights movement had been infiltrated by "weak-minded fanatics" who were detracting attention from the legitimate grievances originally expressed in the Declaration of Sentiments and declared that the efforts of reformers in the past ten years had not accomplished much.[10]

The way that opponents of women's rights insisted that women's proper place in the home was based on natural differences between the sexes and placed women's rights activists outside the bounds of their sex—in effect, exiling them from womanhood—attests to the power of the ideology of separate spheres in American culture in the first half of the nineteenth century. When dress reform became a major concern for women's rights activists and a number of leaders, including Cady Stanton, began to wear the bloomer outfit, a barrage of furious ridicule ensued.[11] The negative response to dress reform also reflected the ideology of separate spheres in that women who chose to adopt a different form of dress were perceived to be moving into the forbidden territory reserved for men and were thereby threatening the very foundations of the ordering of society. Women in the outfit were taunted on the street, cartoons appeared in the newspapers, and songs were even sung about the bloomer costume in music halls.[12] Adhering to the idea that those who did not conform to the prevailing norms of womanhood were abnormal, bitter, and unfeminine, newspapers claimed that women who wore the outfit were advocating an end to marriage and the family and caricatured them as masculine or as unattractive old maids. The adoption of the outfit by women's rights reformers was generally seen as another indication that these women were trying to be men—that they were unsexing themselves by appropriating male dress.

In 1854, during the campaign for married women's property rights in New York, Cady Stanton, Anthony, and Ernestine Rose appeared before the Joint Judiciary Committee of the state legislature to deposit their 10,000 signatures and to address the committee and several hearings in both houses. Cady Stanton's address to the legislature marked the first time that a woman made a major speech to that body. The three women continued their extensive petition campaign for the next six years. Although the campaign culminated in 1860 with legislative reform protecting the property of married women, the New York legislators' responses to the campaign echo the same themes as the responses to the broader campaign for women's rights in the 1850s. For example, Assemblyman Jonathan Burnet commented in 1854, in response to the petitions, that these women "do not appear to be satisfied with having unsexed themselves, but they desire to unsex every female in the land, and to set the whole community ablaze with unhallowed fire."[13] Assemblyman Daniel P. Wood nevertheless presented the petition on behalf of the women, requested that a select committee be formed, and argued that the number of signatures alone demanded a dignified response from the legislature. The New York Assembly created a select committee to which the petitions were referred. Although that committee promised to treat the subject seriously, its report proclaimed that "A higher power than that from which emanates legislative enactments has given forth the mandate that man and woman *shall not be* [equal]."[14] The husband, it continued, was the sovereign head of the family. Marriage, contrary to Cady Stanton's claims, was not a civil contract but one that was "more binding" and with "more solemn specialties." Still, the committee recommended legislation to enable the wife to collect her own earnings if her husband was unable to support her. In 1855, a similar committee recommended a slight change in property laws so that widows would have more control over their husband's property. But, in 1856 the judiciary committee issued a report ridiculing the entire woman's rights movement. Samuel A. Foote, who delivered the report, told the Assembly that the "ladies" who demanded equality between the sexes had "the choicest tidbits at the table," the "best seats in cars, carriages, and sleighs," and "the warmest place in winter and the coolest place in summer." Their dresses cost three times as much and took up three times as much space as male attire. It was men who were oppressed. The report's derision reached its peak when it recommended that couples who had both signed the petition request a law authorizing a clothing switch "so that the husband may wear the petty-coats, and the wife the breeches, and thus indicate to their neighbors and the public the true relation in which they stand to each other."[15]

At the outset of the campaign for reform in the property system, there was substantially more support for married women's property rights than for suffrage. Still, opponents of property rights reform in the 1850s commonly argued that women were incapable of handling their finances and that that the law of nature validated male sovereignty.[16] As the 1850s progressed, however, and women's property rights became more widely accepted, opposition to reform tended to focus more on suffrage. For example, between 1852 and 1860, the *New York Times* came to support bills for married women's property rights while it continued to sneer at suffrage. In 1860, the *Times* supported the married women's property rights bill but declared that it could not see what else Mrs. Lucy Stone might want without waging "war upon human nature itself and the ordinances of high heaven."[17]

The responses to women's rights reform clearly reflected the extent to which the ideology of the separate spheres thoroughly constrained women's lives. Opponents of reform also vociferously and repeatedly renounced the supposedly dominant liberal belief in the equality of individuals. Thus, Cady Stanton, who had based so many of her arguments on the liberal tradition—asking only that the promise of the Declaration of Independence be fulfilled by applying the principles of equality to women—found that she was up against seemingly insurmountable obstacles. Foremost among those obstacles was the absolute refusal on the part of the opponents of reform to consider the possibility of natural equality of men and women.

As we saw in chapter 2 the antebellum woman's rights movement began to develop when some abolitionist women moved out of the domestic sphere to join the struggle against slavery. Women who worked in benevolent associations in the 1830s and 1840s appeared to be engaging in activities that were appropriate, virtuous, and well within their prescribed sphere. By the 1850s, however, many of those women had shifted their efforts to the campaign for suffrage. Nevertheless, a number of socially prominent women worked for benevolent causes and campaigned for improvements in women's education but remained opposed to woman suffrage.[18] Women like Emma Willard, Catharine Beecher, and Sarah Josepha Hale celebrated an idealized domesticity, emphasizing women's moral superiority and their role in protecting the morals of the nation. They remained committed to raising the status of women's domestic role at least in part in an effort to compensate for the relative decline in the status of women that occurred in the early nineteenth century with the transfer of economic production from the household to the factory.[19] Although their goal was to elevate women's domestic role, these women remained dedicated to preserving the boundaries between the separate spheres. Women in the antebellum temperance movement were also opposed to suffrage out of a determination to keep attention focused on the need to improve protections for women and children against the violence and poverty that resulted from men's excessive drinking.

The overwhelmingly negative responses to the antebellum woman's rights movement, particularly to the early demand for the vote, underscore just how deeply embedded the cult of domesticity was in the culture of the United States in the mid-nineteenth century. According to the prevailing wisdom, women's physical and moral qualities rendered them unfit for the public world of politics and business. Maintaining the barriers between the separate spheres was essential to the health of the nation, the family, and the individual because the boundary between the two realms was part of the natural order. Women's natural place was in the domestic sphere where she could maintain the household and shape the morals of her husband and children. Secure in the domestic realm, women would be protected from the competitiveness and corruption of the outside world. Public life lay squarely in man's sphere, and women had no business invading the male realm. The existence of women's natural differences, which mandated that they perform such different functions, also meant that any breakdown of the boundaries between public and private—that is, the prospect of allowing women into the public sphere by giving them the vote—posed a serious threat to the family, to womanhood, and to the future of the nation. If women ventured into the public sphere, they would cease to be women, men would no longer be men, families would disintegrate, and the social order would dissolve. The examination of Cady Stanton's responses to the opponents of woman's rights that follows reveals the extent to which her own framework was immersed in the ideology of separate spheres even though she was determined to repudiate it.

Cady Stanton's Responses

Soon after the Seneca Falls Convention, Cady Stanton began to formulate replies to virtually every objection to women's rights. Her arguments, which she articulated in speeches, articles, and letters, were carefully reasoned and substantive but were often interspersed with passionate and defiant—at times even inflammatory—rhetoric. Her comments frequently reflected her disgust with the rules and customs that kept women's lives so limited and with the people—both male and female—who in various ways were perpetuating the unequal status of women. Her responses during the antebellum period were designed not only to educate critics on women's position but also to emphasize the benefits to society that women's rights would bring. She often focused on women's special qualities, particularly their moral virtues. Moreover, she frequently argued that the prospect of women moving into the sphere that had traditionally been reserved for men did not pose a threat to the family but rather would improve it.

As we saw in chapter 2, Cady Stanton's arguments reflected the multiple traditions insofar as they included a liberal-equal rights perspective as well as the notion of a republican duty to participate in public life for the common good. Her arguments also reflected ascriptive notions concerning both sex and race: women were morally superior to men in general, and educated white women, in particular, were superior to uneducated foreigners and slaves. Fully participating women with equal rights could therefore bring their moral virtues—the natural qualities with which they were endowed—to bear on politics. Although she challenged the cult of domesticity, with its rigidly prescribed separate spheres, and envisioned a transformation of power relations within the family, when she replied to the critics of women's rights she worked squarely within the dominant ideology of the separate spheres. She framed her arguments strategically in order to maximize her chances of garnering support for women's rights and weakening the opposition. Still, the way she devised her rejoinders to the opponents of women's rights also suggests the extent to which the cult of domesticity was so deeply ingrained in the culture of the nineteenth century that it invariably played a major role in her analysis.

Cady Stanton had much to say in response to the biblical argument against women's rights. In the 1840s, she began to use the argument that she would develop fully in *The Woman's Bible* in 1895: that the Bible, interpreted correctly, did not prescribe woman's subordination to man. In 1848, for example, she recommended that those who relied on the scriptural authority to oppose women's rights pay more careful attention to their Bibles.[20] She also frequently drew attention to the way that the church excluded women. In a letter to Susan B. Anthony, for example, she observed that "the Church is a terrible engine of oppression, especially as concerns woman."[21] At the Rochester Convention in 1848, she prefaced her address by expressing the hope that if there were any clergymen present, they would not keep silent during the Convention only to go on Sunday to their pulpits to denounce the women, who would not be allowed to reply.[22]

It was only a few days after the Seneca Falls Convention that Cady Stanton and Elizabeth W. McClintock wrote a letter to the editors of the *Seneca County Courier* in response to a sermon charging the reformers at the Seneca Falls Convention with "infidelity." The two women observed that the Bible was traditionally interpreted to support moral wrongs, and they challenged the prevailing interpretation of Scripture:

> No reform has ever been started but the Bible, falsely interpreted, has opposed it. Wine-drinking was proved to be right by the Bible. Slavery was proved to be an institution of the Bible. War, with its long train of calamities and abominations is proved to be right by the Bible. Capital punishment is taught in the Bible. Now it seems to us, the time has fully

come for this much abused book to change hands. Let the people no longer trust to their blind guides, but read and reason for themselves— even though they thus call down on themselves the opprobrious epithet of "infidel," than which no word in our languages is more misunderstood and misapplied. We throw back the charge of infidelity on the religionists of the present day, for though they assert their belief in the Divinity of Christ, they deny, in theory and practice, his Divine commands.[23]

Cady Stanton and McClintock contended that women had an obligation not to man but rather to "that Divine Being who claims the reverence and obedience of all his sons and daughters." The claims of religious opponents of women's rights were, they argued, "in direct opposition to the spirit of Christianity," as they relied on isolated passages of the Bible, "to destroy the conscience and the sense of moral accountability in one half the people of the earth."[24]

Those "religionists," Cady Stanton charged, were the true infidels. In her letter to the Woman's Rights Convention in 1852, she proclaimed that the most violent enemies of women's rights were to be found among the clergy. Nevertheless, she noted, when in need of money for various missions, most notably their own profit, the same clergymen were always ready to solicit funds from women. She admonished women to organize their own charities and castigated religion for intensifying women's oppression:

> [W]oman, in her present ignorance, is made to rest in the most distorted view of God and the Bible, and the laws of her being; and like the poor slave, "Uncle Tom," her religion, instead of making her noble and free, and impelling her to flee from all gross surroundings, by the false lessons of her spiritual teachers—by the wrong application of great principles of right and justice, has made her bondage but more certain and lasting—her degradation more hopeless and complete.[25]

Cady Stanton's early critique of religion provided her with a way to refute those who relied on the Bible and the church to condemn women's rights. Her analysis of religion, however, was much more than a response to the critics. Over the next thirty years, she developed it into a full-blown critique that challenged all religions on the grounds that they justified and promoted the subordination of women. The way she was willing to attack the organized religion that was at the center of the culture of the United States draws attention to the radical strain in her thought.

As for the charge that women were physically, morally, and intellectually inferior to men, in the address she delivered several times in New York in 1848, Cady Stanton admonished the men who were so convinced of their "natural inborn, inbred superiority both in body and mind and their full complete Heaven descended right to lord it over the fish of the sea, the fowl of the air, the beast of the field and last tho' not least the immortal being called woman" to take more notice of women's demonstrated abilities; they would do well, she said, to pay attention to "historical research, to foreign travel—to a closer observation of the manifestations of mind about them and to an humble comparison of themselves with such women as Catharine of Russia, Elizabeth of England distinguished for their statesmanlike qualities."[26] Those men, she continued, should look at the literary achievements of some noteworthy women and the scientific accomplishments of others and to the Amazons for their physical strength. Thus, she not only defied the perception of woman as morally, intellectually, and physically the inferior of man but also suggested that the men who took such a position were ignorant. Given freedom from the domestic sphere, women would prove themselves equal to men in intellectual ability. As for moral virtue, she argued that women were superior to men "not by nature, but made so by a false education."[27]

Responding to the objection to women's rights based on their purported physical inferiority, Cady Stanton asserted that women's physical potential was as yet untested and that although men might be larger and stronger, the power of the mind was always much more important than either size or physical strength. Women's moral virtues formed an important theme that ran through Cady Stanton's speech. She attributed the ubiquitous moral stagnation in American society, evidenced by war, slavery, drunkenness, licentiousness, and gluttony, to the degradation of women. The "secret of all this woe, [was]—the inactivity of her head and heart. . . . The earth has never yet seen a truly great and virtuous nation, for woman has never yet stood the equal with man."[28]

Just as Cady Stanton praised women's qualities she also attempted to counter the images of homes destroyed by women trying to be men that opponents called to mind:

> We did not as some have supposed assemble to go into the detail of so-
> cial life alone, we did not propose to petition the legislature to make
> our Husbands just, generous and courteous, to seat every man at the
> head of a cradle and to clothe every woman in male attire, no none of
> these points however important they may be considered by humble
> minds, were touched upon in the convention.[29]

Minimizing the implications of the reforms that women's rights advocates were demanding and emphasizing the liberal foundations of proposals for reform, she reminded opponents that the woman's rights conventions were a means of protesting a "form of government existing
without the consent of the governed, to declare our right to be free as
man is free—to be represented in the government which we are taxed to
support."[30]

Cady Stanton also responded to the argument that women's rights
would destroy the family by explaining that it was not women's rights
but the degraded position of women that jeopardized families. Equality
would provide the foundation for strengthening them. Freedom and
equality, she argued, would not "destroy all harmony in the domestic circle." Indeed, she questioned the existence of "harmonious households"
as she described women's subordination and domestic drudgery within
the family and the "Hen-pecked Husband" who "can absent himself
from home as much as possible, but he does not feel like a free man."[31]
She admonished that the only truly happy households were those in
which husband and wife "share equally in counsel and government.
There can be no true dignity or independence where there is subordination, no happiness without freedom."[32] In 1850, she reiterated that argument, rearranging the words only slightly: "there is no true happiness
where there is subordination—no harmony without freedom."[33]

Cady Stanton also explicitly condemned the doctrine of separate
spheres, charging that it failed to take individual abilities and preferences into account:

> If God has assigned a sphere to man and one to woman, we claim the
> right to judge ourselves of His design in reference to us, and we accord
> to man the same privilege. . . .
>   There is no such thing as a sphere for a sex. Every man has a differ-
> ent sphere, and one in which he may shine, and it is the same with every

woman; and the same woman may have a different sphere at different times.[34]

She went on to illustrate her argument that a woman may occupy a different sphere at different times in her life with the examples of Angelina Grimké and Lucretia Mott, both of whom spent time in the public sphere but at another time devoted themselves to their homes and families. Her praise of women's devotion to home and children softened her challenge to the cult of domesticity considerably as she conceded that at a certain time in a woman's life—when she has young children—she must devote herself to the domestic realm and that only when she is free from such responsibilities will public activities be appropriate.

To the argument that women are represented by fathers, husbands, brothers, and sons and therefore do not need the vote, Cady Stanton responded that women were tired of the type of representation in which they were invariably manipulated and deceived and deprived of their rights:

[M]en like to call her an angel—to feed her with what they think sweet food nourishing her vanity, to induce her to believe her organization is so much finer more delicate than theirs, that she is not fitted to struggle with the tempests of public life but needs their care and protection. Care and protection? Such as the wolf gives the lamb—such as the eagle the hare he carries to his eyrie. Most cunningly he entraps her and then takes from her all those rights which are dearer to him than life itself, rights which have been baptized in blood and the maintenance of which is even now rocking to their foundations the kingdoms of the old world.[35]

Among other objections to woman suffrage to which Cady Stanton responded in 1848 was the argument that if women voted, they would soon be joining men in combat, or, as she expressed it, "But if woman claims all the rights of a citizen will she buckle on her armour and fight in defence of her country?"[36] Cady Stanton's response was simple: all war is wrong. "I would not have man go to war. I can see no glory in fighting with such weapons as guns and swords whilst man has in his possession the infinitely superior and more effective ones of righteousness and truth."[37]

She also responded to the ridicule to which supporters of dress reform were subjected.[38] She associated woman's right to choose her attire with her ability to fulfill her potential and to break free of her constraints. When she applauded dress reform in 1851 in an article in the *Lily,* she argued that, far from being the mere whim of a bunch of silly women, it was a change that would put woman in her true position, making her primary and "rags" secondary. She observed that "whatever is comfortable and convenient, and permits the greatest freedom of motion, is the most perfect costume." Clothing should "stand out of the way of the full and perfect development of the woman."[39] When Cady Stanton praised Lucy Stone for wearing the bloomer costume at the Woman's Rights Convention in Syracuse in 1852, she declared that "woman can never be developed in her present drapery, she is a slave to her rags."[40] She also decried the pervasive power of fashion that forced her to give up wearing the bloomer outfit in public, commenting to Elizabeth Smith Miller that "Such is the tyranny of custom, that to escape constant observation, criticism, ridicule, persecution, [and] mobs, one after another went back to the old slavery and sacrificed freedom to repose."[41]

In 1855, Cady Stanton forged an explicit link between dress reform and the natural equality of the sexes when she argued that the dress of men and women should be similar so that it would reflect their common natures. Her cousin, Gerrit Smith, had written to her arguing that the woman's rights movement could not hope to achieve its goals unless women "throw off the dress, which, in the eye of chivalry and gallantry, is so well adapted to womanly gracefulness and womanly helplessness, and to put on a dress that would leave her free to work her own way through the world."[42] Nevertheless, he maintained that women's clothing should be different from men's. Cady Stanton replied that the prerogative to dress as one chooses does not necessarily carry equal rights with it: "We have no reason to hope that pantaloons would do more for us than they have done for man himself. The negro slave enjoys the most unlimited freedom in his attire, not surpassed even by the fashions of Eden in its palmiest days; yet in spite of his dress, and his manhood, too, he is a slave still."[43] She argued nevertheless that given the similarities between men and women, there could be no justification for maintaining distinctions between their attire: "Surely, whatever dress is convenient for one sex must be for the other also. Whatever is necessary for the perfect and full development of man's physical being, must be equally so for woman. I fully agree with you that woman is terribly cramped and crippled in her present style of dress. I have not one word to utter in its defense; but to me, it seems that if she would enjoy entire freedom, she should dress just like man."[44]

Cady Stanton's response to female opponents of women's rights is important to the analysis of her work for the light it sheds on her conception of women both as individuals and as a group and what she perceived as the basis of their obligation to support the campaign for woman's rights. When she responded to female opponents, she initially tried to justify women's failure to understand their own oppression by emphasizing that they had been subjected to injustice for so long that they were not even aware that there was a problem. Those who did realize the unfairness of their subordination could not even begin to contemplate a solution. In her 1848 speech, for example, she lamented, "So long has man exercised a tyranny over her injurious to himself and benumbing to her faculties, that but few can nerve themselves against the storm, and so long has the chain been about her that however galling it may be she knows not there is a remedy."[45] She imagined a future in which women would be "enlightened in regard to their present position, to the laws under which they live—they will not then publish their degradation by declaring themselves satisfied nor their ignorance by declaring they have all the rights they want."[46] At this point, Cady Stanton seemed confident that once women became conscious of the extent of the injustices with which they lived, they would participate in the movement or, at the very least, give it their enthusiastic support.

Although her comments in 1854 in her appeal to women to sign petitions to the New York legislature demanding property rights and suffrage reflected the same themes, she also borrowed from abolitionist rhetoric, comparing the slave's apparent satisfaction to woman's inability to understand her oppression:

It is humiliating to know that many educated women so stultify their consciences as to declare that they have all the rights they want. Have you who make this declaration ever read the barbarous laws in reference to woman, to mothers, to wives, and to daughters, which disgrace our Statute Books? Laws which are not surpassed in cruelty and injustice by any slaveholding code in the United States; laws which strike at the root of the glorious doctrine for which our fathers fought and bled and died. . . .

If, in view of laws like these, there be women in this State so lost to self-respect, to all that is virtuous, noble, and true, as to refuse to raise their voices in protest against such degrading tyranny, we can only say of that system which has thus robbed womanhood of all its glory and greatness, what the Immortal Channing did of slavery, "If," said he, "it be time that the slaves are contented and happy-if there is a system that can blot out all love of freedom from the soul of man, destroy every trace of his Divinity, make him happy in a condition so low and be-nighted and hopeless, I ask for no stronger argument against such a slavery as ours." No! never believe it; woman falsifies herself and blas-phemes her God, when in view of her present social, legal, and political position, she declares she has all the rights she wants.[47]

Women should understand their condition and fight against it. How could they, as Cady Stanton termed it, falsify themselves?

A year later, Cady Stanton had even harsher words for female oppo-nents of reform: any woman who maintains that she has all the rights she wants is either "deplorably ignorant, selfish, or false." She con-tinued to maintain that although they may disparage women's rights, women nevertheless resent being made to pay taxes when they have no voice in government just as they lament their dependence on men. Also, the most privileged women claim they have all the rights they want but "actually suffer for the want of something to do . . . their lives are ob-jectless, their sympathies are shrivelled by being forever confined to themselves and children. They go the senseless round of life, thinking and acting according to the most approved methods, and the soul dies in such trammels." She went on to reiterate that even the life of the most privileged woman could be compared to that of a slave and that even if such women had no problems of their own, they should support women's rights out of sympathy for the many who were not so fortu-nate. They had a duty to help those who "have come down from the pleasant mountains . . . to wander friendless and alone in the valley of sorrow and humiliation. The next turn of fortune's wheel may bring you there too."[48]

Women will never get what they ask for, she wrote in 1856, until the "majority of women are openly with us; and they will never claim their civil rights, until they know their social wrongs." She maintained that women would support reform once they understood that there was hope for significant change. Meanwhile, "she patiently bears all this because in her blindness she sees no way of escape"; the movement should undertake "to show that there is hope for woman this side of heaven, and that there is a work for her to do before she leaves for the celestial city."[49]

Cady Stanton refined and strengthened her argument that no woman could possibly have all the rights she wanted in a revision of the 1856 essay that she published in 1859. Even the most fortunate woman, she noted, is vulnerable to her all-too-powerful husband:

> The soul lives not in the outward, and if the only legitimate object of a woman's pursuit is love and marriage, has she "all the rights she wants," when her love may not be voluntary. When law and gospel, judge and juror, all agree that a man calling himself husband, has the right not only to the custody of her person, but to the guardianship of the holy affections of a young and trusting heart—affection, which, in his grossness, he never seeks to concentrate on himself—satisfied that he holds the outward woman.[50]

She reminded her female critics that women are forbidden to teach in the church and that their literary efforts were denigrated—their books "are popular only so far as they echo back man's thunder." What, moreover, of the widow and the wife whose property is seized to pay the debts of her husband and the woman who manages to discard the "heavy yoke of discordant marriage" but loses her children, property, and home? No woman who has earned her own living—"the Teacher, the Seamstress, the Drunkard's wife, the Outcast"—Cady Stanton admonished, will "underrate the importance of our demands, with the silly motto, 'I have all the rights I want.'" Finally, she conceded that some women may actually have all the rights they wanted, but they should help those who did not: "If I have all I want for body and soul, is it not the best reason in the world why I should generously aid all those who are oppressed, suffering, destitute, friendless and alone? Lives there a woman whose nature is so hard, narrow and selfish, that she can pity no sorrows but those which she has felt in her own person?"[51]

She elaborated in a tract that she published anonymously in 1859.

Even if there are some women who have all the rights they want, she advised, there can be no justification for their refusal to support those who do not:

> Because their soft white hands have never labored, is that a reason why they should not demand a right to wages for those who spend their days in honest toil? When famine has reduced any of the human family almost to starvation, shall I refuse them food because I am not hungry? If I have all I want for body and soul, is it not the best reason in the world why I should generously aid all those who are oppressed, suffering, destitute, friendless and alone? Lives there a woman whose nature is so hard, narrow and selfish, that she can pity no sorrows but those which she has felt in her own person? Or can there be one woman in this nation so ignorant that she really thinks she is already living in the full possession of all the rights that belong to a citizen of a Republic?"[52]

She was increasingly critical of privileged wives who claimed to have all the rights they needed—could anyone be so ignorant? she asked. Cady Stanton's comments reflected more empathy for women who were not so fortunate—those who had to work for minuscule wages, those who were left destitute and with no means to provide for their children by irresponsible, brutish husbands. Yet, she lashed out at working women when female teachers in New York refused to demand equal wages in 1856 even after Susan B. Anthony counseled them to do so. Cady Stanton expressed her disgust privately to Anthony, declaring with disdain, "What an infernal set of fools these school-marms must be!! Well, if in order to please men they wish to live on air, let them. The sooner the present generation of women die out the better. We have jackasses enough in the world now without such women propagating any more."[53] She also responded unequivocally to temperance women who opposed suffrage on the grounds that they needed to keep attention focused on the problem of excessive drinking and the need to convince legislators to protect women and children from intemperate husbands and fathers. Her answer was simply that the vote would enable women to protect themselves so that they would no longer need to rely on the good will of male legislators.

Did Cady Stanton view women as a group with obligations to the other members of that group or as a collection of separate rights-bearing individuals pursuing their own interests? Did she consider it important that they support women's rights in order to help women as a group, to improve society, or did she believe it was more important for each woman to advance her own interests? Her increasingly angry responses to women opponents indicate that she conceived of women as a group with a shared obligation to promote the interests of that group. Also, she often repeated that women's rights would improve society. Thus, it was not for the pursuit of self-interest that women should join the campaign for women's rights reform but rather out of a commitment to the well-being of women as a group.

Cady Stanton's comments concerning women's failure to come to grips with their membership in an oppressed group suggests that she was developing a concept that was akin to the false consciousness that Karl Marx made famous. Women, like workers, could not see that they were subjugated and exploited. The most privileged women, who were supported and protected by their husbands, could not imagine a better life. In other words, women had no consciousness of themselves as a group. Their position had given them a "false consciousness" according to which they "had all the rights they wanted." Until they overcame that false consciousness, they could not become aware of themselves as a group and, therefore, could not unite in the struggle for change.

How does such an analysis comport with liberalism, republicanism, or ascriptivism? It contains a republican theme insofar as it asserts that society will improve as a result of women's contributions to public life. Yet, there is much to her analysis of what might be called woman's false consciousness that does not fit comfortably into any of the three traditions. Instead, it reveals a radical strain in Cady Stanton's work, rejects the individualism of American political culture and transcends the three categories of the multiple traditions.

Conclusion

Among the most prominent themes running through Cady Stanton's responses to the opponents of the antebellum campaign for women's rights were her attack on the biblical argument that God intended women to be subordinate to men and on the notion that separate spheres for males and females were divinely ordained, natural, and inevitable. In her rejection of the biblical argument and her criticism of religion, it is possible to see an early version of the radical critique of religion and of the Bible that Cady Stanton would develop in later years. In addition, as noted earlier, her analysis of women as a group points to another radical element of her thought. In contrast, although she criticized the cult of domesticity, she took care to defend the woman's rights movement against the charges that women reformers were trying to infringe on male territory by venturing into the public sphere, that they were trying to replace men, and that they were intent on destroying the family. She tempered the most far-reaching implications of her agenda by emphasizing the injustices of property law and the absence of political representation for women and underlined the plight of women who found themselves married to financially irresponsible, abusive, or alcoholic men. Moreover, by manipulating the tradition of ascriptivism that posited women's inferior intellectual capacities, Cady Stanton argued that women's ability to resolve problems, though concededly different from men's, was at least as useful as, if not superior to, the male's purported capacity for logical reasoning.

Her comments also underline how deeply ingrained the cult of domesticity was, even in her own thought. Cady Stanton frequently alluded to women's essential role within the family, emphasizing the need for expanding their role in the public sphere so that they could be better wives and mothers. Moreover, if they had political rights, women would be more capable of protecting themselves in the domestic realm. At the same time, however, she was advocating fundamental change in the power dynamic of the family and a radical transformation of society.

5

The Civil War Years

Breaking Down Barriers Between Public and Private

Introduction

With the outbreak of the Civil War, in 1861, Cady Stanton put aside her work for women's rights in order to devote herself to the cause of emancipation and Union victory. Yet she did not really turn away from women's rights but instead thoroughly integrated that cause with abolitionism. Moreover, her work during the war served to undermine the boundary between the public and the private spheres in ways that were enormously important in the struggle for women's rights and in the development of her ideas.

Cady Stanton and the Garrisonians

During the second half of the 1850s, the conflict over slavery moved to the center of national politics and began to encroach on the woman's rights movement. Major developments that captured the attention of women's rights reformers included the passage of the Kansas-Nebraska Act and the birth of the Republican Party, in 1854; the conflict over the settlement of Kansas and the violence between the rival state governments, the controversy over whether Kansas would be admitted to the Union as a free or a slave state, and John Brown's massacre of proslavery settlers at Pottawatomie Creek, in 1856; and his attempt to capture the federal arsenal at Harper's Ferry, Virginia, in 1859.

As we saw in chapter 2, the antebellum woman's rights movement was closely linked to Garrisonian abolitionism. In 1856, the American Anti-Slavery Society engaged Susan B. Anthony as an agent and put her in charge of organizing in New York. After the Supreme Court's decision in *Dred Scott v. Sandford*, in 1857, which held that Congress lacked the power to prohibit slavery in the territories and that black people were not citizens of the United States and, therefore, could not bring suit in federal court, Anthony continued her work for women's rights while also increasing her antislavery activities, organizing lectures for other agents and speaking to audiences herself.[1]

In January 1861, Anthony organized a tour of speakers through towns in upstate New York to condemn any compromise with the South and to demand immediate emancipation.[2] One of those speakers was Elizabeth Cady Stanton. In the early months of the war, Anthony continued to arrange antislavery meetings throughout New York, and Cady Stanton lectured intermittently. When the Anti-Slavery Society made a decision to end the lecture tours, Anthony was outraged, but Cady Stanton conceded that the public meetings should be canceled. Abolitionists began to return to the field, however, as it became clear that President Lincoln was not moving quickly enough against slavery.

Although Cady Stanton was considerably less active in antislavery work during the 1850s than Anthony, she maintained close connections with the Garrisonians.[3] In fact, it was at Garrison's invitation that she spoke at the American Anti-Slavery Convention in 1860. She observed that "this is the only organization on God's footstool where the humanity of woman is recognized, and these are the only men who have ever echoed back her cries for justice and equality."[4] She also was in frequent contact with other abolitionists, including her cousin Gerrit Smith.

Cady Stanton's views concerning secession, the war, and the Lincoln administration's policies regarding the slaves closely paralleled those of the Garrisonians, who welcomed secession and abjured violence but then embraced the Civil War as a means to end slavery. The Garrisonians objected to Lincoln's war policies because they did not make slavery the central issue of the war and did not take decisive action to quickly emancipate the slaves.[5] In 1850, she delivered an address to the Woman's Rights Convention in Worcester, Massachusetts, voicing her general opposition to war: "I believe all war sinful; I believe in Christ; I believe that the command, 'Resist not evil,' is divine; I would not have man go to war; I can see no glory in fighting with such weapons as guns and swords, while man has in his possession the infinitely superior and more effective ones of righteousness and truth."[6]

Like the Garrisonians, Cady Stanton revised her position after the attack on Fort Sumter and rallied to the Union cause. In April 1861, she expressed her agreement with Wendell Phillips's "Discourse on the War," in which he reversed his disunionist position and welcomed the war.[7] She wrote later in 1861, "This war is music in my ears. It is a simultaneous chorus for freedom; for every nation that has ever fought for liberty on her own soil is now represented in our army."[8] Also like the Garrisonians, she condemned the federal government's efforts to compromise with the slave states in order to avoid secession. In a letter to Elizabeth Smith Miller in 1856, she wrote: "My own opinion is that the 'staving off' policy has been fairly tried and I am becoming more and more convinced that we shall be in the midst of violence, blood, and civil war before we look for it. Our fair republic must be the victim of the monster, slavery, unless we speedily rise in our might and boldly shout freedom."[9] Yet, in another letter she wrote that same year concerning the conflict over slavery in Kansas, she declared to the abolitionist Samuel J. May: "I hope the women's rights women will have nothing to do with it. We have been long enough aids to man's sins and follies. If I cannot have a voice in the government of my country, I have no idea of scraping lint for those who are threatening to break it up."[10]

Her departure from the Garrisonian disdain for party politics was apparent, however, in Cady Stanton's letter to Anthony in 1855 in which she expressed her approval of Henry Stanton's activities in the new Republican Party. She wrote, "I am rejoiced to say that Henry is heart and soul in the Republican movement and is faithfully stumping the state once more. I have attended all the Republican meetings."[11] Still, she was to remain much closer to the Garrisonians than to the Republicans. In 1857, after the Supreme Court's decision in *Dred Scott v. Sandford,* she endorsed disunionism and indicated that she agreed with Garrison that the Constitution was a proslavery document.[12] Her comments two years later, however, reflected a more ambivalent attitude when she wrote to Anthony asking her position on the proslavery LeCompton Constitution in Kansas: "You Garrisonians are such a crotchety set that generally, when all other men see cause for rejoicing, you howl the more grievously. How is it now? I desire to know, for as I am one of you, I wish to do what is most becoming to one of the order. Shall I fire off my boys' cannon and a bundle of crackers, or shall I wear sackcloth and ashes?"[13]

Cady Stanton supported Lincoln's candidacy in 1860 in part because of Republican opposition to the extension of slavery into the territories. Like the Garrisonians, however, she was convinced that emancipation should be the goal of the Civil War. In 1863, she exhorted women to understand that the war involved the principles of "liberty or slavery—democracy or aristocracy—equality or caste—and choose, this day, whether our republican institutions shall be placed on an enduring basis, and an eternal peace secured to our children, or whether we shall leap back through generations of light and experience, and meekly bow again to chains and slavery."[14]

Cady Stanton quickly became disillusioned with Lincoln's reluctance to free all the slaves. In December 1861, she wrote to Gerrit Smith expressing her agreement with his assessment of Lincoln's statement in his message to Congress that he would not interfere with slavery in the South as "twattle and trash." She characterized all of the president's messages to Congress as "of the most mamdy-pamby order" and declared, "he certainly does not dignify the office he fills."[15] She wrote in 1862 to Elizabeth Smith Miller, "I do hope the rebels will sack Washington, take Lincoln, Seward, and McClellan and keep them safe in some Southern fort until we man the ship of state with those who know whither they are steering and for what purpose."[16]

The events of the second half of the 1850s and early 1860s concerning slavery, abolitionism, and war had a direct impact on Cady Stanton's life. Her cousin Gerrit Smith, who provided financial support for John Brown's raid on Harper's Ferry in 1859 and was thus implicated in Brown's case, had himself committed temporarily to a mental institution. In 1861, two of Cady Stanton's sons were old enough to serve in the army. Her second son, Henry, ran away and enlisted. Two of her nephews also ran away to enlist, and one died in combat.[17] In addition, as an activist in the Republican Party, Henry Stanton hoped for an appointment in Lincoln's administration as solicitor of the Treasury. That position went to someone else, and Stanton accepted a position as deputy collector of the Customs House in New York City, where he was responsible for supervising and securing the port against smugglers and shippers of Southern goods. The Stanton family moved to New York City in 1862, and, in the summer of 1863, rioters protesting the draft sacked the offices of the *New York Tribune,* hanged some free black men, and burned a black orphanage only two blocks from the Stanton's home. The mob went past their house while the Stanton children hid on the fourth floor, ready to escape to the roof, and Cady Stanton prepared to appeal to the rioters as "Americans and citizens of a Republic."[18] The mob seized the Stanton's oldest son, Neil (Daniel), and accused him of buying his way out of the draft. Cady Stanton reported that he saved himself by inviting some of his assailants to join him in a saloon, where they drank to Jefferson Davis. She later wrote to Nancy Smith, commenting on the incident:

> The riot raged in our neighborhood through the first two days of the trouble largely because the colored orphan asylum on Fifth Avenue was only two blocks away from us. I saw all those little children marched off two by two. A double portion of martyrdom has been meted out to our poor blacks, and I am led to ask if there is no justice in heaven or on earth that this should be permitted through the centuries.[19]

Working for Union Victory and Emancipation

Cady Stanton and Susan B. Anthony had their first major disagreement over the question of whether the campaign for women's rights should continue during the Civil War. When the war began, in April 1861, Anthony had completed arrangements for the National Woman's Rights Convention in May. The American Anti-Slavery Society canceled its scheduled meeting and advised the women's rights leaders to do the same. Cady Stanton and others advised Anthony to postpone the convention, and she did so reluctantly.[20] Anthony wrote to Martha Coffin Wright in late May expressing her resentment over the canceled meetings.

> Our position, to me seems most humiliating—simply that of the political world—one of expediency not principle. . . . I have not yet seen one good reason for the abandonment of all our meetings—& am as time lengthens, more & more ashamed & sad that even the little apostolic number have gone over to the worlds motto that the means must be sacrificed to the end.[21]

Anthony was likewise disappointed in the opposition from other women's rights leaders to calling a convention in the spring of 1862. She was sick at heart, she wrote, that "All our reformers seem suddenly to have grown politic. All alike say, 'Have no conventions at this crisis'! Garrison, Phillips, Mrs. Mott, Mrs. Wright, Mrs. Stanton, etc., say, 'Wait until the war excitement abates'; which is to say, 'Ask our opponents if they think we had better speak, or, rather, if they do not think we had better remain silent.'"[22]

In contrast to Anthony, Cady Stanton was ready to commit herself to emancipation and Union victory, reasoning that the public was so preoccupied with the war that it would pay little attention to anything else. Moreover, she fully expected that, in return for the loyalty and hard work of the women's rights activists, the Republican Party would support woman suffrage once the war ended. So, with the beginning of the Civil War in April 1861, Cady Stanton put aside women's rights. Anthony's fear that if women stopped agitating for their rights, the gains they had made would be reversed turned out to be well founded. In 1862, the New York legislature repealed the provision of the Married Women's Property Act that gave mothers the right to equal guardianship of their children. The legislators also eliminated the right of wives to control their property on the death of their husbands. Many years later, in her autobiography, Cady Stanton conceded that Anthony had been right and that the women's rights leaders had learned an important lesson:

> [N]amely, that it is impossible for the best of men to understand women's feelings or the humiliation of their position. When they asked us to be silent on our question during the War, and labor for the emancipation of the slave, we did so, and gave five years to his emancipation and enfranchisement. . . . I was convinced, at the time, that it was the true policy. I am now equally sure that it was a blunder.[23]

Cady Stanton continued her political activities in New York, joining the Union effort to win the war and to bring an end to the institution of slavery.[24]

In her work during this period, Cady Stanton embraced the Garrisonian natural-rights argument that slavery was a violation of every individual's right to liberty. In her address in 1860 to the American Anti-Slavery Society, for example, she emphasized the conflict between liberty and slavery. The laws that sanctioned slavery, she observed, perverted "man's moral sense and innate love of justice." Slavery had "corrupted our churches, our politics, our press; laid violent hands on

Northern freemen at their own firesides; it has gagged our statesmen, and stricken our Northern Senators dumb in their seats; yes, beneath the flag of freedom, Liberty has crouched in fear."[25] In her address in 1861 to the New York State Anti-Slavery Society, she condemned the mobs that disrupted abolitionist meetings. She declared that abolitionism "cannot be choked down, nor hissed down, nor stomped down, for truth is mighty and must eternally prevail; and in spite of mobs, and bluster, and threats, freedom shall triumph, and crush the reptile slavery beneath her feet." Denouncing compromise with the South once again, she proclaimed that if Northerners had any self-respect, they would have "seceded long ago, from these heathen idolaters."[26]

Undermining the Boundary Between Public and Private

Although Cady Stanton was willing to put aside her work for women's rights for the duration of the war, her speeches and writings during that time show just how thoroughly she integrated abolitionism with women's rights. In so doing, she repeatedly emphasized women's obligation to work for Union victory and the emancipation of the slaves in such a way as to undermine the separation of the public and private spheres.

She frequently linked the problem of slavery to other social problems, thus adapting and expanding the Garrisonian natural-rights approach to the struggle for justice and equality for all human beings. She declared in 1860, for example, that the mission of the Garrisonian abolitionist movement was to liberate not only the African slave but also "the slaves of custom, creed and sex."[27] She also departed from her earlier practice of comparing white women and male slaves when she drew attention to the plight of slave women:

> Are not nearly two millions of native-born American women, at this very hour, doomed to the foulest slavery that angels ever wept to witness? Are they not doubly damned as immortal beasts of burden in the field, and sad mothers of a most accursed race? Are they not raised for the express purposes of lust? Are they not chained and driven in the slave-coffle at the crack of the whip of an unfeeling driver? Are they not sold on the auction-block? Are they not exposed naked to the coarse jests and voluptuous gaze of brutal men?[28]

In "The Slave's Appeal," which she published in 1860, she condemned slavery on biblical grounds and applied the Ten Commandments to slavery. She exhorted New Yorkers to defy the Fugitive Slave Law to "Make New York sacred to freedom, that when the panting fugitive shall touch your soil his chains must fall forever. Give to his exiled countrymen all the rights, privileges and immunities of citizenship, and shut your harbor against the barbarous and Heaven-defying commerce of man in man."[29] While she did not emphasize the plight of slave women in that tract, when she reached the commandment forbidding adultery she warned, "the trembling girl for who thou didst pay a price but yesterday in a New Orleans market, is not thy lawful wife."[30]

In 1863, she returned again to the suffering of slave women:

> Slavery for man is bad enough, but the refinements of cruelty must ever fall on the mothers of the oppressed race, defrauded of all the rights of the family relation, and violated in the most holy instincts of their nature. A mother's life is bound up in that of her child. There center all her hopes and ambition. But the slave-mother, in her degradation, rejoices not in the future promise of her daughter, for she knows by experience what her sad fate must be. No pen can describe the unutterable agony of that mother whose past, present, and future are all wrapped in darkness; who knows the crown of thorns she wears must press her daughter's brow; who knows that the wine-press she now treads, unwatched, those tender feet must tread alone.[31]

By early 1861, Cady Stanton had set the tone that her work would take for the duration of the war. In a speech she delivered as part of Anthony's "No Compromise with Slavery" tour in January, she declared, "It is immensely important that at this hour every woman should understand the true position of this nation & give the whole force of her intellectual & moral power in the right direction."[32] She went on to proclaim that every woman had an obligation "to interest herself in public justice & give to the world the moral laws for the government of nations, for man is so absorbed in outward improvements & material gains that the everlasting principles of right, have been lost sight of buried as they are beneath heaps of gold dust & cotton."[33] She then likened slavery to a tyrannical husband who "holds Freedom in subjection."[34] In her speech in February to the New York State Anti-

Slavery Society, she defended free speech against the mobs who disrupted the antislavery meetings and compared slaveholders to cannibals "who sell babies by the pound, and feed on their flesh—these polygamists, who have many wives, and sell their own children." She also drew attention to women's duty to leave home to "clear the rubbish in the outer world, and pluck the thorns from the paths our sons so soon must tread."[35]

To the Garrisonian refrain that slavery was a moral wrong Cady Stanton added the argument that women had a special role to play in the moral life of the nation and therefore had an obligation to participate in public life in order to aid the struggle against slavery. With that theme, which was reminiscent of the Grimké sisters' arguments in 1836 emphasizing women's special duty to join the abolitionist movement, Cady Stanton combined two approaches. One was based on natural rights and equality—women have the same right to participate as men, just as the slaves have the same right to liberty as white men. The other approach revolved around the idea of women's responsibilities as wives and mothers. In addition, the emphasis she put on women's concern with the moral issue of slavery appealed to women who had not joined the antebellum woman's rights movement and encouraged them to participate in the public realm of politics and war. Her frequent use of images of the family in her discussion of secession and slavery was also likely to draw women's attention to the impact that those issues had on their lives. Thus, Cady Stanton's work during the war, which on the surface put aside women's rights in favor of emancipation and Union victory, actually served to facilitate the breaking down of the rigid boundaries between the public and the private spheres by encouraging women to move beyond the limits of home and family into the world of politics.

After the Emancipation Proclamation went into effect, in January 1863, both abolitionists and antislavery Republicans feared that President Lincoln would modify the Proclamation in the face of conservative pressure. In the spring of 1863, after the Union defeats at Fredericksburg and Chancellorsville, the Copperheads—or Peace Democrats—who opposed emancipation and argued that the goal of the war was simply to restore the Union enjoyed considerable popularity. In response to the Copperhead movement, Republicans started to organize Loyal Leagues or Union Leagues throughout the North, not only to promote loyalty to the goal of Union victory but also to influence Republican policy to place more emphasis on emancipation as a war aim.

In New York, Henry Stanton and Gerrit Smith organized the Loyal National League, upon which Cady Stanton and Anthony modeled their Women's Loyal National League. By the end of Congress's session in the summer of 1864, Anthony and Cady Stanton had collected more than 400,000 signatures calling for a constitutional amendment to abolish slavery. Although the Women's League built on the precedents set by women abolitionist petitioners in the 1830s, its organizers planned to do more. They hoped to create a political pressure group of women who would have an influence on the presidential election in 1864.[36] Thus, Cady Stanton and Anthony endeavored to combine the goals of emancipation of the slaves with women's rights. Indeed, at its first meeting, the Women's League promised "to give support to the government in so far as it makes the war for freedom."[37]

The new organization also passed a series of resolutions, including one proclaiming that "There never can be a true peace in this Republic until the civil and political rights of all citizens of African descent and all women are practically established."[38] The Women's League constantly urged women to move into the public sphere by joining the campaign to end slavery, while it also encouraged women to participate in presidential politics. The organization thereby not only made a contribution to the abolitionist movement but also advanced new ideas about women's role in the political realm and, in turn, had an influence on the woman's rights movement in the postwar era.[39]

In March 1863, Cady Stanton issued "An Appeal to the Women of the Republic," which was printed in the *New York Tribune,* as well as in antislavery journals. She urged Northern women to pledge themselves "loyal to freedom and our country" and to unite against slavery. She appealed to the patriotism of Northern women, as well as to the cult of domesticity and to the old ideology of republican motherhood. She observed that Southern women seemed to be "more devoted to their cause than we are to ours," because "They see and feel the horrors of the war; . . . the foe is at their fireside; while we, in peace and plenty, live as heretofore. The women of the South know what their sons are fighting for." She reminded women that they had always had a special role in shaping the morals of the family and the nation: "The women of a nation mold its morals, religion, and politics."[40]

In her call for the first meeting of the Women's League, Cady Stanton again emphasized women's special role as mothers and urged them to move beyond traditional modes of participation in the war effort:

To man, by common consent, is assigned the forum, camp, and field. What is woman's legitimate work, and how she may best accomplish it, is worthy our earnest counsel one with another. We have heard many complaints of the lack of enthusiasm among Northern women; but, when a mother lays her son on the altar of her country, she asks an object equal to the sacrifice. In nursing the sick and wounded, knitting socks, scraping lint, and making jellies, the bravest and best may weary if the thoughts mount not in faith to something beyond and above it all. . . . Woman is equally interested and responsible with man in the final settlement of this problem of self-government; therefore let none stand idle spectators now.[41]

In the opening speech of that meeting, Cady Stanton emphasized women's important role in the "moral and religious sphere of action," as well as the "double duty" that women must perform during war. She proclaimed, "The women of a nation mold its morals, religion, and politics; not by the sermons they preach, but by the lives they live . . . woman's influence is omnipotent!"[42] Since Southern women could keep the rebellion alive, consider what Northern women could do "to maintain the best government on the earth."[43] Men had failed to impart the basic principles of freedom and equality, but women had the moral power to banish the sin of slavery:

Had all Northern mothers taught these great truths to their sons as sedulously as Southern mothers have the lessons of slavery; we should have crowded slavery into the Gulf long ago, with the almighty power of our free institutions. And here, O woman of the XIXth century! is your work for the future. The nation is to be educated to-day in the first principles of human rights—a hopeless task for man alone never to be accomplished until the mothers of the Republic be galvanized into a new life of religious earnestness and noble purpose, until the eternal principles of justice and mercy have crystallized in their inner souls.
    As I look forward to the true Republic that will surely rise from this shattered Union, I behold the future woman in harmony with its grand

proportions, crowned with new virtue and strength, honor and majesty, adorning the niche it is her destiny to fill.[44]

In 1864, both Republicans and abolitionists were divided over Lincoln's reconstruction policy and his renomination and reelection. Lincoln's reconstruction plan, which he announced in December 1863, offered a full pardon to almost all Confederates if they took an oath of future loyalty to the Constitution, provided for the reestablishment of state governments, and allowed those governments to institute temporary arrangements for the freed slaves that need not include equal political and legal rights.[45] Those who joined Wendell Phillips to form the anti-Lincoln faction of abolitionists helped to start a movement for the nomination of John C. Frémont, while Garrison led the abolitionists who remained committed to Lincoln. In the spring of 1864, abolitionist supporters of Frémont organized Frémont Clubs and called for a nominating convention to be held in May.[46] Although most of the women abolitionists continued to support Lincoln, Cady Stanton and Anthony were both early supporters of Frémont and helped to organize the first Freedom and Frémont Club in the office of the Women's League. They also endorsed the convention and supported the plan for a popular uprising before the Republican convention convened in Baltimore.

Cady Stanton agreed with the other abolitionists in the Phillips group that Lincoln's reconstruction plan was unacceptable and that Lincoln had taken neither swift enough nor adequate steps to abolish slavery and secure political and civil rights for black people. She applauded the Frémont movement as a democratic uprising. Writing to Jessie Frémont, she proclaimed, "It is time to inaugurate an entirely new mode of making Presidents. . . . Let the people place men before the nation and in mass convention make known their choice."[47]

Her political reasons for opposing Lincoln's reelection overlapped with the personal. In late 1863 Henry Stanton, then Deputy Collector of the Port of New York, was accused of accepting bribes to allow goods through the blockade against the Confederacy. He was forced to resign his position and was the subject of a long congressional investigation. It was revealed that the Stanton's oldest son, Neil, who had been working for his father as a clerk, had accepted small bribes and forged his father's signature on several documents. Although the congressional investigation failed to discover any evidence of wrongdoing on the part of Henry Stanton, the committee's report cast him in the most unfavorable light possible. As Cady Stanton knew, the scandal that thoroughly discredited her husband was part of a struggle for power between two rival factions of the Republican Party.[48]

As the meeting to celebrate the first anniversary of the Women's Loyal National League approached, Cady Stanton and Anthony considered using the occasion to officially endorse Frémont. In the advertisement for the meeting, they declared that "The nation's destiny now trembles in the balance, and waits the electric word that shall rouse the women of the Republic to make themselves a POWER FOR FREEDOM in the coming Presidential Campaign."[49] In response, Caroline Wells Healey Dall wrote to Cady Stanton, appealing to the women of the League not to get involved in the presidential campaign—women should interest themselves in political issues, she said, but they should play a modest role and not dictate. She advised Cady Stanton not to turn the meeting into an "electioneering caucus, where all that disgusts us in political strategy shall be repeated, and where those who have had no experience of the actual conflict, . . . proclaim a party purpose, and forfeit forever a moral stand-point which is fully their own."[50] Dall proceeded to defend Lincoln and concluded with a warning that if the women of the League became active political partisans, they would not be able to garner the support of all the loyal women in the country.

In a lengthy reply to Dall, Cady Stanton defended women's right and obligation to participate in politics, religion, and social life. The League, she explained, was the first and only organization of women that had the express purpose of influencing politics, and, as such, it had helped to lift "politics into the sphere of morals and religion."[51] As it turned out, Garrison declined to print Cady Stanton's reply until after the meeting was over.[52] Moreover, Wendell Phillips agreed to speak at the meeting on the condition that it not endorse Frémont, and Cady Stanton agreed. The result was that the Women's League did not endorse Frémont at that meeting, although it passed resolutions that were critical of the Lincoln administration, including one that condemned as evidence of the administration's "heartless character or utter incapacity" to conduct the war the government's failure to protect black troops against confederate atrocities.[53] The meeting also approved a resolution demanding suffrage for black men, as well as a more far-reaching call for a new Constitution guaranteeing liberty and equality for every human being.

In September, Frémont withdrew from the presidential contest and urged his followers to support Lincoln. Most of the abolitionists then threw their support to Lincoln, but Cady Stanton and Anthony refused to do so. Cady Stanton wrote to Anthony,

> After they themselves [the Republicans] have exposed the incapacity and rottenness of the administration, what impudence to ask the people to accept another four years under the same dynasty. I do not believe that either party can block the wheels of progress, and it is certainly a good thing to clean out thoroughly the political sty once in four years. The family of men are amazingly like each other; republicans and democrats, saints and sinners, all act alike and talk, each in his turn, the same cant.[54]

After the election, Cady Stanton continued to disagree with the abolitionists, including Gerrit Smith and Garrison, who maintained their support for Lincoln. At the end of December 1864, she wrote to Anthony complaining about Smith's and Garrison's defense of a proposed apprenticeship system for former slaves and declared, "We say now, as ever, Give us immediately unconditional emancipation, and let there be no reconstruction except on the broadest basis of justice and equality."[55]

The Women's Loyal National League continued the petition campaign for a constitutional amendment prohibiting slavery until the House of Representatives passed the Thirteenth Amendment, in January 1865. Cady Stanton fully expected that, with Union victory, the Republicans would reward the women's rights leaders for their hard work by granting suffrage. She was wrong. As we will see in chapter 6, the Republican and abolitionist betrayal had a profound effect on the subsequent development of Cady Stanton's ideas and strategies.

Conclusion

The most important theme of Cady Stanton's work during the Civil War and of this chapter is that her work defending the right and obligation of women to participate in the struggle to free the slaves and to win the war served to undermine the boundary between the public and the private spheres. As we have seen, she frequently repeated the argument that women's duty to support the Union and the freedom and rights of the slaves mandated that they move into the traditionally forbidden public sphere. Women's right to join the cause, she made clear, went far beyond the immediate contest of the goals of Union victory and emancipation to women's right to participate in public life in general and, in particular, in the struggle for their rights. Cady Stanton also successfully incorporated abolitionism into women's rights by repeatedly emphasizing that liberating the slaves would also bring an end to the slavery of custom and sex, as she put it. In her view, eliminating the institution of slavery embraced a broader principle of equality for all, including women. The abolitionists and the Republicans proved her vision to be mistaken when they abandoned the cause of woman suffrage in order to maximize their chances of securing the vote for black males. Cady Stanton's vision nevertheless undercut the seemingly impermeable boundary between the public and the private spheres by sending a message to women that they had not only a right but also a duty to join the Union cause, to participate in the election campaign, and to join the suffrage movement in the years following the Civil War.

6

The Postwar Years
Reconstruction and Positivism

Introduction

Since the 1960s, scholars have explored the ways in which white women's rights activists in the postbellum years set aside their egalitarian values when it came to rights for African Americans.[1] A number of historians have examined the impact that the male abolitionists' abandonment of woman suffrage had on the movement, noting that the willingness of white reformers to exploit racist arguments to promote women's rights, at least in part, was a result of the dissolution of the alliance between abolitionism and women's rights.[2] More recently, however, scholars have begun to emphasize that discourses of race as well as gender informed the woman's rights movement from its inception; thus, it was not a simple matter of the leaders exchanging liberal egalitarian values for ascriptive racist ideas but rather that white women reformers used different ideological and political strategies at different times to achieve their goals.[3]

During the fifteen years that followed the Civil War, Elizabeth Cady Stanton's arguments began to reflect more ascriptivist and antidemocratic themes than they had earlier. She often linked the virtue, honor, and dignity of women to the right to vote in ways that combined elements of republicanism and ascriptivism: women had a duty to participate in public life and to devote themselves to improving the well being of the community, and, as morally superior beings, they were singularly well qualified to do so. Moreover, she often employed ascriptivism to advance racist arguments. By the 1870s, ascriptivist ideas had gained considerable popularity in the United States. Evolutionary theories of racial hierarchy had begun to find increasing acceptance, and the climate of ideas was growing more hostile to equal rights.

Liberal themes nevertheless continued to run through Cady Stanton's arguments. I argue that, although the politics of Reconstruction help to explain the increased emphasis she placed on ascriptivist arguments. The termination of the alliance between abolitionism and women's rights does not tell the whole story. The changing climate of ideas also had a major influence on the development of her ideas. As racist ideologies grew increasingly popular during the second half of the nineteenth century they began to play an increasingly important role in her work. It is important to keep in mind that, as we saw in chapter 2, ascriptivist themes were present in her arguments as early as 1848. Thus, it should be clear that her ideas did not simply change from liberal egalitarian to inegalitarian ascriptivist but rather that the preexisting inegalitarian elements of her thought became more prominent in her work.

This chapter begins with a discussion of the developments in the postwar woman's rights movement and the role that Cady Stanton played in the organized campaign during that period. It then moves to an examination of the shift in her approach during the years after the Civil War in order to call attention to the connection between the abolitionists' and Republicans' abandonment of the cause of woman suffrage and Cady Stanton's increasingly ascriptivist approach. Finally, I examine the intellectual background of Positivism that sheds light on the changing tone of her arguments during this period.

This chapter has two major objectives. The first is to demonstrate that Cady Stanton's arguments in the postwar years did indeed come to rely more on ascriptive themes, in regard to both sex and race. It was during this period that she unhesitatingly set suffrage for white women against voting rights for black men and immigrants. She shifted the focus of her arguments away from her earlier claim that women and men possess the same natural rights to contend that women have special qualities that render their participation in political life beneficial, indeed, essential to the well-being of society. The second objective is to shed light on the reasons for Cady Stanton's shift to ascriptivist arguments. Accordingly, I examine her arguments against the background of the historical developments of the abolitionist abandonment of the cause of women's rights and the changing character of the woman's rights movement, as well as the more general climate of ideas in the United States during the fifteen years that followed the Civil War.

Cady Stanton and the Postwar Woman's Rights Movement

Cady Stanton played a major role in the development of the postwar woman's rights movement as she and Susan B. Anthony took the lead in reviving it when the war ended. It was also their opposition to the Fourteenth and Fifteenth Amendments that culminated in the division of the movement into two rival organizations, in 1869. Subsequently, the two leaders led the broader, more progressive branch of the campaign for women's rights. But, as conflict among women's rights activists continued and as the Cady Stanton–Anthony branch of the movement grew more conservative, an increasingly alienated, isolated, and disillusioned Cady Stanton went her own way, spending the decade of the 1870s as a paid lecturer. As I examine the role that Cady Stanton played in the postwar revival of the woman's rights movement and her activities in the movement until the end of the 1860s, I attempt to shed light on the ways in which her activities represented a response to Reconstruction politics and, more generally, the changing political context of the postwar years.

The abolitionist and the woman's rights movements were united for some thirty years in their quest to bring an end to slavery. As we saw in chapter 5, women's rights leaders set aside their own goals and dedicated themselves to the cause of emancipation and Union victory during the Civil War. Cady Stanton and Anthony organized the Women's Loyal National League and not only organized a petition campaign that helped to achieve passage of the Thirteenth Amendment but also worked to influence public policy regarding the goals of the war and participated in the presidential campaign of 1864.[4] At the end of the war, abolitionists, allied with Republicans in Congress, led the drive for racial equality in Reconstruction. As women's rights reformers' abolitionist allies emerged as influential actors on the national political scene and as suffrage for blacks became a national political issue, obtaining the vote for women began to seem like a plausible goal.[5] Expecting the abolitionists to support woman suffrage just as the women's rights leaders had worked for abolition and Union victory during the war, activists like Cady Stanton were profoundly disappointed when their former allies, adopting a strategy of maximizing their chances of winning black male enfranchisement, abandoned the cause of woman suffrage.

In 1865, Wendell Phillips assumed leadership of the American Anti-Slavery Society and made clear that abolitionists were going to work for a constitutional amendment prohibiting denial of the vote on the basis of race but not sex. He proclaimed, "I hope in time to be as bold as Stuart Mill and add to that last clause 'sex'!! But this hour belongs to the negro. As Abraham Lincoln said 'One War at a time'; so I say, One question at a time. This hour belongs to the negro."[6] The abolitionists' choice severed the links between the two movements and had a major impact on the development of the postwar campaign for women's rights. One of the consequences was that women's rights activists began to question the dependent position they held among the Garrisonians and to start to formulate their own goals. The result was that the campaign for women's rights began to emerge as a politically autonomous movement.[7] Another consequence was that women's rights leaders, including Cady Stanton, began to turn more to ascriptive arguments, pitting white women against black men.

Cady Stanton commented on Phillips's statement that "This is the negro's hour" in a letter she wrote to Anthony in August 1865. Underlining the need for a woman's rights convention, she noted, "I have argued constantly with Phillips and the whole fraternity, but I fear one and all will favor enfranchising the negro without us. Woman's cause is in deep water."[8] In February 1866, the House of Representatives began to consider a constitutional amendment that would guarantee equal rights to life, liberty, and property to all citizens.[9] Debate began in early May on a provision that introduced the first use of the word "male" in the Constitution. In June, Congress passed the Amendment. Section 2 confirmed that women would be excluded from Reconstruction by providing that states would have their representation in the House reduced to the extent that they denied the vote to any *male* inhabitants.

As Congress began to debate the Fourteenth Amendment, Cady Stanton and Anthony drew up a petition to Congress asking that woman suffrage be included and collected 10,000 signatures in support of that position. In addition, they organized the first postwar woman's rights convention, which met in New York in May 1866. With Cady Stanton presiding, the convention adopted an appeal to Congress asking that it recognize that:

> The only tenable ground of representation is UNIVERSAL SUFFRAGE, as it is only through Universal Suffrage that the principle of "Equal Rights to All" can be realized. All prohibitions based on race, color, sex, property, or education, are violations of the republican idea; and the various

qualifications now proposed are but so many plausible pretexts to debar new classes from the ballot-box.[10]

Anthony presented a resolution to establish the American Equal Rights Association (AERA), an organization that was intended to combine the antislavery and the woman's rights movements and to work to secure a constitutional amendment to enfranchise women and black men.[11] As she explained, the women's rights reformers "wished to broaden [their] Woman's Rights platform, and make it in name—what it ever has been in *spirit*—a Human Rights platform."[12] The convention adopted Anthony's resolution, and the AERA was born. After adopting a constitution for the new organization, the group elected Cady Stanton vice president when she declined the presidency so that Lucretia Mott could take that position. During the meeting, Wendell Phillips reiterated his conviction that black male suffrage should take precedence over woman suffrage. He announced, however, that he was opposed to the insertion of the word "male" into the Constitution.[13]

Only a month after the founding of the AERA, Congress passed the Fourteenth Amendment. Cady Stanton ran for Congress in the fall of 1866 as a gesture of protest against the Republicans' abandonment of woman suffrage and to underline the irony of the situation in which women were denied the vote and yet were eligible to run for office. She nominated herself as an independent candidate and announced her candidacy in a letter that appeared in New York City newspapers. She declared that her intent was to "rebuke the dominant party for its retrogressive legislation in so amending the National Constitution as to make invidious distinctions on the ground of sex."[14]

In 1867, Cady Stanton and Anthony turned their attention to suffrage reform at the state level, campaigning for changes in the New York Constitution and for woman suffrage in Kansas. Appearing before the Judiciary Committee of the New York state legislature prior to the scheduled constitutional convention, Cady Stanton asked that the word "male" be stricken from the section of the state constitutional provisions concerned with qualifications for voting and that women be allowed to vote for delegates to the convention.[15] Noting that the state constitution did not automatically disenfranchise males who had been "kept at any alms-house or other asylum, at public expense; nor . . . confined in any public prison,"[16] she reiterated her argument that women's special qualities rendered them particularly deserving of the ballot:

I claim to understand the interests of the nation better than yonder pauper in your alms-house, than the unbalanced graduate from your asylum and prison. . . . No wonder that with such voters, sex and color should be exalted above loyalty, virtue, wealth and education. I warn you, legislators of the State of New York, that you need the moral power of wise and thoughtful women in your political councils, to outweigh the incoming tide of poverty, ignorance, and vice that threatens our very existence as a nation. Have not the women of the republic an equal interest with yourselves in the government, in free institutions, in progressive ideas, and in the success of the most liberal political measures?[17]

Her reference to the "incoming tide" referred to immigrants who, in her view, should not be allowed to vote if refined, educated, virtuous women were not. Although she did not hesitate to draw on ascriptivist notions of inequality based on nationality, she quickly shifted ground to rely on the individual-rights argument that was very much in tune with the ideas of John Stuart Mill: "Each one of you has a right to everything in earth and air, on land and sea, to the whole world of thought, to all that is needful for soul and body, and there is no limit to the exercise of your rights, but in the infringement of the rights of another; and the moment you pass that limit you are on forbidden ground, you violate the law of individual life, and breed disorder and confusion in the whole social system."[18]

Two separate referenda were scheduled in Kansas for November 1867 to determine whether to remove "male" and "white" from the state constitution. The AERA devoted its resources to the campaign, and workers traveled the state for nine months in support of the referenda. Winning in Kansas was particularly important to the AERA because it would be the first popular test ever made of woman suffrage, and victory would demonstrate that public opinion was not opposed to the enfranchisement of women. Success in Kansas would also help the AERA convince Republicans that woman suffrage would not undermine the campaign for black suffrage.[19] The Kansas Republican Party mounted a formal effort to defeat woman suffrage, while prominent abolitionists, including Wendell Phillips, refused to assist the campaign for the referenda.[20] The Republican press likewise urged voters in Kansas to approve black suffrage while declining to endorse woman suffrage until shortly before the election.

Cady Stanton and Anthony, in Kansas from September until the election in November, directed their efforts at Democrats, who constituted one-quarter of the electorate in the state. George Francis Train volunteered his services to garner votes for the referendum, and Anthony accepted. Train was a wealthy railroad promoter and financier, a nationally known Copperhead, who was mounting an independent campaign for the presidency. A Democrat who was intent on challenging the power of the Republicans, he linked woman suffrage to white supremacy and thereby exacerbated the ascriptivist strains that were already becoming more apparent in the arguments for women's rights. Anthony's and Cady Stanton's alliance with Train alienated other women's rights leaders and played a role in the division of the leadership of the movement between Cady Stanton and Anthony on the one hand and Lucy Stone and Henry Blackwell on the other. Lucy Stone wrote to Olympia Brown that she was "utterly disgusted and vexed" and that "no decent woman should be in [Train's] society."[21] Cady Stanton and Anthony defended their connections to Train by suggesting that they were merely taking the same route that the abolitionists had when they chose not to support suffrage for women:

> So long as opposition to slavery is the only test for a free pass to your platform and membership of your association, and you do not shut out all persons opposed to woman suffrage, why should we not accept all in favor of woman suffrage to our platform and association, even though they be rabid pro-slavery Democrats? Your test of faithfulness is the negro, ours is the woman; the broadest platform, to which no party has as yet risen, is humanity.[22]

Cady Stanton wrote to Martha C. Wright maintaining that Train was "a pure, high-toned man without a vice. He has some extravagances and idiosyncrasies, but he is willing to devote energy and money to our cause when no other man is." She went on to express her opinion that "it would be right and wise to accept aid even from the devil himself, provided he did not tempt us to lower our standard."[23]

Their alliance with Train evidenced Cady Stanton's and Anthony's determination to maintain women's rights—specifically, suffrage—as their highest priority. They were no longer willing to compromise, and they would never again postpone their own goals to help another group achieve its objectives. Cady Stanton wrote many years later of her certainty that the movement's decision to put aside its goals and work for Union victory and an end to slavery had been a "blunder." She noted that if male reformers were to ask women's rights leaders to keep silent a second time, "we would not for a moment entertain the proposition. The women generally awoke to their duty to themselves. They had been deceived once and could not be again. If the leaders in the Republican and abolition camps could deceive us, whom could we trust?"[24]

While their willingness to accept Train's assistance reflects the paramount importance that Cady Stanton and Anthony attached to the enfranchisement of women, it was also a response to the abolitionists' betrayal. Abandoned by their former allies, they looked elsewhere for support. On the surface, Cady Stanton's and Anthony's new alliance with Train seemed to signal a departure from the principles of the previous twenty years of the campaign for women's rights. Considering that Cady Stanton's arguments had always contained ascriptivist elements, however, the alliance may be viewed as a continuation, albeit in more pronounced form, of her ascriptivist sentiments regarding race.

The strategic aspect of the alliance with Train was important. Abandoned by the Republicans, the woman suffrage movement needed new allies. Cady Stanton may well have hoped to establish connections with individual Democrats in such a way as to challenge Republicans and attract Northern voters to the cause of woman suffrage. After the defeat of both black and woman suffrage in Kansas, she lamented the split between the Republican campaign for black suffrage and the effort to enfranchise woman. She placed the blame on the Republicans: "I believe both propositions would have been carried . . . but with a narrow policy, playing off one against the other, both were defeated."[25] An alliance between Republican abolitionists and women's rights supporters might have succeeded in securing the vote for blacks and women in Kansas, but, as it was, the Democrats were able to use woman suffrage as a tool to help bring about the defeat of suffrage for black men. Also, as Cady Stanton and Anthony began to look for new alliances outside the ranks of the abolitionists and Republicans, they explored the possibility of joining woman suffrage to Democratic politics. Writing in the *Revolution* in 1868, for example, Cady Stanton claimed that Democrats supported women's rights.[26] But it became clear where the Democrats stood when the party convention in July of the same year rejected Anthony's appeal for the party to support woman suffrage.

In what may have been only a post hoc rationalization, both Cady

Stanton and Anthony argued that Train's efforts had a positive impact on the election in Kansas.[27] As they continued to work with Train after that election, conflict within the movement escalated. Lucy Stone and Henry Blackwell argued that Anthony had made the decision to work with Train without consulting the other members of the AERA. Not only had Anthony behaved undemocratically, they contended, but she had also mismanaged Association funds in Kansas by spending excessive amounts on Train. Cady Stanton and Anthony nevertheless continued to work with him. They joined him on a speaking tour for woman suffrage and accepted financing from him for their newspaper, the *Revolution.*

The Kansas campaign in 1867 has been viewed as an important turning point in the woman's rights movement.[28] Alienated from the abolitionists and at odds with many of the other women's rights leaders, Cady Stanton and Anthony distanced themselves from the AERA and began to seek new allies and to develop new ideas and strategies. In effect, they began to organize an autonomous movement for women's rights.[29] One indication of their independence from their old allies was their newspaper, the *Revolution,* which first appeared in January 1868 with Anthony as business manager and Cady Stanton as one of the editors. Although Train initially funded the paper, he left for England shortly thereafter, and the two women assumed financial responsibility, as well as editorial control of the paper. By the end of the year, Train had severed his connection to the paper. The *Revolution* reported on individual women's accomplishments and published articles and editorials, including many authored by Cady Stanton, on a variety of subjects, such as problems of working women, marriage and divorce, and prostitution. The editors also reprinted excerpts from the work of Mary Wollstonecraft, Frances Wright, and August Comte. The central impulse of the *Revolution,* however, was its opposition to the Fifteenth Amendment, which Congress submitted to the states in February 1869. Cady Stanton wrote editorials condemning the Amendment and argued that the policy of keeping the issues of female and black male suffrage separate would lead to defeat for both, just as it had in Kansas.[30]

Although the AERA continued until the movement formally divided in May 1869, after the Kansas campaign it ceased to be a forum for much women's rights work and became increasingly dominated by the tensions within the movement.[31] Conflict over whether the woman's rights movement should support the Fifteenth Amendment dominated the organization's convention in May 1869.[32] Cady Stanton, as vice president of the organization, presided over the meeting. The abolition-ist Stephen Foster spoke, condemning the *Revolution* for publishing ar-ticles opposing the Fifteenth Amendment and charging Cady Stanton with "repudiating the principles" of the AERA, namely universal man-hood suffrage; he argued that she was thereby ineligible to hold office in the organization.[33] Frederick Douglass then made a plea for securing black male suffrage first, on the grounds that black men needed it more than women did:

> When women, because they are women, are hunted down through the cities of New York and New Orleans; when they are dragged from their houses and hung upon lamp-posts; when their children are torn from their arms, and their brains dashed out upon the pavement; when they are objects of insult and outrage at every turn; when they are in danger of having their homes burnt down over their heads; when their children are not allowed to enter schools: then they will have an urgency to ob-tain the ballot equal to our own.[34]

Amid the discussion over whether women should fight for black male suffrage if they were not also to be given the franchise, Lucy Stone tried to forge a compromise, admonishing that "[w]e are lost if we turn away from the middle principle and argue for one class."[35] An angry Cady Stanton responded that she did not believe in allowing "ignorant ne-groes and foreigners" to make laws that she would have to obey.[36]

As the meeting continued, Ernestine Rose proposed that the name of the AERA be changed to the Woman's Suffrage Association. Lucy Stone opposed such a move, maintaining that it was imperative to wait until the "colored man gained the right to vote" before making such a change. Otherwise, she feared, the group would "lose the confidence of the public."[37] Stone thereby aligned herself with the members of the AERA who supported the Republican Party and the Fifteenth Amend-ment and accepted the abolitionists' argument that suffrage for black men must precede woman suffrage. The result was that, by the end of the convention, Cady Stanton and Anthony realized that the AERA had become a forum for securing suffrage for black men without in-cluding women, and they decided to sever all connections with the orga-nization.[38]

Only two days after the AERA convention adjourned, Cady Stanton and Anthony took the lead in founding the National Woman Suffrage

Association (NWSA) at a reception for the women delegates to the AERA convention given by the editors of the *Revolution*. The new organization was committed to securing a Sixteenth Amendment that would guarantee that the vote would not be denied on the basis of sex and to a movement that would be controlled by women.[39] Cady Stanton, who was elected president of the new organization, proposed that only women be allowed to join. Although her proposal was defeated, only women held office in the organization. A few of the other reformers followed Cady Stanton into the NWSA, including Parker Pillsbury, Lucretia Mott, Martha C. Wright, Olympia Brown, Paulina Wright Davis, and Ernestine Rose. Under Cady Stanton's leadership, the NWSA's goals included not only woman suffrage but also reform in divorce laws, more rights for women in marriage, an eight-hour workday, and increased pay for women. Other women's rights leaders, including Stone and Blackwell, joined the members of the New England Woman Suffrage Association and organized the American Woman Suffrage Association (AWSA).

Although their organization focused on woman suffrage and the campaign for a Sixteenth Amendment, Cady Stanton and Anthony and the others who joined them in the NWSA considered woman suffrage to be but one element in the struggle to end women's oppression, whereas the AWSA focused solely on the goal of obtaining the vote for women. The AWSA also continued to support the Republican Party and the Fifteenth Amendment and had the support of powerful abolitionists such as Frederick Douglass, William Lloyd Garrison, and Wendell Phillips, as well as Republican leaders. Henry Ward Beecher, the pastor of Plymouth Church in Brooklyn, became the president of the AWSA.

The reformers who formed the AWSA were willing to wait until the Reconstruction questions on the status of blacks and the conditions for readmission of the Southern states were resolved before pressing Republicans for woman suffrage. In contrast, Cady Stanton and Anthony were convinced of the strategic necessity of demanding woman suffrage before the process of Reconstruction was completed on the grounds that the opportunity for securing the vote for women would vanish once the controversy over Reconstruction was settled.[40]

While Congress was considering the Fifteenth Amendment, in late 1868, Cady Stanton and Anthony tried to influence its terms so that it would include women as well as black males. Cady Stanton went to Washington to lobby for an amendment that would enfranchise women.

Possibly as a result of her efforts, one senator, Samuel Pomeroy of Kansas, submitted a proposal that defined suffrage as a right of citizenship and enfranchised women as well as black men. When Congress passed the Fifteenth Amendment without a provision prohibiting denial of the franchise on the basis of sex, Cady Stanton refused to support it. She charged that the Amendment was "an open, deliberate insult to the women of the nation."[41]

After Congress passed the Fifteenth Amendment, Cady Stanton and Anthony traveled in the Midwest for six weeks, reaching out to suffragists in Chicago, as well as in Missouri, Wisconsin, and Ohio.[42] They rallied support among Midwestern women for the suffrage amendment, and some of those women attended the AERA convention in May 1869. Nevertheless, the group that opposed Cady Stanton and Anthony and continued to support the Fifteenth Amendment prevailed at the meeting that culminated in the split in the woman's rights movement into the NWSA and AWSA.

Although it was overshadowed by the controversy over the Fifteenth Amendment in 1869, disagreement within the woman's rights movement over divorce reform that had surfaced in 1860 continued to divide the movement. Some of the reformers, including Lucy Stone and Antoinette Brown Blackwell, not only opposed Cady Stanton's efforts to place divorce reform on the movement's agenda but also disagreed with her conception of marriage as a voluntary contract between two equal partners. Cady Stanton's opponents on the issue took the position that was more common in the nineteenth century: marriage protected women; easier divorce would allow men to abandon their wives and would thus be harmful to the overwhelming majority of women who were financially dependent on their husbands. Although Cady Stanton did not oppose marriage per se, she was far ahead of her time in her belief that it was an institution that needed fundamental reform. Thus, while her ideas about marriage did not fully comport with the free-love movement's view that marriage was an inherently oppressive institution, the connections she established with that movement set her apart from most of the other leaders of the woman's rights movement.

After the division of the movement into the NWSA and the AWSA, the NWSA's position on marriage and divorce, shaped by Cady Stanton and Anthony, distinguished it from its more traditional rival. While both organizations increasingly focused on the vote, shaping the woman's rights movement into a single-issue political movement for woman suffrage,[43] Cady Stanton continued to advocate a wide range of reforms that she considered crucial to achieving equality for women. Disaffected with the organized movement's narrow focus on suffrage, in the fall of 1869 she began to establish her independence from the movement when she took a position as a paid lecturer for the New York Lyceum Bureau. She remained on the lecture circuit until 1880, spending eight months out of every year traveling from New England to the Midwest. On each tour, she would travel to as many as thirty-six cities and small towns in six weeks and then return to New York or Chicago to start again. She usually spoke once a day and twice on Sundays, and some afternoons she would meet with the women in the community.[44] Her lectures covered a variety of topics, including "Home Life," "The Subjection of Women," "Marriage and Divorce," "Marriage and Maternity," "Prison Life," and "The Bible and Women's Rights." Women's need to establish their independence in their relations with men was a constant theme that ran through her speeches.

She continued to participate in some activities of the NWSA. In 1876, for example, she drafted a declaration of rights for the Association's exhibit for the centennial celebration in Philadelphia, though she declined to participate in the woman's rights protest at Independence Hall. Also, she worked with the NWSA, lobbying Congress for a constitutional amendment that would guarantee women's right to vote. Although she presided at several conventions of the NWSA and assumed the presidency in 1878, she had grown sufficiently disaffected and disconnected that she served largely as a figurehead, while Anthony took over the actual power in the organization. As a result of various developments in the 1870s, which are discussed in some detail in chapter 7, including her association with Victoria Woodhull, the Beecher-Tilton scandal, as well as her ideas about marriage and divorce, Cady Stanton kept herself at a distance from the organized women's rights movement for the rest of her life.

Growing Ascriptivism in the Postwar Years

Scholars have examined the ways in which white women's rights leaders responded to the enfranchisement of black men—more generally, the politics of Reconstruction—by developing arguments that emphasized differences between white women on the one hand and black men and immigrants on the other.[45] By the 1870s, these leaders were drawing from theories of evolution to support ascriptive arguments that white women were the "rightful, natural protectors of uncivilized races" whose enfranchisement would not challenge sexual difference and would promote the progress of civilization.[46] Thus, rationales for woman suffrage that emphasized the importance of bringing the "feminine element" into politics for the good of the nation to combat the corruption of men and utilized overtly racist arguments became increasingly common. Cady Stanton's arguments during this period exemplify such developments. Although she was making more use of ascriptivist themes by the end of the 1860s, she continued to draw from liberal theories of natural rights and equality. Thus, she was able to shift the ideological foundations of her arguments gradually from liberalism to ascriptivism. The following discussion, which traces the changes in her arguments between 1865, when Wendell Phillips proclaimed that "this is the Negro's hour," and 1869, when Congress passed the Fifteenth Amendment, suggests that the politics of Reconstruction had a definite impact on the development of her ideas.

In July 1865, shortly before she learned that the Republicans were planning to exclude women from the suffrage provision in the Fourteenth Amendment, Cady Stanton published an article in which she emphasized natural rights and equality in her demand for universal suffrage. She condemned "class legislation," linking it to monarchy and "rotten aristocracy," and charged that it was a "form of government and social life directly opposite to the genius of true republican institutions."[47] She went on to observe, "All this talk about education and property qualifications is the narrow assumption of a rotten aristocracy."[48]

After she learned about the terms of the Fourteenth Amendment, however, her arguments began to assume a racially divisive tone and to emphasize the differences between men and women. For example, she wrote to Martha C. Wright suggesting that intelligence and education should be a qualification for suffrage. She commented that:

> We have fairly boosted the negro over our heads, and now we had better begin to remember that self-preservation is the first law of nature. Some say, "Be still, wait, this is the negro's hour." But I believe this is

the hour for everybody to do the best thing for reconstruction. A vote based on intelligence and education for black and white, man and woman—that is what we need.[49]

She may have been more candid in a private letter than she was in her public statements. Still, her published work had also begun to evidence a more racially antagonistic tone by the end of 1865. In a letter she published in the *National Anti-Slavery Standard* in December, she grounded her argument in the notion of universal suffrage while also alluding to evolutionary theory and introducing comparisons between black men and white women. She wondered whether women should "stand aside and see 'Sambo' walk into the kingdom first." Rather,

> As self-preservation is the first law of nature, would it not be wiser to keep our lamps trimmed and burning, and when the constitutional door is open, avail ourselves of the strong arm and blue uniform of the black soldier to walk in by his side, and thus make the gap so wide that no privileged class could ever again close it against the humblest citizen of the republic?[50]

After offering that metaphor for universal suffrage, however, she proceeded to condemn class legislation in a way that emphasized differences and conflicts between men—both black and white—and women:

> "This is the negro's hour." Are we sure that, he, once entrenched in all his inalienable rights, may not be an added power to hold us at bay? Have not "black male citizens" been heard to say they doubted the wisdom of extending the right of suffrage to women? Why should the African prove more just and generous than his Saxon compeers?[51]

She then proclaimed that if the rights "of person, property, wages, and children" for black women are not secure, "their emancipation is but another form of slavery . . . it is better to be the slave of an educated white man, than of a degraded, ignorant black one." She concluded by returning to an explicit appeal to universal suffrage:

> This is our opportunity to retrieve the errors of the past and mould anew the elements of Democracy. The nation is ready for a long step in the right direction; party lines are obliterated, and all men are thinking

for themselves. If our rulers have the justice to give the black man suffrage, woman should avail herself of that new-born virtue to secure her rights; if not, she should begin with renewed earnestness to educate the people into the idea of universal suffrage.[52]

She was still focusing on universal suffrage at the first Woman's Rights Convention after the war, in May 1866—the meeting at which the AERA was created—when she made the following plea in support of merging the campaign for black and woman suffrage:

> Has not the time come . . . to bury the black man and the woman in the citizen, and our two organizations in the broader work of reconstruction? They who have been trained in the school of anti-slavery; they who, for the last thirty years, have discussed the whole question of human rights, which involves every other question of trade, commerce, finance, political economy, jurisprudence, morals and religion, are the true statesmen for the new republic-the best enunciators of our future policy of justice and equality. Any work short of this is narrow and partial and fails to meet the requirements of the hour.[53]

Likewise, in the preamble to the constitution of the new AERA, Cady Stanton reiterated the natural rights-equality approach when she wrote:

> Whereas, by the war, society is once more resolved into its original elements, and in the reconstruction of our government we again stand face to face with the broad question of natural rights, all associations based on special claims for special classes are too narrow and partial for the hour; Therefore, from the baptism of this second revolution-purified and exalted through suffering—seeing with a holier vision that the peace, prosperity, and perpetuity of the Republic rest on EQUAL RIGHTS TO ALL, we, to-day, . . . bury the woman in the citizen, and our organization in that of the American Equal Rights Association.[54]

Further, the petition that Cady Stanton and Anthony addressed to Congress in December 1865 asking that woman suffrage be included in the Fourteenth Amendment included a mixture of liberal-egalitarian and ascriptive approaches. It began by pointing to women's superior qualifications: "we represent fifteen million people—one-half the entire population of the country—intelligent, virtuous, native-born American citizens; and yet stand outside the pale of political recognition."[55] The petition then proceeded to appeal to the natural rights-universal suffrage argument with the assertion that:

> The Constitution classes us as "free people," and counts us whole persons in the basis of representation; and yet are we governed without our consent, compelled to pay taxes without appeal, and punished for violations of law without choice of judge or juror. The experience of all ages, the Declarations of the Fathers, the Statute Laws of our own day, and the fearful revolution through which we have just passed, all prove the uncertain tenure of life, liberty, and property so long as the ballot—the only weapon of self-protection—is not in the hand of every citizen.
>
> Therefore, as you are now amending the Constitution, and, in harmony with advancing civilization, placing new safeguards round the individual rights of four millions of emancipated slaves, we ask that you extend the right of Suffrage to Woman—the only remaining class of disfranchised citizens—and thus fulfill your constitutional obligation "to guarantee to every State in the Union a Republican form of Government." . . . we would pray . . . in order to simplify the machinery of Government and ensure domestic tranquillity, that you legislate hereafter for persons, citizens, tax-payers, and not for class or caste.[56]

Cady Stanton maintained the universal-suffrage approach in her letter declaring her candidacy for Congress in the fall of 1866, in which she proclaimed, "Not one word should be added to that great charter of rights to the insult or injury of the humblest of our citizens. I would gladly have a voice and vote in the Fortieth Congress to demand universal suffrage, that thus a republican form of government might be secured to every State in the Union."[57] She also included the ascriptive claim that white women were more deserving of the franchise than black men and immigrants when she admonished that most of the

> Freedmen of the South and the millions of foreigners now crowding our shores, . . . represent neither property, education, or civilization, [but] are all in the progress of events to be enfranchised, the best interests of the nation demand that we outweigh this incoming pauperism, ignorance, and degradation, with the wealth, education, and refinement of the women of the republic.[58]

Then, at the meeting of the AERA in 1867, she turned back to universal suffrage:

> As the greater includes the less, an argument for universal suffrage covers the whole question, the rights of all citizens. In thus relaying the foundations of government, we settle all these side issues of race, color, and sex, end class legislation, and remove forever the fruitful cause of the jealousies, dissensions, and revolutions of the past. . . . Here black men and women are buried in the citizen. As in the war, freedom was the key-note of victory, so now is universal suffrage the key-note of reconstruction.[59]

Later in that speech, however, she relied on the claims of racial superiority and nativism, charging that white women had far more to contribute to the progress of civilization than black men:

> With the black man we have no new element in government, but with the education and elevation of woman we have a power that is to develop the Saxon race into a higher and nobler life, and thus, by the law of attraction, to lift all races to a more even platform than can ever be reached in the political isolation of the sexes.[60]

Thus, while she was still basing her arguments on the idea of universal suffrage, Cady Stanton introduced ascriptive racial themes, pointing to white women's superiority to black men and immigrants. Those themes would assume an increasingly prominent role in her arguments in subsequent years.

In 1868, Gerrit Smith declined to sign the petition in which Cady Stanton and Anthony asked Congress not to amend the Constitution to expand suffrage unless women were included. Cady Stanton responded in an essay that was published in early 1869 in the *Revolution*. Her comments were consistent with others that she made during the late 1860s—she combined the natural-rights claim for universal suffrage with assertions of white women's superiority to black men and immigrants. Her essay began and concluded with references to suffrage as a "natural, inalienable right of every citizen." She admonished that "there is to be no reconstruction of this nation, except on the basis of Universal Suffrage, as the natural, inalienable right of every citizen to its exercise is the only logical ground on which to base an argument."[61] Yet, when she accused her cousin of supporting class legislation that would benefit men at the expense of women, she speculated that he must believe it to be in the best interest of the country "that every type and shade of degraded, ignorant manhood should be enfranchised, before even the higher classes of womanhood should be admitted to the polls."[62]

Later in the same essay, she underlined the benefits of woman suffrage, emphasizing the special qualities of women and alluding to theories that emphasized natural differences between men and women, rather than their common humanity. She also included a particularly racially divisive comparison between black men and white women;

> While philosophy and science alike point to woman, as the new power destined to redeem the world, how can Mr. Smith fail to see that it is just this we need to restore honor and virtue in the Government? When society in California and Oregon was chiefly male and rapidly tending to savageism, ship loads of women went out and restored order and decency to life. Would black men have availed anything among those white savages? There is sex in the spiritual as well as the physical, and what we need today in government, in the world of morals and thought, is the recognition of the feminine element, as it is this alone that can hold the masculine in check.[63]

Even more overtly ascriptive, in the contexts of both race and sex, was the argument she presented in the same essay by relating the story of a young girl, who was working on a farm when "a negro . . . effected her ruin" and who subsequently gave birth to a child whom she was then accused of smothering. Cady Stanton asked, How will Saxon girls fare in courts with "judges and jurors of negroes"?[64] She then moved away from explicit references to race but continued to emphasize the virtues of women, denouncing society run by men as

> one grand rape of womanhood, on the highways, in our jails, prisons, asylums, in our homes, alike in the world of fashion and of work. Hence, discord, despair, violence, crime, the blind, the deaf, the dumb, the idiot, the lunatic, the drunkard, all that was "inverted" and must be so, until the mother of the race be made dictator in the social realm. To this end we need every power to lift her up, and teach mankind that in all God's universe there is nothing so holy and sacred as womanhood.[65]

An essay entitled "Manhood Suffrage," which Cady Stanton published in the *Revolution* in December 1868, provided the basis for several speeches in which she expressed her opposition to the Fifteenth Amendment in 1869. She subsequently modified her comments to express her support for a woman suffrage amendment.[66] She was still framing her argument in terms of universal suffrage: "Because a government based on the caste and class principle, on the inequality of its citizens, cannot stand. . . . There is only one safe sure way to build a government, and that is on the equality of all of its citizens, male and female, black and white."[67]

From there, she turned abruptly to ascriptivist themes, emphasizing differences between men and women She objected to "man's government" because the male element is a destructive force, "stern, selfish, aggrandizing; loving war, violence, conquest, acquisition; breeding discord, disorder, disease and death."[68] She also relied on class arguments, calling for "government of the most virtuous, educated men and women [who] would better represent the whole humanitarian idea, and more perfectly protect the interests of all, than could a representation of either sex alone."[69] The lowest classes of men, she reminded her audience, are the ones who are most hostile to women's rights. Would senators, she asked, put their own mothers, wives, and daughters "below unwashed, unlettered ditch-diggers, boot-blacks, hostlers, butchers, and barbers?"[70] She also included racial and nativist comments, for example:

> Just so if woman finds it hard to bear the oppressive law of a few Saxon fathers, the best orders of manhood, what may she not be called to endure when all the lower orders, natives and foreigners, Dutch, Irish, Chinese and African, legislate for her and her daughters?[71]

Certain men, who know nothing about government and have not even read the Declaration of Independence, would be making laws for women like Lucretia Mott. Driving home her nativist and racial point, Cady Stanton labeled such men as Patrick, Sambo, Hans, and Yung Tung.[72]

Clearly, her arguments had become more overtly racist, nativist, and elitist by the end of the 1860s as her call for universal suffrage began to recede into the background with the increasing prominence of references to the superiority of educated white women over men in general and specifically foreigners, blacks, and men of the lower classes. At the same time that she condemned the "aristocracy of sex" that existed by virtue of women's exclusion, she also repeatedly contended that educated, cultured women—white and native born—possessed the requisites of citizenship, whereas uneducated poor men—black or white—and immigrants did not. Such arguments also carried the elitist, antidemocratic implication that only women who occupied the higher social and economic ranks of society were entitled to the vote, not by virtue of their sex but rather because of their highly developed intellectual qualities and superior moral values. Other women—black, working class, and immigrants—remained absent from her analysis.

It stands to reason that Cady Stanton's shift to more ascriptive arguments for woman suffrage is partly attributable to the politics of Reconstruction. Anger and frustration stand out clearly in her arguments after the passage of the Fourteenth Amendment, the defeat in Kansas, and the exclusion of women from the Fifteenth Amendment. Her outrage at the powerlessness of women like herself—with backgrounds of wealth and privilege—who were denied the fundamental right to vote while suffrage was bestowed on all men, regardless of economic, social, or educational qualifications is unmistakable and clearly helps to explain her increasing reliance on ascriptive arguments.

As journalist Vivian Gornick described it, the inability of so many people to understand the meaning of Cady Stanton's insistence on universal suffrage drove her "to the wall" as she came to understand just how deeply rooted was the resistance to equality for women.[73] Her mounting frustration as the campaign for woman's rights continued to meet with resistance and derision after more than twenty years undoubtedly encouraged Cady Stanton to shift to arguments that might have a better chance of succeeding. She expressed such sentiments in a letter to Lucretia Mott in 1876:

> Our demands at the first seemed so rational that I thought the mere statement of woman's wrongs would bring immediate redress. I thought an appeal to the reason and conscience of men against the unjust and unequal laws for women that disgraced our statute books, must settle the question. But I soon found, while no attempt was made to answer our arguments, that an opposition, bitter, malignant, and persevering, rooted in custom and prejudice, grew stronger with every new demand made, with every new privilege granted.[74]

Still, her shift cannot be fully explained as a response to the politics of Reconstruction or to the failure of liberal arguments to convince the opponents of women's rights. It is important to be aware that, while her racist and nativist rhetoric clearly became more prominent and more overt during this period, she did not entirely abandon her previous liberal equal-rights-based arguments. Nor were the ascriptivist themes completely absent from her earlier work. As we saw in chapter 2, in the antebellum years her arguments were predominantly liberal but were interspersed with combinations of republican and ascriptive claims that women's moral superiority would make them particularly virtuous citizens—voting women would greatly improve the political life of the nation. The improvements would result not only from the redress of the imbalance of power of the male monopoly—a republican claim—but also from the introduction of women's moral influence, which would combat men's self-seeking, corrupt approach to politics—an ascriptive claim. Her frequent assertions of women's moral superiority and her emphasis on the need to protect women in the domestic realm reflected the dominant ideas of the cult of domesticity. In short, her ascriptivism did not emerge solely from the circumstances of Reconstruction politics. In fact, it is discernible in her earliest work, where her arguments emphasizing the differences between the sexes and the races appear alongside liberal demands based on natural rights and equality.

Thus, the shift in Cady Stanton's arguments to a more predominantly ascriptive approach during the Reconstruction years did not represent a major departure from her earlier work. Indeed, the racist strains in her arguments were consistent with her earlier beliefs and represented a change in emphasis rather than a break with the way in which she had earlier blended the different traditions. Her earlier beliefs, combined with her frustration and disillusionment with Republicans and abolitionists, are likely to have helped make it easier for her to adopt the racially divisive approach of pitting woman suffrage against the enfranchisement of black men.

The extent to which Cady Stanton's ideas continued to move toward a more ascriptive approach is further substantiated by her public endorsement in 1877 of an amendment to the Constitution that would require compulsory education and educational qualifications for suffrage. She proposed that only those who could read and write in English be admitted to citizenship. Although Cady Stanton claimed that the requirement would not conflict with the theory that suffrage is a natural right because it would not deny suffrage to any class, she nevertheless noted that it "would also be our most effective defence against the ignorant foreign vote."[75]

Intellectual Currents: The Influence of Positivism

Although the politics of Reconstruction played a role in Cady Stanton's growing ascriptivism, the specific political circumstances of the postwar years cannot fully explain the increasing prominence of illiberal themes in her work. First, as we have seen, those themes were present in the arguments she constructed before the Civil War. Second, the impact of new and increasingly popular ideas and ideologies that operated within the framework of evolutionary theory and that embraced ascriptivist values is particularly clear in her work during the second half of the 1860s and throughout the 1870s. The ideas of the French Positivist Auguste Comte and his followers in the United States had a major impact on Cady Stanton's work during this period. She read Comte's work, wrote articles about it for the *Revolution,* and, although his theory was conservative and inconsistent with the goals of the woman's rights movement, adapted it to suit her needs. Influenced not only by Comte but also by the English philosopher Herbert Spencer, Cady Stanton's arguments by the end of the 1860s had begun to reflect an evolutionary understanding of the development of individuals, as well as the progress of political and social institutions. It was later, however, that her ideas began to manifest more explicitly the ideas of social Darwinism, heavily influenced by Herbert Spencer, an ideology that was growing increasingly popular during the last twenty years of the twentieth century and came to displace Positivism. The discussion that follows is limited to the influence of positivism on Cady Stanton's thought. I save the examination of social Darwinism for chapter 9.

Comte's overarching goal was to discover a positive science of society based on what he perceived to be immutable scientific laws. Indeed, he coined the term "sociology," which he viewed as closely connected to the natural sciences.[76] Comte's belief in a universal human nature developing through a process of interaction with appropriate social conditions transmitted through communication and socialization led him to envision society as evolving to the point where it would eventually be organized scientifically and in which egoism and conflict would be replaced by cooperation and harmony. In his view, the mind, as well as science, ideas, and institutions, all proceeded through three stages—theological, metaphysical, and scientific or positive, with each stage representing different points in the evolution of human beings. Humankind, Comte argued, had evolved to the point where social organization based on scientific principles and a new moral consensus could eliminate all problems of modern society, including warfare, colonial conquests, class conflict, and excessive individualism.[77] Thus, the importance of social institutions, including language, religion, and the division of labor, lay primarily in the contribution they made to the wider social order.[78]

Cady Stanton was particularly attracted to the prospect of a society governed by scientific principles, as opposed to religion or custom. In 1868, she proclaimed her belief in government "as a fixed science, controlled by laws as immutable as those that govern the planetary world."[79] Similarly, in 1871, she remarked that "the fundamental conditions of life" must be "based on science."[80] Four years later, she wrote, "Instead of leaving every thing in the home to chance as now, we should apply science and philosophy to our daily life."[81] Her arguments about marriage and divorce reform can be understood as a manifestation of the influence of Positivism insofar as such reforms would not only benefit individual women but would promote the progress and well-being of society. Alcoholic fathers, she so often repeated, produced defective offspring. Thus, she proposed in 1870 that the government should prohibit the marriage of those she referred to as morally, physically, and mentally unfit.[82] The Positivist argument that society should be governed by scientific principles also comes through clearly in her argument that government should be "scientific," guided by the most intelligent members of the population, who are "gifted with the genius of coordination or the power to harmonize, organize and direct. . . . If the average ability were raised a grade or two," Cady Stanton declared in 1882, "a new class of statesmen would conduct our complex affairs at home and abroad, as easily as our best business men now do their own private trades and professions. The needs of centralization, communication and culture call for more brains and mental stamina than the average of our race possesses."[83]

Although Cady Stanton embraced the Positivist vision of a society governed by scientific principles, there were other aspects of Comte's philosophy with which she did not agree. The aspects of Positivism that concerned the role of women she adapted to suit her purposes. The division of labor in advanced societies, Comte argued, was marked by specialization. A central aspect of that specialization revolved around sexual differences. Thus, women and men, according to the Positivists, must perform distinctly different roles. Women's unique nature, according to Comte, gave them an essential role but one that was nevertheless limited to the domestic sphere; he insisted that they should remain dependent on men and maintain their charming "infantile" qualities.[84] Comte found the "feminine element" to be essential to the ordering of society. As he stated, "The original source of all moral influence will be far more effectual when men have done their duty to women by setting them free from the pressure of material necessity, and when women on their side have renounced both power and wealth."[85] According to this view, blurring the distinction between the sexes in any way would represent a step backward for society.

Cady Stanton embraced the notion of sexual difference but rejected the idea that women's sphere should be limited. After spending an afternoon with "some Positivists" in 1880, she noted in her diary that she "found many of them narrow in their ideas as to the sphere of woman. The difference of sex, which is the very reason why men and women should be associated in every circle of activity, these Positivists make the strongest argument for the separation of the two sexes."[86]

The growing popularity of Positivism, and more generally of evolutionary theory, in the United States put Cady Stanton, as well as other women's rights leaders, in a difficult position. Given the so-called scientific principle of sexual differences, defenders of women's rights needed to move beyond the liberal framework of natural rights and equality to an approach that relied on sexual difference, rather than similarity. There was also a racial strain to the positivists' view of the importance of sexual difference. Because sexual difference was linked to civilization, the prospect of blurring the distinction between white women and white men appeared to threaten the advancement of white civilization. Thus, white women's rights leaders needed to construct their arguments so that women's rights would not appear to diminish the sexual difference between white men and white women.[87]

Cady Stanton exploited the Positivist notion of sexual difference, using it to justify expanding rather than limiting women's lives. Referring to Comte's argument about the importance of the "feminine element," she wrote, in an editorial in the *Revolution,* "When Comte asserts that recognition of woman's thought is primal to the reconstruction of the state, the church, and the home, he grants all we have ever asked. He disposes of every question he discusses on the basis of social harmony."[88] Rejecting Comte's prescription for a limited role for women, however, she emphasized the need for their influence in all areas of society and politics.

There can be little doubt that Cady Stanton's reading of Comte reinforced her inclination to emphasize that the differences—rather than the similarities—between the sexes made women's participation in public life essential to the well-being of society. She frequently relied on Comte's conception of the "feminine element" to support her argument that women's influence in all sectors of public life would improve society. She wrote a letter in 1867, for example, in which she expressed that idea: "when philosophers come to see that ideas as well as babies need the mother soul for their growth and perfection, that there is sex in the mind and spirit, as well as body, then they will appreciate the necessity of a full recognition of womanhood in every department."[89] In an editorial in the *Revolution* in 1869, she referred to the "feminine element" or the "love element which is woman" as indispensable in counteracting the selfish force of men:

> We insist . . . that Comte's principles, logically carried out, make women the governing power in the world. . . . Comte makes man a personal, selfish, concentrating, reasoning force. He makes woman impersonal, unselfish, diffusive, intuitive, a moral love power. He divides society into three classes, Intellect, Affection and Activity. He says intellect and activity, capital and labor, ruler and ruled, can only be harmonized through affection, which is the feminine element in woman, and this he exalts above the intellect and activity, conception and execution. "Love for others," he says, is the great law on which society . . . is to be reorganized. This can only be done by the cultivation of the unselfish, the moral, the diffusive, the woman; and thus we actually reverse the present order of things.
>
> In the restoration of the love element, which is woman, capital and labor will be reconciled, intelligence and activity welded together, forming a trinity that shall usher in the golden age.
>
> We have thus far lived under the dynasty of force, which is the male element, hence war, violence, discord, debauchery. From this we can

only be redeemed by the recognition and restoration of the love element which is woman.[90]

In a speech to medical students in 1871, she reiterated the essential but nevertheless distinct role she envisioned for women:

> I hope women are not to enter this profession as men, merely to follow in their footsteps and echo their opinions, but to bring the feminine element into this science, which in its greater tenderness, caution, and affection, naturally seeking to ward off evils, will teach the laws of hygiene rather than different systems of therapeutics. It would be a proud record for our sex if the page of history should show that simultaneously with the scientific education of woman, and her practice in the healing art, there arose among mankind a conscientious observance of the laws of health, a religious creed requiring of its disciples faith in pure air, simple, nutritious diet, regular exercise, daily baths, a dress for girls adapted to a free use of the lungs and limbs, and a holy preparation in both sexes of body and soul for the high duties of parenthood.[91]

Clearly, Cady Stanton drew from Positivism to support her argument that women's influence—or womanhood as a principal organizing force—was vital to modern society, or, as she expressed it, the "restoration of the love element" based on "immutable" principles "governing not only the solar system, the vegetable, mineral and animal world, but the human family, all moving in beautiful harmony together."[92] In her view, in the final stage of human history that Comte anticipated, women would reconcile all the antagonistic elements of the modern world into a new, harmonious social order.

Positivism, in short, encouraged Cady Stanton's shift away from a liberal approach to one that was less individualistic and more concerned with—in republican terms—the public good. Or, in the terms of Positivism, she became more interested in the ways in which women's rights would contribute to the progress of society toward one in which harmony and altruism would prevail over egoism and competition. Likewise, Positivism goes far to explain her increasing emphasis on sexual difference as the basis for women's rights, rather than the liberal argument that women were similar to men and were therefore entitled to the same rights.[93] Positivism was also consistent with Cady Stanton's shift to more elitist, ascriptive arguments. Not only were women inherently different from men—and, as she often argued, morally superior—but also the scientific organization of society mandated government by experts who could understand what was needed for achieving harmony and social order.

Conclusion

Why did Cady Stanton in the years following the Civil War increasingly support her demands for women's rights with undemocratic and inegalitarian arguments? The explanation lies in the dynamics of historical and intellectual forces with which Cady Stanton was interacting. Moreover, the fact that her own ideas from the beginning contained strains of illiberalism is important insofar as the context of the politics of Reconstruction and the dominant intellectual currents worked in conjunction with her early predilections to produce an approach that was less liberal and more ascriptive than it had been before the Civil War.

It is clear that her arguments, particularly in the late 1860s, frequently reflected the resentment and isolation engendered by the abolitionists' and Republicans' desertion of the cause of women's rights. Suzanne Marilley noted that, "As their message was ignored or rejected, the women turned to nativist Americanist ideas about the inferiority of black men and immigrants."[94] Cady Stanton's increasing willingness to utilize ascriptivist arguments reflects her frustration as the woman's rights movement continually encountered ridicule and resistance. Her anger at men in general—not just the abolitionists—helps to account for her growing tendency to emphasize women's special qualities. She wrote in 1871, for example, of her fury with "white males": "When I think of all the wrongs that have been heaped upon womankind, I am ashamed that I am not forever in a condition of chronic wrath, stark mad, skin and bone, my eyes a fountain of tears, my lips overflowing with curses, and my hand against every man and brother."[95]

The shift in her emphasis also reflects the increasing popularity of ascriptive ideas in American political culture after the Civil War. Evolutionary theories such as Auguste Comte's Positivism and, only a few years later, social Darwinism challenged claims of natural rights and equality by positing natural sexual differences, as well as a racial hierarchy in which white women's superiority not only entitled them to participate in politics but also made it essential for them to do so to counteract the influence of African Americans and immigrants. Thus, by drawing on popular political and social theories to support women's rights, Cady Stanton developed arguments that made sense to her and that, given the intellectual climate, seemed most likely to succeed.

Moreover, if Cady Stanton's growing ascriptivism is attributed solely to external factors, important facets of her political thought are likely to be excluded from the analysis. Although her elitism and ascriptivism grew more pronounced as the political and intellectual climate became more hospitable to such ideas, there was an illiberal strain in Cady Stanton's earliest work. If she had not been amenable to such a perspective, the growing ascriptivism in the ideology of the late nineteenth century would most likely not have had such a pronounced effect on her work in the post–Civil War years. Clearly, ascriptivist arguments did not suddenly appear in Cady Stanton's work when the effect of Reconstruction politics became clear, nor did they emerge solely as a result of the influence of Positivism or other intellectual currents.

7

The Postwar Years

The New Departure, the Alliance with Labor, and the Critique of Marriage

Introduction

The goal of this chapter is to delineate the radical dimension of Cady Stanton's thought by examining her attempt to forge an alliance with labor, her vision of marriage, and her determination to enlighten women about their position within the family. Although the radical strain of her work is apparent in those areas, the fact that she was still relying on liberal principles is evidenced by her legal argument for woman suffrage that she embraced during this period. I begin with an examination of that argument, the "New Departure," and then turn to her alliance with labor, her arguments concerning women's subordinate position in marriage, and her concept of self-sovereignty. Her work in those last three areas illustrates how she rejected the dimensions of the liberal paradigm that both posited a dichotomy between the public and private and focused on the efficacy of legal and political reforms to eliminate women's subordinate status. Although Cady Stanton was committed to reforms that would allow women to function on an equal basis with men in the public sphere, she was also intent on changing women's status within marriage and the family. Her arguments in this context support the contention that although much of her work operated within the boundaries of the traditions of liberalism, republicanism, and ascriptivism, her thought also contained a radical dimension.

In addition, the approach she took portended those of radical feminists in the 1960s and dominance feminists in the 1980s and 1990s who argued that the "personal is political" and that woman's lack of power in relationships with men and in the family guaranteed that she would remain at a disadvantage both economically and politically. Thus, the private realm of the home and family that liberalism placed beyond the bounds of politics was at the center of demands for reform for those twentieth-century feminists, as well as for Cady Stanton's campaign for women's rights.

Cady Stanton and the New Departure

The approach that became known as the New Departure, which provided the basis for the strategy adopted by some women's rights leaders in the 1870s, was grounded in the legal argument that the Constitution, properly interpreted, gave women the right to vote.[1] The constitutional argument advanced by women who attempted to register and vote in ten different states in the elections of 1872 was that the Fourteenth Amendment conferred suffrage upon women as one of the privileges and immunities of national citizenship.[2] Missouri suffragists Virginia and Francis Minor posited that the Fourteenth Amendment, with its conferral of national citizenship, considered in conjunction with the Fifteenth Amendment, which removed control of suffrage from the states and placed it in the hands of the national government, rendered suffrage a right of national citizenship. Also, in 1871, Victoria Woodhull, who is discussed at length in the next section of this chapter, appeared before the House Judiciary Committee to argue that women had the constitutional right to vote and proposed that Congress pass legislation declaring that all U.S. citizens possessed that right. Woodhull contended that the Fifteenth Amendment gave the right to vote to all citizens and forbade the states to deny that right "on account of sex or otherwise."[3]

Adopting the New Departure approach, the NWSA in 1871 advised women that it was their duty to try to register to vote, and, if officials refused to allow them to do so, the organization recommended that they bring suit in federal court. In 1875, when the issue reached the U.S. Supreme Court, the justices ruled unanimously that citizenship does not include the right to vote. Finding that suffrage is not among the privileges and immunities of citizens of the United States, the Court soundly rejected the New Departure argument.[4]

With the defeat of the New Departure, the NWSA turned to a constitutional amendment to secure woman suffrage, formally introducing an amendment specifically prohibiting disfranchisement on the basis of sex at the Tenth Washington Convention of the NWSA in January 1878. The amendment was introduced in the Senate and referred to the Committee on Privileges and Elections, which granted a hearing to a number of representatives of the NWSA. Cady Stanton, one of those who delivered comments to the committee, took the opportunity to reiterate her support for the New Departure approach—"that our constitution, fairly interpreted, already secures to the humblest individual all the rights, privileges and immunities of American citizens."[5] The fundamental law "should be so framed and construed as to work injustice to none, but to secure as far as possible perfect political equality among all classes of citizens."[6] She conceded that an amendment was needed because there were widely varying interpretations of the Constitution.

Cady Stanton outlined the New Departure argument extensively, relying on the Fourteenth Amendment's grant of citizenship to all persons born or naturalized in the United States and the protection of "national" privileges and immunities against state infringement. Because the right to vote, she argued, is a privilege and immunity of citizens of the United States, although the Constitution leaves the qualifications for voters to the states, it does not give them the "right to deprive any citizen of the elective franchise; the State may regulate but not abolish the right of suffrage for any class."[7] Consequently, provisions in state constitutions that exclude citizens from voting on account of sex violate the Constitution in both "spirit and letter."[8]

She also referred to various other constitutional provisions to buttress her argument, including the Preamble, the prohibition on bills of attainder and titles of nobility, the Privileges and Immunities Clause in Article IV, Section 2,[9] the guarantee in Article IV, Section 4, to every state of a republican form of government, and the Supremacy Clause in Article VI.[10] The thrust of her references to the various constitutional provisions was that women were included in the category of "people" who came together to establish the Constitution and that they were also citizens whose privileges and immunities, including the right to vote, were protected against state infringement. Singling out women for exclusion from the franchise amounted to a bill of attainder, and a government run by one class of citizens constituted a nobility. A republican form of government could not exist so long as more than half of the population was excluded from the franchise. Finally, the Supremacy Clause reinforced Cady Stanton's argument that the states had no authority to withdraw the franchise from citizens of the United States.

Despite the fact that the Constitution already protected women's right to vote, an amendment was needed because of the Supreme Court's failure to interpret the document impartially or, for that matter, consistently. Cady Stanton castigated the Court on both grounds, noting:

> [H]owever the letter and spirit of the constitution may be interpreted by the people, the judiciary of the nation has uniformly proved itself the echo of the party in power. When the slave power was dominant the Supreme Court decided that a black man was not a citizen . . . and when the constitution was so amended as to make all persons citizens, the same high tribunal decided that a woman, though a citizen, had not the right to vote. An African, by virtue of his United States citizenship, is declared, under recent amendments, a voter in every State of the Union, but when a woman, by virtue of her United States citizenship, applies to the Supreme Court for protection in the exercise of this same right, she is remanded to the State, by the unanimous decision of the nine judges on the bench, that "the Constitution of the United States does not confer the right of suffrage upon any one." Such vacillating interpretations of constitutional law must unsettle our faith in judicial authority, and undermine the liberties of the whole people.[11]

As Cady Stanton continued her address to the Senate Committee, she reiterated the principle of national supremacy over states rights and the need for the national government to exercise its power to protect the inalienable rights of individuals.

Cady Stanton's speech in 1878 not only reveals her thoroughgoing understanding of the legal arguments set forth by proponents of the New Departure but, more important for present purposes, reveals her continuing commitment to the principle of equal rights. Her argument that the Constitution already protected women's right to vote seems incongruous with the purpose of her address, which was to convince the members of the Committee of the need for a constitutional amendment to guarantee women the vote. Indeed, she seemed unwilling to abandon the New Departure even after the Supreme Court rendered it untenable. One of the other women's rights leaders who addressed the Committee, in contrast to Cady Stanton, emphasized women's unique qualities that would allow them to improve government at all levels. Still another offered an anecdote about her black servant's inability to understand how to cast his ballot when he arrived at the polls.[12]

Although Cady Stanton's speech underlined her commitment to liberal principles, the fact that she had so frequently turned to republican and ascriptive ideologies lends further support to the argument that she blended the different traditions and frequently switched approaches. In the context of the New Departure, her defense of liberal principles stands out so clearly because she appeared to be defending an approach that had already proved to be ineffective. That the New Departure had been defeated meant that she would have to change her approach by embracing even more ascriptivist arguments, and she did so increasingly in the last twenty years of the nineteenth century.

The Alliance with Labor

In their search for new allies, Cady Stanton and Anthony turned to the labor reform movement, proposing an alliance with the National Labor Union (NLU), a federation of national trade unions founded in 1866. The NLU represented the first attempt to organize a national federation of labor in the United States and proposed a variety of far-reaching reforms. The proposed reforms included the eight-hour day, a major overhaul of the currency and banking system as well as the tax structure and the federal government's land distribution policy, a federal agency to aid in the education of workingmen, and cooperative endeavors that would unite the interests of labor and capital. Turning to direct political action in 1868, the NLU decided to establish its own political party, the National Labor Party. As a result, individual trade unions, primarily concerned with promoting improved working conditions and wages for workers and opposed to direct political action, began to withdraw from the NLU. Moreover, the trade unions disagreed with the NLU's decision to include blacks in order to promote unity among all workers and refused to admit blacks to their unions. By 1872, both the organization and the labor party were defunct.[13]

Meanwhile, Cady Stanton and Anthony were attracted to the NLU because of its egalitarian agenda and its interest in creating a new political party. In addition, the first congress of the organization adopted a resolution declaring its support for women workers and inviting their cooperation. Cady Stanton and others, writing in the *Revolution* in the summer of 1868, called for a new political party that would combine the campaign for woman suffrage with the labor reform movement.

Because of the apparently overlapping goals of woman's rights and labor reform, an alliance between the two groups seemed to be exactly what Cady Stanton and Anthony needed. The alliance between the two groups proved to be short-lived—it lasted only a little longer than a year. The NLU, dependent on trade unions made up of white male workers who saw women (as well as black males) as a threat to the solidarity that provided their only chance of attaining leverage with their employers, rejected the goal of woman suffrage.[14]

In 1868, Cady Stanton attended the third annual congress of the NLU and was seated as a delegate despite some objections from other delegates. She delivered an address in which she focused on labor reform. Her comments reflected empathy for the poor that contrasted with her growing elitism and ascriptivism during the postwar years. She spoke of "surging multitudes, ragged, starving, packed in dingy cellars and garrets where no ray of sunshine or hope ever penetrates," of factories where "young and old work side by side with tireless machines from morn til night," of men who must steal or starve. She asked whether the "conditions of different classes [could not] be more fairly established." And "is it right that a large majority of the race should suffer all their days the cruel hardships of poverty that a small minority may enjoy all life's pleasures and benefits?"[15] Everyone, she asserted, at least in the abstract, has the equal right to life, liberty and the pursuit of happiness. The conditions of northern workers, she admonished, were not much different from the lives of slaves under the southern plantation system. Abstract rights mean little if they are overcome by necessity: the natural right to travel is meaningless to a man who must stay in one place and work in order to survive. She also expressed the idea that "the highest good of the individual is the highest good of society"[16] and that poverty, a result of human ignorance and selfishness, can be remedied. She alluded to the idea that a man's labor is his own and criticized the church for teaching the poor to be patient and wait for the next life rather than seeking a solution to poverty.

Although many of Cady Stanton's comments in that address echoed the liberal-egalitarian ideas of the Garrisonians, the emphasis she placed on the horrors of poverty and her contention that poverty was not natural but created by society reflect a radical perspective. Nevertheless, Cady Stanton pulled back from the radical implications of her comments when she called on the "educated classes" to fight for the freedom of the laborer: "There is no hope of any general self-assertion among the masses. The first steps for their improvement must be taken by those who have tasted the blessings of liberty and education."[17]

In September 1868, in an attempt to gain delegate status at the NLU congress that year, Anthony organized the Working Women's Association with a group of newspaper typesetters who worked in the offices of the *Revolution*. Subsequently, the Working Women's Association, which was dominated by printers, grew to more than one hundred members and became central to Cady Stanton's and Anthony's efforts to organize women to demand the vote. There were major differences, however, between the suffragists and the typesetters over the priority that the Working Women's Association should give to suffrage. Although Cady Stanton argued that the vote was crucial to improving the economic position of working women, the typesetters remained unconvinced that suffrage would bring about any significant improvements for them. Still, because both groups shared the goals of ending economic discrimination against women and achieving equality in the labor force, the working women joined the suffragists to fight for inclusion of women in the unions, an end to the sexual division of labor, and equal pay. With Anthony's encouragement, they organized the Women's Typographical Union and began to work to establish a producer's cooperative. Although Cady Stanton hoped that "Out of the present Association will be formed cooperative unions in every branch of industry,"[18] the Working Women's Association failed to organize women in trades other than typesetting.[19]

The Working Women's Association then turned to investigating and publicizing the problems of women workers, and Cady Stanton, Anthony, and others took on the cause of Hester Vaughn, a twenty-year-old domestic servant in Philadelphia who had been sentenced to hang for infanticide. As a result of either an affair with or a rape by a man she declined to identify, Vaughn had become pregnant. She gave birth alone and after several days was found in her room with her dead baby. Although there was no evidence that she had killed the child—or even that the child was alive at birth—she was imprisoned, tried without proper defense, and convicted.[20] The Working Women's Association adopted resolutions demanding a new trial or pardon for Vaughn, and Cady Stanton and Elizabeth Smith Miller presented the resolutions to the governor of Pennsylvania.

Hester Vaughn's case came to represent the dangers that working women faced and the injustices that issued from a judicial system from which women were completely excluded. Writing in the *Revolution*, Cady Stanton took the opportunity to condemn the double sexual standard and the law of infanticide, as well as women's exclusion from the legal and political process. She implored the mothers of Pennsylvania to

> rescue that defenceless girl from her impending fate. Oh! make her case your own, suppose your young and beautiful daughter had been thus betrayed, would it not seem to you that the demands of justice should take the life of her seducer rather than her own? Men have made the laws cunningly, for their own protection; ignorantly, for they can never weigh the sorrows and sufferings of their victims. So long as by law and public sentiment maternity is made a disgrace and a degradation, the young and inexperienced of the poorer classes are driven to open violence.[21]

Vaughn remained in jail for six months until the governor released her on the condition that she depart immediately for England.[22]

The alliance between woman's rights and women's labor reform dissolved after only a year. Working-class, wage-earning women withdrew from the Working Women's Association as it became increasingly an organization of middle-class career women. While it would have promoted egalitarian goals, the coalitions between women's rights advocates and labor reformers and then between women's rights supporters and women workers was so radical and so at odds with any of the traditions of American political culture that it was untenable. Although neither the NLU nor the Working Women's Association made any explicit claims, the proposed alliance reflected ideas about class consciousness and solidarity and the proposition that unity among the oppressed could lead to liberation for all of mankind that radical labor organizers would take up later in the nineteenth century and that Karl Marx and Friedrich Engels had made famous in *The Communist Manifesto,* in 1848.[23] Cady Stanton and Anthony, however, extended the analysis to women. That approach reappeared in the twentieth century when the New Left and, subsequently, Marxist feminists attempted to forge alliances among workers, intellectuals, and racial minorities and constructed the category of women as an oppressed class that could work with other subordinated groups to overcome that oppression.

A document she composed in 1872 indicates Cady Stanton's continuing support for labor as well for as a number of other reforms that involved uniting women across class lines. She again expressed her support for a new party, for uniting reforms and accomplishing them with "women's method." Among the reforms she advocated were replacing wage labor with cooperation, ending capital punishment, enacting prison reform, extending charity and common sisterhood to prostitutes, reforming the criminal justice system, and working for international peace. She also argued for child care for working mothers and a system of public education in which students at all levels would become "cadets of the state"—that is, they would receive financial support for their studies. She stated that the "mission is to recognize the bond of humanity between all the peoples, the human solidarity deeper and prior to the national."[24]

More New Alliances: Free Love

"Free love" was a radical movement from which the antebellum woman's rights movement took particular care to disassociate itself, as evidenced by the debate at the woman's rights convention in 1860. Ideas that Cady Stanton expressed about marriage and sex, however, intersected at major points with those of the free-love movement—something that added to her controversial position in the woman's rights campaign in the 1870s.

The free-love movement that emerged in the early 1850s had close ties to the earlier perfectionist reform groups, to the utopian communities, and to spiritualism. One of the most prominent proponents of free love, Stephen Pearl Andrews, founded a community, Modern Times, to put his philosophy into practice and organized the New York Free Love League to advance his views. Andrews based his concept of free love on the notion of individual sovereignty, abjuring all interference in relations between the sexes. Church and state sanctions on marriage, he maintained, created an artificial relationship between husband and wife that was particularly harmful to the wife. Arguing that sexual purity could exist only in a relationship that contributed to the fullest development of both parties, he condemned marriage as a "house of bondage and the slaughterhouse of the female sex."[25] The abolition of marriage, Andrews argued, had to take place in a context of reform of the entire society. Two other free-love advocates, Thomas Nichols and Mary Grove Nichols, linked free love to women's health. One requirement for health was limiting sexual indulgence. Thus, it was essential for women to be freed from the sexual demands of men. The Nicholses contended that "if a woman has any right in the world, it is the right to herself; and . . . she has a right to decide . . . who shall be the father of her children. She has an equal right to decide whether she will have children, and to choose the time for having them."[26] Inverting conventional understanding of the institution, the Nicholses maintained that true marriage was the "union of two persons in mutual love," while adultery was any sexual gratification without love.[27] At the beginning of the twentieth century, it was common for radicals to express similar views about marriage. The anarchist Emma Goldman, for example, asked, "Free love? As if love is anything but free!" In the same vein, she admonished,

> Some day, some day men and women will rise, they will reach the mountain peak, they will meet big and strong and free, ready to receive, to partake, and to bask in the golden rays of love. What fancy, what imagination, what poetic genius can foresee even approximately the potentialities of such a force in the life of men and women. If the world is ever to give birth to true companionship and oneness, not marriage, but love will be the parent.[28]

In 1870 Lucy Stone accused Elizabeth Cady Stanton "of holding free love doctrines."[29] Stone alleged that the NWSA had been infiltrated with "loose women" and "free lovers" who wanted to include "easy divorce" in their platform.[30] Moreover, at the meeting in 1869, which ended in the split in the woman's rights movement, the Stone-Blackwell group introduced resolutions disavowing attempts to "undermine or destroy the sanctity of the marriage relation" and stating that they "abhorrently repudiate Free Loveism as horrible and mischievous to society, and disown any sympathy with it."[31] In the hands of the more conservative AWSA, free love was a weapon to be used against Cady Stanton and the others who formed the NWSA, a means of discrediting that group and convincing more women to join the Stone-Blackwell organization. In addition, Victoria Woodhull's involvement with the NWSA and the Beecher-Tilton scandal in the early 1870s had the effect of linking woman's rights to free love in the public mind, which exacerbated the tensions between the two organizations and seriously damaged the campaign for suffrage.

Cady Stanton expressed sympathy for and an interest in the free-love movement.[32] In a speech she delivered to a private club of men and women in 1870, she called not only for suffrage and the "social recognition of the equal rank of the sexes" but also for "freedom from all unnecessary entanglements and concessions, freedom from binding obligations involving impossibilities, freedom to repair mistakes, to express the manifoldness of our own natures, . . . to advance to higher planes of development."[33] Linking free love to the progress of humanity, she proclaimed, "We are one and all free lovers at heart, although we may not have thought so. We all believe in a good time coming, either in this world or another, when man and woman will be good and wise, when they will be 'a law unto themselves,' and when therefore the external law of compulsion will be no longer needed."[34] Appealing to elitist sensibilities, she suggested that the best people—"the most enlightened and the most virtuous"—were supporters of free love, while

the criminal classes feel the necessity of law and would resist social enfranchisement more than anybody else. It is the refined natures of delicate sensibilities and tender consciences who loathe the compulsory adulteries of the marriage bed, and it is the men of rigorous logic and love of justice who insist on the same freedom for others as for themselves even when the freedom may be used to do what they think wrong.[35]

In 1870, Victoria Woodhull, an outspoken advocate of free love, announced that she would be a candidate for the presidency of the United States in the next election. Earlier that year, she had begun to provide financial support for Stephen Pearl Andrews and his group of spiritualists. Andrews's ideas about free love had a major influence on Woodhull. In fact, Andrews was reputed to have written her speeches on the subject.[36]

In May 1871, Woodhull joined Cady Stanton on the platform of the NWSA convention. Woodhull not only demanded the vote for women but also called upon government to cease "to interfere with the rights of adult individuals to pursue happiness as they choose . . . or with contracts between individuals of whatever kind . . . which will place the intercourse of persons with each other upon their individual honor."[37] She delivered a speech later that year to a large audience in New York City in which she asserted that if all individuals have the right to life, liberty, and the pursuit of happiness, the law has no power over marriage. Proclaiming herself to be a "free lover," she asserted her *"inalienable, constitutional, and natural* right to love whom I may, to love as *long* or as *short* a period as I can; to *change* that love *every day* if I please and with *that* right neither *you* nor any *law* you can frame have *any* right to interfere.[38]

Although a number of members of the NWSA had begun to challenge Woodhull's involvement with the woman's rights movement by early 1872, Cady Stanton continued to support her.[39] She also favored Woodhull's plan to inaugurate a People's Party at the NWSA convention in May 1872 to support Woodhull's candidacy for president. The call for the meeting, signed by Cady Stanton, Isabella Beecher Hooker, and Matilda Joslyn Gage, stated in part that "we believe the time has come for the formation of a new political party whose principles shall meet the issues of the hour, and represent equal rights for all."[40] Anthony, who vehemently disagreed, insisted at the business meeting the day before the convention that Woodhull's group could not use the hall that the NWSA had reserved. An angry Cady Stanton then resigned as president of the NWSA and refused to preside at the convention. But she delivered the keynote address and, over Anthony's objection, asserted that women should vote in the coming election as members of Woodhull's People's Party.

Cady Stanton's views on marriage clearly overlapped with the doctrine of free love. Her sympathy for free love is suggested not only by her support for Victoria Woodhull but also by her defense of the free-love proponent Francis Barry in the *Revolution* in 1868 against readers' outraged responses to his assertion that the position of mistress was less degrading than that of wife.[41] Cady Stanton and the free-love advocates nevertheless differed in an important respect. The "free lovers" condemned the institution of marriage per se as an infringement on individual sovereignty and advocated its abolition. In contrast, Cady Stanton condemned marriage in its present state as "man-marriage" and advocated that it be reformed to take women's interests into account. In 1869, in the *Revolution,* she outlined her position on marriage. She noted that marriage and divorce laws bore unequally on woman and man. "But so far from abolishing the institution of marriage, I would have it more pure and holy than it is to-day, by making woman the dictator in the whole social realm."[42] She elaborated later in the same issue of the journal, noting that woman had never given her consent to the creeds, codes, and customs of marriage. She objected not only to laws concerning marriage but also to the teachings of the church. as well as to the social customs that were so degrading to women. Summarizing the defects of marriage, she proclaimed,

> Marriage today, is in no way viewed as an equal partnership, intended for the equal advantage and happiness of both parties. Nearly every man feels that his wife is his property, whose first duty, under all circumstances, is to gratify his passions, without the least reference to her own health and happiness, or the welfare of their offspring; and so enfeebled is woman's judgment and moral sense from long abuse, that she believes so too, and quotes from the Bible to prove her own degradation.[43]

Cady Stanton's differences with the proponents of free love, as well as with athe institution of marriage in its late-nineteenth-century form, are captured by a letter she wrote in 1875:

> You ask if I believe in "free love." If by "free love" you mean promiscuity, I do not. I believe in monogamic marriage, and for men as well as women. Everything short of this makes a mongrel, sensual, discordant progeny. . . . I do not believe in man having a wife for breeding purposes and an affinity [mistress] for spiritual and intellectual intercourse. Soul-union should precede and exalt physical union. Without sentiment, affection, imagination, what better would we be in procreation than the beasts? If by "free love" you mean woman's right to give her body to the man she loves and no other, to become a mother or not as her desire, judgment and conscience may dictate, to be the absolute sovereign of herself, then I do believe in freedom of love.[44]

Although Cady Stanton took great care to distance herself from the free-love advocates, her vision of what marriage should be was very similar to theirs. While she did not actually embrace the legal abolition of marriage as they did, she wanted to see marriage improved so that it would raise the position of the wife to one of equality with the husband and so that it would be consistent with the principle of individual sovereignty. Moreover, she looked forward to a future in which women would have the economic independence that would give them the freedom to marry out of love rather than necessity. Such ideas were consistent with liberal principles of individual autonomy and equality. Nevertheless, making her conception of marriage a reality would have required a major transformation of the institution of marriage and relations between men and women that were grounded in long-established cultural and religious traditions. Moreover, her association with the free-love doctrine and its proponents, like her attempts to forge alliances with the labor movement, points to a radicalism that transcends the liberal, republican, and ascriptive traditions. It was also that radicalism that set her apart from the other women's rights leaders and played such an important role in her increasing isolation from the organized movement.

The Critique of Marriage: Self-Sovereignty, Female Sexuality, and Voluntary Motherhood

A particularly detestable aspect of "the Husband's right of property in the wife,"[45] in Cady Stanton's view, was his legal prerogative to force her to have sex with him. Cady Stanton frequently lamented that this dimension of inequality in marriage not only deprived women of their dignity but also—because it often resulted in unwanted pregnancy—threatened women with physical harm. Moreover, Cady Stanton often pointed to the detrimental effects on society of brutish, drunken men fathering children who ended up in "lunatic asylums." Men's uncontrolled sexual appetites, in her view, impeded the progress of civilization. One of her goals for women was what she called "self-sovereignty," or control of their own sexual lives. Women—not their husbands—should have the power to determine how often they would engage in sex. Or, as she explained, "the mother of mankind" should have the prerogative to "set the bounds to his indulgence."[46] With her own self-control and the power to say "no" to her husband, a wife could control her reproductive life. Self-sovereignty would thus be a crucial step in transforming marriage into an equal partnership. Suffrage and legal reform would encourage such a development—by removing the husband's legal rights over his wife's body, for example—but would not be sufficient. Cady Stanton's discussions with women on the Lyceum circuit in the 1870s emphasized the importance of raising their awareness of their right and responsibility to seize control of their sexual lives. Legal reform was important, but women's individual and personal action would also be crucial in the transformation of marriage.[47]

She argued that a woman should not have sex with a drunken, brutal husband—or any husband she did not love—and often suggested that women had more control over their sexual appetites than men. Still, Cady Stanton, along with the advocates of free love, recognized the existence of a female sexual drive. She wrote in her diary in 1883, for example, complaining that Walt Whitman did not understand women's sexuality: "he speaks as if the female must be forced to the creative act, apparently ignorant of the great natural fact that a healthy woman has as much passion as a man, that she needs nothing stronger than the law of attraction to draw her to the male."[48]

A prominent theme of Cady Stanton's on the Lyceum circuit was what she called "enlightened motherhood." She spoke to women-only audiences of "the gospel of fewer children & a healthy happy maternity."[49] Closely connected to her notion of self-sovereignty, enlightened motherhood revolved around the idea that women would gain control over their reproductive lives not by means of artificial contraception, which was considered unnatural and dangerous, but by virtue of their ability to control their sexual lives. Her advice to women to "turn over a new leaf, and make a race of gods and poets and statesman," and her comment that "it is more important what kind of a child we raise than how many. *It is better to produce one lion than a dozen jackasses*"[50] referred to women's ability to choose when to become mothers.

Cady Stanton's efforts to impart her ideas of self-sovereignty and voluntary motherhood to as many women as possible add force to the claim that her thought transcended the traditional liberal distinction between the public and the private. Aware that the two were invariably intertwined, she argued that it was essential for a woman to be able to control her sexual and reproductive life by virtue of her ability to refuse to have sex with her husband. In order to give women the power to say "no" and for them to achieve equality in domestic relations, the laws regarding marriage had to be reformed. Clearly, women needed the vote in order to bring about legal change. In short, legal and political equality were essential if marriage was to become an equal partnership between a man and a woman. Still, reform in the public sphere would not be sufficient, as changes would be necessary at the level of the most intimate relations between men and women. Cady Stanton's determination to change women's lives by imparting to them a consciousness that they had the potential to control their own sexual lives was another dimension of her work that reflected her extremely broad reform vision that went beyond the multiple traditions and points to the radical dimension of her ideas.

Two Scandals: Cady Stanton and the Sexual Politics of the 1870s

The woman's rights movement became embroiled in two sexual scandals in the postwar years: the McFarland-Richardson murder, in 1869, and the Beecher-Tilton case, which lasted for several years and ended in 1875.[51] The manner in which the press portrayed the events and the way the public perceived them reveal a great deal about the sexual politics of the nineteenth century, particularly the reality that women were invariably blamed for men's transgressions. In fact, as the details of the Beecher-Tilton affair unfolded, not only was Lib Tilton blamed for forcing herself on Henry Ward Beecher but also the woman's rights movement was condemned for promulgating the ideas of free love.

Most important for present purposes, however, Cady Stanton became involved in both scandals, enthusiastically defending the women who were involved. Each scandal gave her an opportunity to speak out about the problems of marriage and divorce, not only in the context of the need for legal reform but also to condemn the inequality that pervaded the relationships between men and women—an inequality that legal reform could never overcome. While the following discussion may appear to be somewhat of a digression, as it recounts a number of the details of the scandals, my primary concern here is to draw attention to the way that Cady Stanton's comparison of the reality of marriage, with all of its flaws, to her ideal of marriage as an equal partnership between two willing parties highlights the radical dimension of her ideas.

On November 25, 1869, Daniel McFarland shot the journalist Albert Richardson in the office of the *New York Tribune*. The reason: Richardson's love affair with McFarland's wife, Abby Sage McFarland. Daniel McFarland drank heavily, beat his wife, and abandoned her when she was pregnant. They reconciled, and he continued his pattern of abuse and neglect. When Richardson learned of Abby McFarland's situation, he determined to rescue her. In 1867, Daniel McFarland shot Richardson for the first time, was arrested, and agreed to a separation from Abby. Abby went to Indiana to establish the year's residency required for a divorce there, returning to New York in November 1869. After McFarland learned that Richardson had purchased a farm in New Jersey and expected to live there with Abby after their marriage, he shot Richardson again. As Richardson lay dying, Henry Ward Beecher performed a wedding ceremony uniting Richardson and Abby McFarland. The press and then the clergy launched an attack on Beecher for performing the ceremony because New York had refused to recognize her Indiana divorce and therefore she was still legally married to Daniel McFarland.

McFarland was subsequently tried for murder and found not guilty by reason of insanity by an all-male jury. He was also granted sole custody of his and Abby's young son. On May 17, 1870, Cady Stanton and Anthony called a meeting for women in Apollo Hall, in New York City, to protest the decisions. Two thousand women gathered to condemn the judge and jury and to demand that the governor commit McFarland to an insane asylum. An outraged Cady Stanton identified the "the husband's right of property in his wife" as the central problem in marriage. The jury, she contended, was able to acquit McFarland because "neither woman nor slave can testify against their supposed masters." By declaring Abby's divorce illegal, the court permitted any "bloated drunkard or diseased libertine" to possess and coerce a woman sexually. She called for "an entire revision of the laws of New York on marriage and divorce. . . . Marriage as it existed [is] . . . nothing more or less than legalized prostitution. . . . I rejoice over every slave that escapes from a discordant marriage."[52]

At their respective conventions in May 1870, the rival women's rights organizations chose new presidents. The AWSA selected Henry Ward Beecher, and at the NWSA convention a resolution was introduced providing that Cady Stanton and Anthony resign their offices and a "popular man" take their place. Theodore Tilton was then elected president of the NWSA.[53] For present purposes, the importance of the election of Beecher and Tilton to head the two organizations lies in the fact that these two men played major roles in the second scandal.

In July 1870, Lib Tilton confessed to her husband, the newspaper editor Theodore Tilton, that she had been having an affair with his friend Henry Ward Beecher. Initially, Tilton accepted the affair, decided to extend to his wife the open marriage that he had been enjoying, and maintained his close personal relationship with Beecher.[54] But, when he learned that his wife was pregnant with Beecher's child, he reacted violently, condemning Beecher as a "damned lecherous scoundrel" and physically threatening Lib. Both Anthony and Cady Stanton were meeting with Tilton, who was then editing the *Revolution,* and thus witnessed his explosion. Anthony, in fact, spent the night in the Tiltons' house barricaded with Lib in the bedroom, where Lib related the details of her affair with Beecher.

Lib Tilton lost the baby either to a miscarriage or an abortion. Theodore lost his positions as contributor to the *Independent,* a popular religious weekly, and as editor of the *Brooklyn Daily Union.*[55] When Beecher learned that Lib Tilton had confessed the affair to her husband, the minister persuaded her to write a letter revoking that confession. At the urging of her husband, however, she subsequently renounced that letter. As Beecher maneuvered to prevent the exposure of the affair, he began to shift the blame to Lib Tilton, complaining, "I don't understand how *she* could have done this to me."[56]

When the AWSA and then Horace Greeley's *New York Tribune* attacked Victoria Woodhull in 1871, she threatened to make the Beecher-Tilton affair public to reveal the hypocrisy of the people who condemned her for practicing free love while secretly engaging in it themselves.[57] Tilton proceeded to ingratiate himself with Woodhull—he wrote her biography and became infatuated with her, and they may even have become lovers.[58] Woodhull tried to blackmail Beecher by threatening to reveal the affair unless he publicly endorsed her position on free love. He refused and kept his distance, particularly after she delivered her speech in November 1871 in which she not only endorsed free love but also admitted to practicing it. In the spring of 1872, Tilton began to distance himself from her, as well, joining the liberal Republicans to nominate Greeley for president and reporting for the *New York Tribune.*

Woodhull had to suspend publication of *Woodhull & Claflin's Weekly* but was able to restart the presses for the issue dated November 2, 1872, which carried the story of "The Beecher-Tilton Scandal Case" in the form of an interview with Victoria Woodhull by an unnamed reporter. She named Cady Stanton and two other woman's rights leaders, Isabella Beecher Hooker and Paulina Wright Davis, as her sources. She related the details of Beecher's affair with Lib Tilton, took the opportunity to endorse free love, and described Beecher as one of its practitioners. Beecher publicly denied Woodhull's charges.

Cady Stanton was drawn into the scandal when a story appeared in a number of newspapers incorrectly quoting her as denying the truth of Woodhull's story. Beecher's sister, Isabella Beecher Hooker, in an effort to convince Cady Stanton to come forward to correct the story, wrote an article in the *Hartford Times* in which she not only alleged that Cady Stanton had known of the affair but also revealed a number of confidences, including Cady Stanton's love for her own brother-in-law.[59]

The scandal dragged on for three years. Beecher was cleared first in a church investigation. To protect himself, Beecher impugned not only Woodhull but also Cady Stanton and Anthony, calling them "human hyenas" with a "greedy and unclean appetite for everything that was foul and vile."[60] One witness implied that both women had been involved with Theodore Tilton. Cady Stanton responded in an interview in which she reviewed the events of the night that Anthony spent barricaded with Lib Tilton and confirmed that Lib Tilton had truthfully confessed her "criminal intimacy" with Beecher. When Anthony expressed her annoyance with her for making public comments, Cady Stanton responded, lamenting the way that the scandal had unjustly and cunningly "rolled on our suffrage movement." She cautioned that "When Beecher falls, as he must, he will pull all he can down with him. But we must not let the cause of woman go down in the smash."[61]

The church committee issued a report concluding that Beecher was the victim of Theodore Tilton's "vicious and revengeful designs" and that Lib Tilton was guilty of plaguing the preacher with her "inordinate affection." The committee reprimanded Beecher for allowing his "great generosity" to blind him to the falseness of the Tiltons.[62] An angry Cady Stanton took the opportunity to reiterate her ideal of marriage in a letter to the *Chicago Daily Tribune*: "In spite of the various relations in which men and women of all ages have lived, and still live, there must be a true condition; and, to my mind, it seems that might be found, with *love and quality,* in a true marriage of one man and one woman."[63] Coming to Lib Tilton's defense, she observed that, "like a withered flower, 'the Great Preacher' casts her aside, and tells the world 'she thrust her affections on him unsought.'"[64]

The day after the Plymouth Church committee issued its report, Theodore Tilton filed suit for alienation of affection against Beecher and asked for $100,000 in damages. The sensational trial—"an American obsession, a supershow, far transcending the question of innocence or guilt"—lasted for six months, finally ending in a mistrial when the jurors could not agree on a verdict.[65] As he had done before the church committee, Beecher maintained his innocence and insisted that if there was any fault in the matter, it lay with Lib Tilton, who had developed a passion for him and created the problem by not warning him that Theodore Tilton suspected him of being the object of her unwanted affections.[66] Beecher emerged unscathed from the scandal, while Theodore Tilton went bankrupt and Lib Tilton, rapidly losing her sight, was left with little money and with four children to raise. She eventually wrote a public letter in which she reaffirmed the truth of her affair with Beecher.

Cady Stanton's, Anthony's, and Isabella Beecher Hooker's entanglement in the scandal, Henry Ward Beecher's repeated condemnation of the NWSA and its leaders, including his own sister, and Victoria Woodhull's involvement in the organization had damaging consequences for the woman's rights movement. The scandal pushed the two already divided organizations further apart. Moreover, by implicating the NWSA in what to the public had become an odious doctrine of free love, the scandal prompted the leaders to sever all ties to anything that might contain even the slightest hint of free love. Thus, the NWSA followed the AWSA in narrowing its focus to the single cause of woman suffrage.

Independent and determined as always, Cady Stanton continued to advocate fundamental changes in the relations between men and women. In an interview in 1875, she pointed to three positive effects of the trial. First, it "knocked a great blow at the priesthood," particularly in the eyes of women. Second, it served to emphasize the importance of strong, independent-minded women:

> It has taught men the need of women being strong minded and self-poised for men's own protection. . . . It has knocked a blow at the subordination of the state of wifehood. . . . Men will not forget that for their own safety, that in all association of men with women, better a strong, self-poised woman than the weakling who is to-day domineered by this man's magnetism, and to-morrow by that.[67]

Third, she contended that the trial had a "strong pull" toward equalizing the standard of tolerated and reputable behavior of women and men.[68] In another interview, she commended Victoria Woodhull for doing something for women that no one else had: "Leaping into the brambles that were too high for us to see over them, she broke a path into their close and thorny interstices with a steadfast faith that glorious principle would triumph at last over conspicuous ignominy, although her life might be sacrificed."[69]

Conclusion

Elizabeth Cady Stanton's reluctance to give up the New Departure argument even after the U.S. Supreme Court rejected it suggests the extent to which she continued to rely on liberal egalitarian legal principles into the 1870s, even as ascriptivist themes were playing an increasingly prominent role in her arguments. As we have seen, there are also major aspects of her thought that fall outside the multiple traditions into a fourth category of radicalism. Her attempt to forge an alliance with labor, her lectures and writings on self-sovereignty, and her critique of marriage as reflected in her pronouncements on the McFarland-Richardson and Tilton-Beecher scandals underline the radical dimension of Cady Stanton's thought. Her arguments in all of those areas suggest that she recognized the need for a fundamental transformation in culture and society—in attitudes toward women and their proper role, in relations between workers and employers, in the institution of marriage, and in women's ability to control her own reproductive life—that went far beyond the campaign for legal and political reform.

8

Not the Word of God
But the Work of Men
Cady Stanton's Critique of Religion

Introduction

By the 1880s, the United States was drastically different from the country that it had been in 1848, when Cady Stanton organized the first woman's rights convention at Seneca Falls. The industrial revolution had transformed the country, bringing large-scale industry, heavily populated urban areas, large businesses and corporations, and nationwide systems of transportation. Moreover, the United States was soon to become one of the world's great powers. The United States's war with Spain in 1898 ended in victory and the acquisition of Cuba, the Philippines, Puerto Rico, and Guam. Accompanying the massive economic growth and rapid industrialization was an increasing concentration of wealth in the hands of a small percentage of the population. As the "Captains of Industry" devised ways to gain control of whole industries and combine all the processes of production and distribution under a single management, smaller businesses were destroyed. Amid the vast wealth of the new industrialists, a growing urban working class lived in crowded tenements with, at best, inadequate water and sanitation. Working conditions included long hours at dangerous machines in unventilated (even locked) rooms where children who were barely large enough to work the machines made up part of the workforce. Often all members of a family, who lived in a single room, worked in a factory owned by one of the new corporations.

As the new corporations came to control the political as well as the economic life of the country and politics at all levels became increasingly corrupt, various reform movements emerged to advocate regulations aimed at limiting the power of business in the interest of rescuing democracy and preserving the integrity of American government. At the same time, defenders of the status quo drew on popular evolutionary theory to support their argument that laissez-faire was the only policy that was consistent with the principle that life was invariably a difficult struggle in which only the most "fit" could survive. While evolutionary theory was challenging traditional religious beliefs, there was also an upsurge in fundamentalist Protestantism.

One of the accomplishments of the woman's rights campaign was the modification of the doctrine of separate spheres to expand women's role not only within the family but also in the realm of education and charitable work. But, by the 1880s, religious conservatives had resurrected the old, much more rigid doctrine to curb women's opportunities.[1] As Kathi Kern has noted, although the rhetoric of separate spheres allowed women some moral authority, particularly because of the association of religion with the female sphere, the doctrine also served as an obstacle to women's progress. A number of defeats in the campaign for woman suffrage at the state level in the late 1880s, as well as the persistence of limited opportunities for women to study in colleges and universities at both the undergraduate and the graduate levels, attest to the problem. Moreover, there was a backlash against divorce reform beginning in the 1880s as conservatives called for more stringent divorce laws to counteract women's "selfishness" in seeking divorces.[2] In part as a strategic response to the conservative climate, the woman's rights movement had become respectable and conservative and focused on the campaign for suffrage to the exclusion of other reforms to end women's oppression.

It was in such a context that Cady Stanton's ideas evolved during the last twenty years of her life. Industrialization and urbanization, the reform movements and their opponents, the resurgence of conservative Protestantism, challenges to orthodox religious beliefs, and the conservative direction that the organized woman's rights movement all had important effects on her activities and the development of her ideas.

I begin this chapter by considering Cady Stanton's activities during the period in which she grew even more isolated from the increasingly conservative suffrage-focused woman's rights movement; as she commented, she had outgrown the suffrage movement. I then turn to her campaign against organized religion, which culminated in *The Woman's Bible*. As we will see, Cady Stanton's critique of religion and her commentary on the Bible reveals the extent to which, in the later years of her life, she developed her earlier views of religious institutions in the

United States into a full-blown condemnation of what she understood to be one of the major sources of women's oppression. Her critique underlines her understanding that women's oppression lay at the core of American culture and traditions and that fundamental change would be necessary for women to achieve equality.

From Leader to Dissident: Independence and Isolation

Cady Stanton turned sixty-five in 1880, the year she retired from the Lyceum circuit. Her independence from the organized woman's rights movement and freedom from other commitments that had dominated her earlier years increased as she grew older. She spent a great deal of time with her family both in the United States and in Europe but was no longer responsible for home and child care. Henry Stanton passed away in early1887, at the age of eighty-one. Though they had spent much of their married life apart, they had been living together for a few years toward the end of his life. Cady Stanton had already carved out an independent career for herself outside the organized woman's rights movement during the 1870s, but in the 1880s and 1890s she further distanced herself from the NWSA and then, after the merger of the two organizations, from the National American Woman Suffrage Association (NAWSA)

During this period she embarked on and completed several major writing projects. From 1880 until 1886, she and Anthony, with some help from Matilda Joslyn Gage, compiled the first three volumes of *The History of Woman Suffrage.* The disagreements over strategy that marred the relationship between Cady Stanton and Anthony during the 1870s continued, but the two women were able to work closely on the project, spending the bulk of their time together in Cady Stanton's home, where they organized the documents from the beginning of the woman's rights movement. In 1882, Cady Stanton traveled to France, where she helped her son, Theodore, complete his book, *The Woman Question in Europe.* She published Part I of her commentary on the Old Testament, *The Woman's Bible,* in late 1895 and Part II of *The Woman's Bible,* which covered both the Old and the New Testaments, in 1898. Her autobiography, *Eighty Years and More: Reminiscences, 1815–1897,* also appeared in 1898. In 1901, she began to compile her speeches and other papers—a project that she was unable to complete.

An essay she wrote on divorce reform was published in the *New York American* in October 1902 just weeks before her death, on October 26. In a final letter, which she dictated a few days before her death, she asked President Theodore Roosevelt to endorse a constitutional amendment for woman suffrage in his next address to Congress.[3]

Organizations made up of middle- and upper-middle-class women multiplied in the 1870s and 1880s. As these organizations became increasingly interested in various types of reform in the mid-1880s Anthony worked to form alliances with them in an attempt to increase support among women for suffrage. In taking this approach, she moved away from her earlier goal of forging a movement of women committed to the transformation of society and women's place in it to focus on uniting women around the goal of suffrage.[4] Cady Stanton vehemently disagreed with Anthony's new strategy.

In 1888, the NWSA organized the International Council for Women. Although, several years earlier, Cady Stanton had devised a plan to bring together suffragists from different countries, the NWSA decided to expand the Council to include "women working along all lines of social, intellectual or civil progress and reform."[5] The theme of the opening speech that Cady Stanton delivered to the Council was that all the gains that women had made were a result of the campaign for suffrage. Although Anthony reputedly carefully supervised Cady Stanton's writing of that speech, the latter managed to mention issues in addition to suffrage: "these great moral struggles for higher education, temperance, peace, the rights of labor, religious freedom, international arbitration."[6] She also took the opportunity to condemn proposals for a constitutional amendment that would "recognize the Christian theology of the Constitution and introduce religious tests into political parties and platforms."[7] In addition, she acknowledged that voting women would have differences of opinion but would support laws that protect the "interests of the many rather than the few."[8] Finally, she alluded to the broader goals and the importance to society of freedom for women when she stated, "The true woman is as yet a dream of the future. A just government, humane religion, a pure social life await her coming. Then and not till then, will the golden age of peace and prosperity be ours."[9]

In the closing session, Cady Stanton departed even more drastically from the intended tone of the Council when she admonished that the question of women's freedom would eventually be settled with violence if it did not receive "serious consideration" from men in power. Women, she said would "strike hands with Nihilists, Socialists, Communists, and Anarchists, in defense of the most enlarged liberties of the people."[10] Her comments, so out of tune with the sentiment of the Council, suggest the extent to which Cady Stanton disagreed with Anthony's conciliatory approach. Her comments also bolster the assertion that her ideas included a radical element in addition to liberalism, republicanism, and ascriptivism.

The leading role that Anthony took in the negotiations for the merger of NWSA with AWSA was consistent with her goal of unifying as many women as possible around the demand for the vote. Although Anthony asserted that the AWSA wanted to merge with the NWSA because the latter was stronger and more successful, most of the terms of the merger were set by the AWSA.[11] The creation of the NAWSA, in February 1890, resulted in the woman suffrage movement becoming even more conservative and less tolerant of dissent.

Cady Stanton, fundamentally at odds with Anthony's strategy of organizing women around the issue of suffrage, continued to envision broader social change. She remained determined to "lead women to the most comprehensive and challenging interpretation of what it meant to be free."[12] Consequently, she withdrew from the merger negotiations between NWSA and AWSA and did not take part in the founding of the NAWSA. It was at Anthony's insistence, and with much disagreement from the membership, that Cady Stanton was elected to the presidency of NAWSA in 1890. As president she was essentially a figurehead, without allies or power, and spent a good deal of her time in England until she resigned her position in 1892. After that, she never attended another meeting.

Unlike Anthony and the other leaders who took the conservative path by seeking to ally all women's groups around the campaign for the vote, Cady Stanton preferred alliances with more radical and democratic movements, such as the Populists in the early 1890s, and she later spoke favorably of the socialist movement in the United States. She took the position that women should align themselves with other political movements, rather than limit themselves to the issue of suffrage. Such a move, she was convinced, would broaden the issues beyond suffrage, as well as bring more strength to the fight for women's rights. She wrote, in 1894, "If the Prohibitionists, the Populists, the labor organizations and the women would all unite, we should be in the majority."[13]

At the same time that the suffrage movement moved increasingly toward an emphasis on unity and ideological harmony, Cady Stanton urged women's rights advocates to acknowledge and debate their differences. In her address to the first meeting of the NAWSA, she alluded to the political differences among women and contended that there were pressing concerns in addition to suffrage that needed to be addressed. Indeed, she suggested that women could use the vote not only to institute divorce reform but also to maintain the separation of church and state and to solve the "race problem." She urged the organization to address such issues and not allow the movement to isolate itself from the broader political context by excluding all issues other than suffrage: "when any principle or question is up for discussion, let us seize on it and show its connection, whether nearly or remotely, with woman's disfranchisement. There is such a thing as being too anxious lest someone 'hurt the cause' by what he or she must say or do; or perhaps the very thing you fear is exactly what should be done."[14] She expressed her conviction that the movement should not narrow its focus to suffrage in a set of suggestions for the next NAWSA convention that she sent to Anthony in 1899:

> To my mind our Association cannot be too broad. Suffrage involves every basic principle of republican government, all our social, civil, religious, educational and political rights. It is therefore germane to our platform to discuss every invidious distinction of sex in the college, home, trades, and professions, in literature, sacred and profane, in the canon as well as in the civil law.[15]

In short, Cady Stanton's position was that the movement should be as broadly focused as possible and that women should be a force for major change in society.

Cady Stanton's critique of Christianity, discussed at length in the next section, which culminated in the publication of *The Woman's Bible* in 1895, seriously clashed with the woman suffrage movement, whose leaders by then were intent on maintaining respectability and avoiding giving offense to the political and religious establishment. To most of the suffrage leaders, including Anthony, Cady Stanton was attacking the religious beliefs that were helping to bring increasing numbers of people to the campaign for suffrage. Indeed, the NAWSA formally condemned Cady Stanton's commentary on the Bible.

A final disagreement occurred between Cady Stanton and her few remaining followers in the movement and Anthony when the latter announced, in 1898, that she would resign as president of NAWSA in 1900 and designated Carrie Chapman Catt as her successor.[16] Cady Stanton opposed Catt, who had led the move to condemn *The Woman's Bible,* and urged Lillie Devereux Blake to run against her. Blake had been head of the New York Suffrage Association, had won suffrage for women in local school elections, and had managed to get matrons in police stations and women doctors in mental institutions. She had also participated in the writing of *The Woman's Bible.* Anthony opposed Blake, who at the last minute withdrew her candidacy.

In sum, the last years of Cady Stanton's career were distinguished by her growing isolation from the organized woman's rights movement. Though she remained close to Anthony, who generally tried to defend her despite their own differences, she had almost no support among the younger generation of leaders, who took the conservative approach. Despite the absence of support for her broader approach, Cady Stanton refused to compromise and continued to distance herself from the organization. She wrote to Blake of her indignation:

> They refused to read my letters and resolutions to the conventions; they have denounced *The Woman's Bible* unsparingly; not one of them has ever reviewed or expressed the least appreciation of *Eighty Years and More.* . . . For all this I make no public protest, I propose no revenge. Because of this hostile feeling I renounced the presidency and quietly accept the situation, and publish what I have to say in the liberal papers. . . . I have outgrown the suffrage association, as the ultimative [*sic*] of human endeavor, and no longer belong in its fold with its limitations.[17]

After she failed to obtain financial backing for compiling a volume of her speeches and writings, she expressed her frustration and disappointment even more candidly: "If my suffrage coadjutors had ever treated me with the boundless generosity they have my friend, I could have scattered my writings abundantly. . . . They have given Susan thousands of dollars, jewels, laces, silks and satins, and me criticisms for my radical ideas."[18] Clearly, the woman's rights movement would have been fundamentally different had Anthony and the other leaders followed Cady Stanton's lead. Still, even without followers, she refused to compromise and continued her work outside the organization.

The Woman's Bible: *Religion and the Oppression of Women*

With her critique of religion, which culminated in *The Woman's Bible,*
Cady Stanton put herself in the middle of a major controversy of the
nineteenth century that concerned not only the authority of the Bible
but also the relationship between women's rights and religion. In fact,
The Woman's Bible presented a major challenge to the dominant social
and religious values of the period. But, although her analysis of the
Bible was controversial and radical, it was actually very little more than
an elaboration of her earlier ideas. It was fully consistent with her long-
held views of the source of women's subordination and with her earlier
criticisms of Christianity, for example. Moreover, the ideas that she articulated in *The Woman's Bible* reflect the way she used the ideas of
Positivism to support her arguments for women's rights. In an important sense, however, *The Woman's Bible* marked a departure from Cady
Stanton's earlier work insofar as it emphasized her thoroughgoing rejection of the argument that women's rights derive from the moral purity,
or the natural piety, of women.[19] In the context of the present study of
Elizabeth Cady Stanton's thought, her attack on religion is important
primarily for the light it sheds on the way she presented her arguments,
with regard to both strategic concerns and the way that those arguments reflected the intellectual trends of the final years of the nineteenth
century.[20]

In her autobiography, Cady Stanton explained that her differences
with organized religion went back to the days when, as a teenager, she
had become anxious and depressed after attending a series of revivals
and had recovered only when she "found [her] way out of the darkness
into the clear sunlight of Truth [as] . . . religious superstitions gave place
to rational ideas based on scientific facts."[21] The juxtaposition of rational thought and science on the one hand with religious superstition
and orthodoxy on the other was a constant theme in Cady Stanton's
work and played an important role in her critique of religion. In addition, and more specifically, she found religion to be a major source of
women's oppression. The statements she made in the Declaration of Sentiments in 1848 criticizing organized religion for its treatment of women
represent an early articulation of the ideas that she would develop more
fully later in her life and that would culminate in *The Woman's Bible.*

In the 1880s, amid the resurgence of conservative religious views and
the backlash against women's rights, Cady Stanton grew increasingly

interested in analyzing the web of connections between organized religion and women's subordination. It was then that she embarked on the project that became *The Woman's Bible*. Although the two-volume work is commonly described as a revision of the Bible, it was actually a commentary in which Cady Stanton and the members of her revising committee reprinted selected passages and, at the end of each, provided an interpretation and criticism.

The critique of religion that Cady Stanton presented in *The Woman's Bible* is yet another example of one of the major themes in her understanding of the source of and the solution to women's oppression. For her it was not simply the lack of political and legal rights that kept women in a subordinate position but the entire culture that indoctrinated women to see themselves as naturally self-sacrificing and obedient and thereby to accept their dependent status, their position within the family, and their role in the church and, indeed, in all the institutions that relegated women to roles that rendered them powerless and dependent. With her critique of religion, Cady Stanton elaborated on that view, demonstrating that it was not nature, destiny, or a divine plan that placed women in a subordinate position but rather men's monopoly on the interpretation of religious doctrine and the Bible.

Accordingly, in Cady Stanton's view, the vote in and of itself would not end women's oppression. A major transformation of society was necessary, and women could bring this about if and only if they could break free of the cultural and religious bonds that kept them in subjection. They had to reach the point where they would see that their subordination was not divinely sanctioned but created and perpetuated by men. Anthony captured Cady Stanton's sentiment when she explained their fundamentally different approaches:

> You say "women must be emancipated from their superstitions before enfranchisement will be of any benefit," and I say just the reverse, that women must be enfranchised before they can be emancipated from their superstitions. . . . So you will have to keep pegging away, saying, "Get rid of religious bigotry and then get political rights;" while I shall keep pegging away, saying "Get political rights first and religious bigotry will melt like dew before the morning sun."[22]

Thus, from Cady Stanton's perspective, freeing women from the constraints placed on them by religion by analyzing the Bible as a major source of their oppression would represent a major accomplishment in the struggle to eliminate the vast array of obstacles to equality.

A number of developments in the 1880s converged to encourage Cady Stanton to undertake her systematic analysis of the Bible. First, during this period, Protestant denominations, using modern business techniques to attract followers, proliferated.[23] The resurgence of Protestantism took place in the midst of the growing popularity of science and, more specifically, evolutionary theory, which posed a threat to the power of religion. Second, Cady Stanton's frequent trips abroad during the 1880s exposed her to the intellectual critiques of religion that were beginning to appear in Europe. German scholars, engaged in "higher criticism" of the Bible, were treating it as a historical artifact by trying to determine the date, author, and authenticity of its texts.[24] While such work was profoundly disturbing to American churchmen, it manifested a growing interest in critical analysis of the Bible and, as such, must have encouraged Cady Stanton to embark on her own project. Third, revisions of the Bible were appearing—a group of conservative theologians published a Revised New Testament in 1881. Cady Stanton remarked that the revision had done nothing to bring dignity, respect, or equality to women.[25] Such developments not only made it easier for her to develop her critique of religion but also all but guaranteed that her work would be at the center of a major controversy.

Women, including many suffragists, were particularly active participants in the spread of the religious revival. The emphasis on unity in the suffrage movement helped to bring many of these women into the ranks of the NAWSA. The Women's Christian Temperance Union, under the leadership of Frances Willard, for example, joined the suffrage campaign. While Cady Stanton identified religion as a major source of women's oppression, Willard praised traditional Christian values and linked them to women's rights. Women like Willard supported many of the things Cady Stanton opposed, including Sunday closing laws, the teaching of the Bible in schools, a constitutional amendment recognizing Christianity as the religion of the United States, and restrictions on divorce. In short, the suffrage movement came to have a much stronger religious basis than it had in earlier years, which reinforced its increasing conservatism and which, in turn, alarmed Cady Stanton and spurred her to undertake her critique of organized religion.

One of the major contentions of the religious suffragists was that Christianity had elevated women's position. Cady Stanton used that as her starting point to set out her opposing view in an article she published in 1885. She asserted that all religions "taught the headship and superiority of man, the inferiority and subordination of woman . . . they have all alike brought to woman but another form of humiliation."[26] Nevertheless, she directed the bulk of her criticism at Christianity, drawing on historical data to demonstrate that women have "enjoyed in some periods greater honor and dignity and more personal property rights than have been accorded her in the Christian era."[27] It was the concept of original sin, she noted, that dishonored womanhood and brought the entire sex to "a depth of moral degradation that it had never known before."[28] Christianity imposed celibacy on women, and the church persecuted women for witchcraft: they were "hunted down by the clergy, tortured, burned, drowned, dragged into the courts, tried, and condemned for crimes that never existed but in the minds of religious devotees."[29] After the Reformation, she noted, Protestantism eliminated the feminine element, the Virgin Mary, from religion and made "god exclusively male and man supreme."[30] Cady Stanton characterized the church as the most enthusiastic and powerful opponent of women's rights, noting that the clergy opposed legal reforms in relation to women even as secular institutions were slowly allowing change. The church refused to allow women into the ministry and in some churches prohibited women from preaching. This was the case, she noted, even in England and the United States, which "can boast the highest type of womanhood, and the greatest number in every department of art, science, and literature."[31]

In her 1885 article, Cady Stanton lamented that when the Scriptures were collected and printed by men with "monstrous ideas, emanating from [their] bewildered brains . . . in the dark ages," their work was "declared to be the word of God, penned by writers specially inspired by his Spirit."[32] Those Scriptures, she declared, made "women an afterthought in the creation, the author of sin, in collusion with the devil, sex a crime, marriage a condition of slavery for woman and defilement for man, and maternity a curse to be attended with sorrow and suffering that neither time nor knowledge could ever mitigate, a just punishment for having effected the downfall of man."[33] In short, Christianity had not benefited woman; indeed, it was just the opposite: the church had done its worst to degrade women.

An additional problem with organized religion and another source of its denigration of women was, as Cady Stanton explained, "a belief in a trinity of *masculine* gods from which the *feminine* element is wholly eliminated." Because God was an ideal, "the infinite ideal of humanity," it was a "preposterous ridiculous absurdity of supposing God . . . to be of the male sex, and of calling God *him* only." God as an ideal encompassed both male and female qualities, and what humanity needed to do was "reconcile and combine the fractional life of man and woman into complete unions: then shall we become like gods, knowing all truth."[34]

In 1886, intent on expanding her critique of Christianity into a thorough analysis of the Bible, Cady Stanton attempted to form a committee of women biblical scholars to interpret the passages that would be of interest to women. Failing to find any women who were willing to participate, she dropped the project. Taking it up again in 1894, she relied on a group of Theosophists, New Thought leaders, and Freethinkers. Matilda Joslyn Gage, Clara Colby, and Olympia Brown also worked with her. Although a number of other women were formally members of the Revising Committee, Cady Stanton wrote most of *The Woman's Bible* herself.

In general, Cady Stanton argued that the Bible, which the clergy, lawyers, legislators, and even women themselves had so often used to counter women's claims of equality, was not "The Word of God." It was instead, the work of men—something she repeatedly underlined by referring to the author as the "historian." She proclaimed, "The time has come to read it as we do all other books, accepting the good and rejecting the evil it teaches."[35] Moreover, male translators and church historians had interpreted it in such a way as to further rationalize the subordination of women. Cady Stanton believed that the Bible "taught the subjection and degradation of women"[36] and that the "'true' interpretation of the Scriptures" opposed any change in the status of women.[37] In her Preface to Part II of *The Woman's Bible,* she wrote that no special skill was needed to show that the Bible "degrades the Mothers of the Race."[38] She went on to summarize her view:

The Old Testament makes woman a mere after-thought in creation; the author of evil; cursed in her maternity; a subject in marriage; and all female life, animal and human, unclean. The Church in all ages has taught these doctrines and acted on them, claiming divine authority therefore. "As Christ is the head of the Church, so is man the head of woman." This idea of woman's subordination is reiterated times without number, from Genesis to Revelations; and this is the basis of all church action.[39]

Clearly, Cady Stanton's assessment of the Bible was overwhelmingly negative. Nevertheless, in some of her commentaries, she reinterpreted passages of the Bible to demonstrate "that they really portrayed woman as man's equal."[40]

She explained that of the two contradictory accounts of the creation in the Book of Genesis, only the first, which posited the simultaneous creation of man and woman, was credible. It was "in harmony with science, common sense, and the experience of mankind in natural laws."[41] The second version, positing that God made woman out of Adam's rib, reducing women to a "mere afterthought," was "a mere allegory symbolizing some mysterious conception of a highly imaginative editor," someone who was a "wily writer," who felt it important for the dignity and dominion of man to effect woman's subordination in some way."[42] She noted that it would be inconsistent with the sublime process of "bringing order out of chaos; light out of darkness; giving each planet its place in the solar system; oceans and lands their limits" to reduce the creation of the mother of the race to a "petty surgical operation."[43]

Overall, Cady Stanton's commentary presented the Bible as an historical document that was consistently biased against women. For example, she noted that although Eve and her daughters apparently devoted all their energies to childbearing, "the entire credit for the growth of the race is given to Adam and his male descendants."[44] The male perspective consistently extolled violence and war and neglected the important role that women had played in the development of civilization:

Indeed the Pentateuch is a long painful record of war, corruption, rapine, and lust, Why Christians who wished to convert the heathen to our religion should send them these books, passes all understanding. It is most demoralizing reading for children and the unthinking masses, giving all alike the lowest possible idea of womanhood, having no hope nor ambition beyond conjugal unions with men they scarcely knew, for whom they could not have had the slightest sentiment of friendship, to say nothing of affection. There is no mention of women except when the advent of sons is announced.[45]

Cady Stanton confronted a well-known passage, the first Epistle to the Corinthians, in which Paul admonished men to "Let your women keep silence in the churches; for it is not permitted unto them to speak; but they are commanded to be under obedience, as also saith the law."[46] She professed that Paul was advising women to consult their husbands at home, rather than in the church, where controversial issues often arose. She concluded, however, "There is such a wide difference of opinion on this point among wise men, that perhaps it would be as safe to leave women to be guided by their own unassisted common sense."[47] Although her analysis of Paul's injunction was less condemnatory than it might have been, she had more to say about his treatment of women in her commentary on Genesis. She claimed that he had spoken of equality as the very soul and essence of Christianity when he said, "There is neither Jew nor Greek, there is neither bond nor free, there is neither male nor female; for ye are all one in Christ Jesus." She went on to observe, "With this recognition of the feminine element in the Godhead in the Old Testament, and this declaration of the equality of the sexes in the New, we may well wonder at the contemptible status woman occupies in the Christian Church of to-day."[48]

The Woman's Bible is also replete with parallels between customs and behavior in the Old Testament and those of the nineteenth century. Those parallels consistently drew attention to the injustice and, indeed, the inconsistency that ran through the exalted view of the production and care of children, a responsibility of women, and the degrading treatment of women and the low position to which they were assigned. For example, in regard to Rachel's wish for a son, in Genesis, Chapter 25, Cady Stanton remarked on the paradox of the importance of children in society and the essential role of women in their bearing and rearing, on the one hand, and, on the other, the denigration of women:

[W]omen who had no children were objects of pity and dislike among the Jewish tribes. The Jews of to-day . . . believe in the home sphere for all women, that wifehood and motherhood are the most exalted offices. If they really so considered, why does every Jew on each returning Holy Day say in reading the service, "I thank thee, oh Lord! That I was not born a woman!"? And if Gentiles are of the same opinion, why do they consider the education of boys more important than that of girls? Surely those who are to fill the most responsible offices should have the most thorough and liberal education.[49]

Cady Stanton also frequently took the opportunity to draw a practical lesson from her interpretation of biblical passages for women in the nineteenth century. Concluding her commentary on Rachel's death after the birth of her son, she admonished that, although most women prefer the "home sphere" and a "strong right arm on which to lean,"

> Even good husbands sometimes die, and the family drifts out on the great ocean of life, without chart or compass, or the least knowledge of the science of navigation. In such emergencies the woman trained to self-protection, self-independence, and self-support holds the vantage ground against all theories on the home sphere.[50]

In addition, her commentary on Exodus underlined one of the fundamental contradictions in the lives of women, who "have had no voice in the canon law, the catechisms, the church creeds and discipline," yet are expected to obey the rules of a "strictly masculine religion, that places the sex at a disadvantage in all life's emergencies."[51] Thus, in matters of religion just as in secular affairs, women were excluded from participating in the creation of the laws that they were forced to obey.

In response to a letter the Revising Committee received claiming that it was ridiculous for women to attempt to revise the Bible, Cady Stanton, in the Introduction to Part I, drew attention to the parallels between the treatment of women in the Scriptures and their condition under the laws of the nineteenth century. Both needed to be changed to take women into account:

> Why is it more ridiculous for women to protest against her present status in the Old and New Testament, in the ordinances and discipline of the church, than in the statutes and constitution of the state? Why is it more ridiculous to arraign ecclesiastics for their false teaching and acts of injustice to women, than members of Congress and the House of Commons? Why is it more audacious to review Moses than Blackstone, the Jewish code of laws, than the English system of jurisprudence?[52]

Cady Stanton's tone throughout *The Woman's Bible* was acerbic and irreverent. For example, she compared the combatants in the Civil War with the Jews, noting that they both used the Bible to support their position:

In making a God after their own image, who approved of whatever they did, the Jews did not differ much from ourselves; the men of our day talk too as if they reflected the opinions of Jehovah on the vital questions of the hour. In our late civil war both armies carried the Bible in their knapsacks, and both alike prayed to the same God for victory, as if he could be in favor of slavery and against it at the same time.[53]

She also spoke disparagingly of the people of the Old Testament who had no written language and were, therefore, "fitting subjects for all manner of delusions and superstitions." Why, she wondered, should the religious thought of her time be influenced by the customs and opinions of "this ignorant people"?[54]

Cady Stanton's attack on organized religion and her commentary on the Bible represent a further development of her earlier ideas about the foundations of women's subordination that was fully consistent with her argument that the vote was only one of a vast array of reforms that were needed to end women's subordination. Her critique of the Bible was also consistent with the radical strain of her thought. Unlike most of the other woman's rights activists, she believed that for women to achieve equality, fundamental cultural, social, and political change would be necessary, including basic reform in organized religion that would end the tradition of assigning women a secondary role.

There was also a strategic element to Cady Stanton's revision of the Bible. She essentially agreed with the clergy and with women who were opposed to suffrage that the Bible prescribed a limited and subservient role for women—it was, indeed, an obstacle to progress for women. Accordingly, she did her best to make clear that there was no reason to respect the Bible any more than any other book written by men, any laws written by men, or any customs established and perpetuated by men. Consequently, it was quite easy for her to dismiss passages in the Bible that trivialized or ignored women's contributions. For example, as she wrote of the account of the birth of Moses in Exodus, she could dismiss the ideas of the authors of the Bible regarding the role of women:

The only value of these records to us is to show the character of the Jewish nation, and make it easy for us to reject their ideas as to the true status of woman, and their pretension of being guided by the hand of God, in all their devious wanderings. Surely such teachings as these, should have no influence in regulating the lives of women in the nineteenth century.[55]

In spite of the NAWSA's condemnation of *The Woman's Bible* and the negative reaction from the religious establishment, it was a bestseller—it went through seven printings in six months and was translated into several other languages.[56] Most of the substance of the commentary is generally accepted today. But if women had read it in the 1890s and had been empowered to take action, it could have had a transforming impact on organized religion in the United States. *The Woman's Bible* was, at any rate, as one of Cady Stanton's biographers noted, "most important as another declaration of Stanton's independence, representing her intellectual freedom from religious authority and the culmination of her personal theology."[57]

In regard to the multiple traditions, *The Woman's Bible* generally took a liberal approach in attacking the ascriptivist religious tradition that had, as Cady Stanton noted, dishonored womanhood.[58] Moreover, her repeated comparisons of the stories in the Bible with contemporary issues concerning women comported with liberal ideas insofar as she assumed the position that women should strive to be more like men in order to achieve success. In her commentary on the parable of the ten virgins in the Book of Matthew, for example, she emphasized the importance of self-improvement, development through education, and the ability to be self-supporting. The wise virgins—those who brought oil to light their lamps—"are the women who to-day are close upon the heels of man in the whole realm of thought, in art, in science, in literature and in government. . . . They fill the editors' and the professors' chairs, plead at the bar of justice, walk the wards of the hospital, and speak from the pulpit and the platform."[59]

Like her other work, however, *The Woman's Bible* also reflected republican themes when it emphasized the need for women—"the mothers of the race"—to participate in public life in order to redress the imbalance of power that the male monopoly in both church and state had created. The extent to which Cady Stanton criticized the customs and morals of the people of the Bible was consistent with her purpose of revealing it as a document that was written by men interested in establishing and maintaining their power over women. Her willingness to attack an institution that was at the center of American culture points to the radical element of her thought. The tone of her commentary, insofar as it underlined men's determination to establish their own power at the expense of women, was similar to the position that radical feminists would take in the twentieth century. In addition, her depiction of the characters of the Old Testament as ignorant, primitive people lent her commentary an ethnocentric—even anti-Semitic—ascriptive flavor.

Conclusion

Cady Stanton's increasing isolation from the woman's rights movement was in large part a result of her refusal to limit her agenda for reform to woman suffrage, as the other leaders had done by the end of the nineteenth century. Thoroughly convinced that legal reform alone would never be sufficient to end women's oppression, she remained committed to a wide range of reforms that would improve women's position. Her critique of religion and *The Woman's Bible* reveal the depth of Cady Stanton's understanding of the profound cultural sources of women's subordination. Her commitment to multiple reforms, her condemnation of organized religion, and her critique of the Bible confirm the radical element of her thought insofar as they exemplify not only her willingness to challenge the legitimacy of the most respected religious institutions but also her thoroughgoing conviction that women's equality could be achieved only through fundamental social, cultural, and political change.

9

"In the Long Weary March, Each One Walks Alone"

Evolution and Anglo-Saxonism at Century's End

Introduction

This chapter continues to examine Cady Stanton's work during the last twenty years of her life. Here I turn to the impact that the doctrines of social Darwinism and Anglo-Saxonism had on her arguments. The growing popularity of evolutionary theory had a double-pronged impact on the development of her ideas during the last twenty years of the nineteenth century. First, it raised serious questions about the viability of the literal interpretation of the Bible and thus encouraged some scholars and members of the clergy to begin to analyze Scripture so that it could coexist with Darwin's arguments about the origins of life. Such developments in religious thought also encouraged Cady Stanton, who had long been critical of the way organized religion contributed to the oppression of women, to embark on her project to analyze the Bible as a history written by men who were intent on glorifying members of their sex and disempowering women. That project, as we saw in chapter 8, culminated in *The Woman's Bible* and led to Cady Stanton's complete separation from the organized movement for women's rights.

The second prong of the impact of Darwinism, and the subject of this chapter, was to bring more ascriptivism to Cady Stanton's thought from the 1880s until her death. Many of the legal and political developments during this period, such as the end of Reconstruction, the legalization of Jim Crow, the disfranchisement of black men in the South and the virtually complete exclusion of black people from economic life there, and restrictions on immigration were fully consistent with the inegalitarian ideas that dominated intellectual, legal, and political life during the last twenty years of the nineteenth century. Evolutionary theory, in combination with the Anglo-Saxonism that posited the superiority of white, native-born Americans over black people and foreigners, lent credibility to ascriptive doctrines and helped to justify racially exclusionary policies. As we saw in chapter 6, the growing popularity of evolutionary theory encouraged women's rights leaders to emphasize sexual as well as racial difference in an attempt to lessen the threat of woman suffrage to white control of the political system.[1]

Social Darwinism and Anglo-Saxonism: Evolution and Hierarchy

The social Darwinism that became a major intellectual force during the last twenty years of the twentieth century diverged in major ways from the Positivism of August Comte that had influenced Cady Stanton's thought in the second half of the 1860s and throughout the 1870s. Although Comte's system of thought included a theory of evolution, it was one that was much different from that which came to be a central element in social Darwinism. Comte's Positivism focused on change through cultural transmission, rather than through biological change. Without specifying the process by which it would occur, he argued that actions could become fixed in an individual and in humanity and that, if the actions were constantly repeated, they could reproduce themselves spontaneously.[2] Also absent from Comte's system were the mechanisms of natural selection and survival of the fittest that were so important to social Darwinism. In Comte's theory of the evolution of society, since human society was moving toward altruism and harmony, there was no room for warfare, colonialism, or class conflict—phenomena that were central to the worldview of social Darwinism.

At the same time that the ideas of social Darwinism were gaining popularity, thereby supplanting Positivism, Cady Stanton's arguments began to shift. Although her ideas retained elements of the earlier Positivism, particularly with regard to the importance of science and the important role of the "feminine element," by the 1880s they had begun to reflect more clearly the principles of social Darwinism. Indeed, she mentioned reading Darwin and Herbert Spencer in 1882.[3] She was by then, however, apparently already familiar with Spencer's work. In April 1866, she wrote to Robert Dale Owen praising Spencer's "grand philosophy of life." She referred to him as a friend who had sent her "the program of his 'System of Synthetic Philosophy'" and averred that his ideas were "teaching us to lose sight of ourselves and our burdens in the onward march of the race."[4]

In the remainder of this section, I consider some of the most important aspects of social Darwinism and its racial variant, as well as the set of overlapping beliefs that came to be known as Anglo-Saxonism. I examine these doctrines at some length because of the enormous influence they had on Cady Stanton's work during the last years of the nineteenth century. In part because they were purported to be based on immutable principles of science, theories positing hereditary differences in intelligence and the capacity for self-government based on race, ethnicity, sex, and national origin easily supplanted the tradition of democratic egalitarianism and natural rights. Rogers M. Smith noted that this new form of ascriptive inegalitarianism was so widely accepted that "More and more, evolution made old notions of unchanging individual natural rights seem like reassuring fairy tales. The hard truth seemed to be that all individuals and groups were engaged in a bitter struggle to survive amid an unfriendly nature."[5]

Darwin's biological theory about how species change over long periods of time, published in *The Origin of Species,* in 1859, marked the beginning of a revolution in ideas in American thought.[6] While earlier thinkers, including Comte, had worked within an evolutionary framework, Darwin's theory was far more specific about the role of heredity, more scientific, and thus it commanded more respect. According to his theory of natural selection, individuals within a single species differed slightly. Some individuals possessed traits that proved to be advantageous in the competitive struggle for survival against other members of their own as well as other species, as measured by their survival and reproductive success. These useful characteristics were transmitted to descendants, producing gradual change—evolution. Darwin did not apply his theory of natural selection to human beings in *The Origin of Species,* but in *The Descent of Man,* which he published in 1871, he made it explicit that human beings, no less than animals, are shaped by natural selection. It was also in *The Descent of Man* that Darwin expressed the view that some races were superior to others and that the "more civilized" Anglo-Saxons would eventually prevail over others who were savages and who were arrested in a primitive stage of development.[7]

The ideology that came to be called social Darwinism posited that the principles of Darwin's theory of natural selection extended to humans' social existence. Although it was derived from Darwin's basic principles, social Darwinism included the ideas of a number of other philosophers and popularizers in the United States as well as abroad.[8] The English philosopher Herbert Spencer coined the phrase "survival of the fittest," which came to replace Darwin's own "natural selection" in the lexicon of social Darwinism. Spencer's first book, *Social Statics,* which he published in 1850,[9] presented an evolutionary approach that preceded Darwin's publication of his own work. In Spencer's initial conception, evolution was a process by which, through mechanical forces and scientific laws, organisms adapt to their environment. That adaptation was leading toward an ideal, a perfect equilibrium: "evolution can end only in the establishment of the greatest perfection and the most complete happiness."[10] As humans and society evolved, harmony and peace would replace the struggle for existence.

In his later work, however, Spencer replaced the idea that society was evolving toward an ideal with a conception of man and nature in a state of continual and endless flux. Struggle, suffering, and pain became recurring themes in Spencer's work by the 1870s, and he treated them as suitable punishments for the unwise governmental policies that attempted to assist large numbers of people who had not adapted to the requirements of modern social life. Thus, in his view, England's Poor Laws were simply hindrances to the survival of the fittest. He argued that governments should not interfere with the natural process of the social order: "To aid the bad in multiplying is, in effect, the same as maliciously providing for our descendants a multitude of enemies."[11] And even more explicitly: "If left to operate in all its sternness the principle of the survival of the fittest . . . would quickly clear away the degraded."[12] When applied to individuals and groups in society, the themes of "struggle for existence" and "survival of the fittest" suggested that nature, rather than government, "would provide that the best competitors in a competitive situation would win and that this process would lead to continuing improvement."[13] Thus, in Spencer's scheme, struggle was a natural phenomenon that provided the means for progress and that was, consequently, both inevitable and beneficial in human society.

In a time when reformers, most notably the Populists during the last decade of the nineteenth century, were challenging the policy of laissez-faire, social Darwinism became an enormously influential ideology that supported free markets and opposed doctrines of equality. It reinforced the status quo by placing the force of scientific theory behind beliefs that were already widely held. Widely disseminated, social Darwinism became a conservative ascriptive ideology that was extremely effective in justifying the extreme economic inequality of the late nineteenth century.

William Graham Sumner, a former Episcopalian minister who, in 1872, became a professor of political and social science at Yale, was the most influential popularizer of social Darwinism in the United States. He spread the ideas to his large following of students and the academic community by publishing essays in scholarly journals and to a wider audience with his contributions to newspapers and popular magazines. In 1883, Sumner published *What Social Classes Owe to Each Other*, utilizing Darwinian concepts to support a policy of laissez-faire. Life is a never-ending struggle against nature for existence, he explained. There are certain "ills" that are a natural part of that struggle. Consequently, Sumner admonished, efforts to use the government to improve the conditions of those who have not been successful in the struggle—the weak and the poor—are useless. Indeed, efforts at reform are worse than useless because they threaten to disturb the natural order of society. Government regulation to improve the lives of the most unfortunate would infringe on the rights of the successful, industrious members of society, pulling down the fit and lifting up the unfit.

An uncompromising extreme individualism ran through Sumner's thought. He imagined an ideal, unfettered individual—responsible only to himself and his family:

> [E]very man and woman in society has one big duty. That is, to take care of his or her own self. This is a social duty. For fortunately, the matter stands so that the duty of making the best of one's self individually is not a separate thing from the duty of filling one's place in society, but the two are one, and the latter is accomplished when the former is done.[14]

A fundamental opposition between liberty and equality was also central to Sumner's system of ideas. From his perspective, liberty is possible only if government maintains a policy of laissez-faire and allows the resulting inequality to persist, for "if we lift any man up we must have a fulcrum, or point of reaction. In society that means that to lift one man up we push another down."[15] As he explained, if there is liberty, everyone has a chance, but many will not make use of that chance. "Therefore, the greater the chances the more unequal will be the fortune of these two sets of men. So it ought to be in all justice and right reason."[16] Liberty, he contended, guarantees the "general and steady growth of civilization and advancement of society by and through its best members."[17] In contrast, equality among individuals does not exist, and if the government were to try to impose it, the result would be survival of the least fit and the destruction of liberty. In short, there are two alternatives: "liberty, inequality, survival of the fittest; [or] not-liberty, equality, survival of the unfittest. The former carries society forward and favors all its best members; the latter carries society downwards and favors all its worst members."[18]

Progress was natural, according to Sumner. Civilization had evolved from a system of slavery through serfdom to the modern capitalist system. That modern system had been reached through a gradual process of emancipation from the old bonds of nature and society. The modern industrial system was by far superior to older arrangements insofar as it offered opportunities for happiness to everyone, but every individual had to earn that happiness. Moreover, according to Sumner, no one could be assured of success—there could be no guarantees "unless we go back to slavery, and make one man's effort conduce to another man's welfare."[19] Finally, there was a harsh determinism running through Sumner's thought, as well as that of other social Darwinists. It was inevitable that there would always be winners and losers in society, he maintained. Those who were not equipped with the natural qualities that rendered an individual fit to survive the conditions of existence were destined to fail.

The ideology that came to be known as Anglo-Saxonism in the late nineteenth century maintained that there were superior and inferior races and that the latter would be eliminated in the never-ending struggle for survival. Anglo-Saxonism was commonly used to support claims that the government needed to limit the number of people arriving in the United States whose appearance was strange, language incomprehensible, and customs unfamiliar to most Americans. Consequently, America's previous tradition of open immigration gave way to exclusionary policies, backed by "scientific" theories of the inferiority of nonwhite people, that were blatantly racist. Anglo-Saxonism grounded the perception of Americans as a chosen people—part of the American political tradition since the Puritans arrived in the seventeenth century —in ascriptivist notions of racial superiority. Prominent historians claimed that modern democratic institutions could be traced to Anglo-Saxons who brought their understanding and instinct for democracy from northern Europe to New England. The assertion that the instinct for democracy and liberty was hereditary was consistent with Darwinian theory and came to be a major tenet of Anglo-Saxonism. It stood to reason, therefore, that because of the hereditary nature of the capacity for liberty and democracy, those who were not Anglo-Saxons could never acquire it.[20]

Various proposals for restrictions on immigration relied on the theory of Anglo-Saxon superiority. For example, Senator Henry Cabot Lodge introduced bills in both houses of Congress to exclude from the United States those who could not read and write in their own language. In a speech he made in 1895 before the Senate, Lodge claimed that the literacy requirement would exclude primarily those who were "most alien" to the people of the United States—Italians, Russians, Poles, Hungarians, Greeks, and Asians. One race is clearly distinguishable from another, he asserted, by its moral and intellectual characteristics, which "make the soul of the race, and which represent the product of all its past, the inheritance of all its ancestors, and the motives of all its conduct."[21] Unrestricted immigration posed a threat to the Anglo-Saxon race, he explained, because "[i]f a lower race mixes with a higher in sufficient numbers, history teaches us that the lower race will prevail."[22] Although Cady Stanton explicitly disagreed with Lodge's literacy bill, characterizing it as arbitrary and detrimental to the interests of women, she supported a literacy test for suffrage, and, as we will see in the next section, made a number of statements that echoed the anti-immigrant sentiment of Anglo-Saxonism.

In *The Descent of Man,* Darwin pointed to the policy implications of hereditarian theory when he complained that the principles of natural selection were not operating in modern society insofar as "the weak members of civilized society propagate their kind."[23] It was Darwin's cousin, Francis Galton, however, who would develop those implications fully. He coined the term "eugenics" in 1883, hypothesizing that heredity determined the mental and physical characteristics of human beings, and argued that social controls should be used to reduce the numbers of undesirable elements in the population and to encourage the reproduction of the more positive elements. The eugenics movement did not take hold until the beginning of the twentieth century, when eugenics societies were established in the United States. Nevertheless, as we will see in the following section, a number of Cady Stanton's arguments in the 1880s and 1890s incorporated principles of eugenics.

It was also in the 1880s that American academics, building on European work in criminology, began to develop a new field of scholarly study—criminal anthropology—that added fuel to the hereditarian thesis. Most simply, it asserted, criminality was biologically determined —it was inherited. By the beginning of the twentieth the century social scientists were claiming that there was a link between lower intelligence (weak minds) and weak morals. Criminals had inherited their defects. The policy implications were clear. No efforts to improve the life chances for such individuals by changing their environment had a chance of succeeding, so no such efforts should be made. Moreover, since criminal traits were inherited, such people should not be allowed to reproduce.

Cady Stanton's earlier associate and friend Victoria Woodhull published a series of essays in 1870 in which she argued that evolution was central to an understanding of society. She wrote: "The same laws that govern the growth and multiply the plant also govern society and multiply it. The same laws that bring fruit to perfection and dissolution perfect and dissolve societies. The same laws that produce and control the units of the animal kingdom produce and control the units of society."[24] Later, in the early 1890s, when she was living in England, Woodhull published a number of essays in which she expressed views that would later be advanced by eugenicists. For example, she advocated governmental policies that would put the "first principle of the breeder's art" into practice. That is, governments should prevent the birth of unfit people and encourage the breeding of the fit. She averred that "A humanitarian government would stigmatise the marriages of the unit as crimes; it would legislate to prevent the birth of the criminal rather than legislate to punish him after he is born."[25]

Cady Stanton saw Woodhull for the last time in London in 1882 when Woodhull called on her in her hotel.[26] Woodhull's writings on eugenics are worth noting because they anticipated the arguments that later eugenicists would promulgate, but, more important for present purposes, they attest to the spread of hereditarian thinking. Although

Cady Stanton was likely to have been familiar with Woodhull's writings in the 1870s because the latter was at that time associated with the NWSA, she may or may not have run across Woodhull's later work.

Darwinian Theory and Sexual Difference

In the late nineteenth century, Darwinian theory elevated the traditional belief that women and men had different natures to the level of scientific theory. In *The Descent of Man,* Darwin observed that "Woman seems to differ from man in mental disposition, chiefly in her greater tenderness and less selfishness." Men were more competitive, ambitious, and selfish—qualities that "seem to be his natural and unfortunate birthright." He pointed to a marked disparity in intellectual power demonstrated by "man's attaining to a higher eminence, in whatever he takes up, than can woman—whether requiring deep thought, reason, or imagination, or merely the uses of the senses and the hands."[27] Darwin's theory of sexual selection accounted for what he considered to be women's inferiority. The rivalry between men over the centuries had made them superior to women; even though in the nineteenth century men no longer had to engage in physical contests over women, men "generally undergo a severe struggle in order to maintain themselves and their families; and this will tend to keep up or even increase their mental powers, and as a consequence the present inequality between the sexes."[28] Similarly, social Darwinists maintained that sex differences were immutable, rooted as they were in the long process of sexual selection. Evolution had produced strong, energetic, competitive men suited for public life. Women, according to the theory, lagged behind men in evolutionary development, were childlike, delicate, and passive, needed men's protection, and functioned well only in the home.

Darwinism seemed to place the doctrine of separate spheres beyond question—nature had limited women's capabilities to those that revolved around caring for home and children, whereas it had endowed men with the energy, creativity, and intellect to run businesses and governments. Indeed, antisuffrage arguments commonly reflected the influence of social Darwinism. Spencer himself declared women unfit for political participation on the grounds that their mental development was limited—arrested by nature to preserve their energy for reproduction.[29]

At the same time that evolutionary theory was purporting to raise traditional beliefs about women's inferiority to the level of immutable scientific laws, social scientists and woman's rights leaders were using the Darwinian framework in a subversive way to challenge those beliefs. Charlotte Perkins Gilman, who is best known for her book *Women and Economics,* which she published in 1898, worked within the evolutionary framework to challenge women's subordination. Conceding that men were far ahead of women, Gilman traced the cause to a time in human prehistory when females became dependent on males for food and shelter. Thereafter, a woman's survival rested on her ability to attract and hold a husband, and marriage became a female's economic way of life.[30] Women's dependence over the centuries, she contended, had rendered them stunted, crippled, deformed, contaminated, and imbalanced. Their personalities had become distorted in the process of cultivating the characteristics that were needed to attract and retain male support. The debased state of women was harmful to them, Gilman emphasized, rendering it impossible for them to grow into mature human beings capable of living full, productive lives. The shift in the woman's rights movement in the last years of the nineteenth century away from a reliance on ideas of natural rights and equality to support their demand for the vote toward arguments based on women's special qualities that rendered their participation essential to the progress and health of society reflects the same subversive use of popular views, including evolutionary theory.

Cady Stanton's Ideas in the Final Years

Those intellectual currents had a profound impact on Cady Stanton's work during the last twenty years of her life. She adopted the evolutionary framework of social Darwinism, the hereditarian understanding of social pathologies that the eugenics movement would later employ, an extreme individualism that was akin to Sumner's, and the prejudices of Anglo-Saxonism. In addition, the increasing emphasis she placed on arguments that women were morally superior to men and were, consequently, needed in the public sphere coincided with the rise of first Positivism and then social Darwinism, with its contention that women and men had immutable differences rooted in the evolutionary past. She did not, however, adopt social Darwinism's insistence on the necessity of laissez-faire and continued to argue that government had an important role to play in bringing an end to women's oppression. Indeed, she continued to adhere to the Positivist insistence that society should be ordered according to scientific principles. Thus, Positivism and social Darwinism both had a major influence on Cady Stanton's work in the last twenty years of the twentieth century.

In the terms of the Multiple-Traditions Thesis, Cady Stanton's work from the 1880s until her death continued to reflect an interaction among liberal, republican, ascriptive Americanist, and radical arguments. But, while liberal principles of natural rights and equality were still discernible in her arguments, the illiberal strains continued to grow more pronounced.[31] As I have emphasized from the outset, like the multiple traditions that constitute American political culture, the various strands of Cady Stanton's political thought were far from consistent. The way she employed the ascriptivist ideas of social Darwinism, for example, clashed with her earlier liberal, egalitarian ideas, as well as with other arguments she made in the 1880s and 1890s.

Her work during the last twenty years of her life also reveals the importance of the fourth strand of Cady Stanton's thought: radicalism. One of the sources of her disagreement with the organized suffrage movement was her commitment to the need for women to establish connections with other movements, particularly those that were democratic and radical, so that they could forge alliances to work for the fundamental social and political change that was necessary if women were to achieve equality. It was crucial, in her view, that women become a force for radical political change.[32] She applauded the Populists in the 1890s and identified herself with the socialist movement in the United States. She wrote to the NAWSA meeting in 1898: "Those who have eyes to see recognize the fact that the period for all . . . fragmentary reforms has ended. Agitation of the broad question of philosophical socialism is now in order. This next step in progress . . . is now being agitated by able thinkers and writers in all civilized countries."[33] Cady Stanton was also influenced by Fabian socialism, which advocated community ownership of production. In addition, she applauded cooperative industry and cooperative unions and was interested in experiments in cooperative living in communities like Brook Farm. She also emphasized the sharing of cleaning, cooking, and child care as essential to cooperative living and advocated apartment complexes with communal restaurants and recreation rooms.[34] Populism, socialism, cooperation, and radical social change were all fundamentally out of tune with the extreme individualist spirit of social Darwinism.

Departing from the ascriptive racial approach she had used in earlier years and returning to liberalism, Cady Stanton made a number of statements in which she expressed her support for the rights of all classes and races of women. In 1890, for example, addressing the founding meeting of the NAWSA, she proclaimed:

> Wherever and whatever any class of women suffer whether in the home, the church, the courts, in the world of work, in the statute books, a voice in their behalf should be heard in our conventions. We must manifest a broad catholic spirit for all shades of opinion in which we may differ and recognize the equal right of parties, sects and races, tribes and colors. Colored women, Indian women, Mormon women and women from every quarter of the globe have been heard in these Washington conventions and I trust they always will be.[35]

Identifying the source of the "race problem" as a failure to apply the principle of emancipation, she admonished, "[W]e had better make a stand on the Freedman and demand justice for him as well as ourselves. It is justice, and that alone that can end the impossible conflict between freedom and slavery going on in every nation on the globe."[36]

The predominance of the liberal egalitarian theme in her comments at the 1890 NAWSA meeting is noteworthy for several reasons. First, as Suzanne M. Marilley has argued, Cady Stanton may have been attempting to revive the more egalitarian, natural rights emphasis of the antebellum woman's rights movement—though clearly her effort was unsuccessful.[37] Second, her admonition to the suffrage activists to keep the movement broadly focused underlines her irreconcilable differences with the organized suffrage movement, which had already chosen the strategy of narrowing its focus to women's enfranchisement. Finally, when considered in conjunction with many of the other arguments she used during this period, her comments at the 1890 meeting underscore the extent to which her arguments included multiple and conflicting strands of ideas.

Generally, when Cady Stanton spoke or wrote in support of woman suffrage in the 1880s, she began with a claim that suffrage is a natural right. But she quickly moved to other kinds of arguments. In a paper she addressed to the Senate Committee on Woman Suffrage in 1884, for example, she emphasized the theme of individual autonomy and natural rights: "The right of suffrage is simply the right to govern one's self. Every human being is born into the world with this right, and the desire to exercise it comes naturally with the feeling of life's responsibilities."[38] But she then shifted to a republican argument that women's public spiritedness had earned them full citizenship: "[A]nd yet, under all circumstances she has shown her love of individual freedom, her desire for self-government, while her achievements in practical affairs and her courage in the great emergencies of life have vindicated her capacity to exercise this right."[39] Just as in the earlier periods, Cady Stanton's republican themes appeared alongside liberal arguments. For example, she asserted, "The right of suffrage in a republic means self-government, and self-government means education, development, self-reliance, independence, courage in the hour of danger. That women may attain these virtues we demand the exercise of this right."[40] She concluded her address on an ascriptive note with a reference to the dangers of granting privileges to the wrong kind of men—"a lower type of manhood."[41] The pattern of her speeches—moving from liberal and republican and then to ascriptivist arguments—suggests that she was using language of liberalism, yet had more interest in the other approaches that reflected the dominant ideology of the last twenty years of the nineteenth century.

The ascriptivist spirit of Anglo-Saxonism is a clear theme running through her demands for suffrage during the 1880s, and, in fact, she continued to engage in antiforeign rhetoric for the rest of her life. One of the most telling examples is in her address before the Senate Committee on Woman Suffrage in 1888, in which she compared educated women—who despite their superiority could not vote—with immigrants who were clearly unworthy of the political rights they had been given:

Landing in New York one week ago, I saw 400 steerage passengers leave the vessel. Dull-eyed, heavy-visaged, stooping with huge burdens and oppressions endured in the Old World, they stood in painful contrast with the group of brilliant women on their way to the International Council here in Washington. I thought, as this long line passed by, of the speedy transformation the genial influences of equality would effect in the appearance of these men, of the new dignity they would acquire with a voice in the laws under which they live, and I rejoiced for them; but bitter reflections filled my mind when I thought that these men are the future rulers of our daughters; these will interpret the civil and criminal codes by which they will be governed; these will be our future judges and jurors to try young girls in our courts, for trial by a jury of her peers has never yet been vouchsafed to woman. Here is a right so ancient that it is difficult to trace its origin history, a right so sacred that the humblest criminal may choose his juror. But alas for the daughters of the people, their judges, advocates, jurors, must be men, and for them there is no appeal.[42]

The antiforeign rhetoric continued in the address Cady Stanton wrote for the NAWSA convention three years later, in 1891. She lamented, "That all orders of foreigners also rank politically above the most intelligent, highly-educated women—native-born Americans—is indeed the most bitter drop in the cup of our grief which we are compelled to swallow."[43] The theme of Anglo-Saxonism is even more pronounced in the address she wrote for the House Judiciary Committee in 1896. Although she began with a liberal-based reference to women's "natural right to self-government," she quickly turned to reiterate the notion of white women's superiority in her image of "two classes of citizens"—ignorant, drunken, corrupt, voting immigrants:

[A] multitude of coarse, ignorant beings, designated in our constitutions as male citizens—many of them fresh from the steerage of incoming steamers. There, too, are natives of the same type from the slums of our cities. Policemen are respectfully guiding them all to the ballot box. Those who can not stand, because of their frequent potations, are carefully supported on either side, each in turn depositing his vote, for what purpose he neither knows nor cares, except to get the promised bribe.[44]

In contrast to those degraded, ignorant males were the native-born, refined women, with the education and experience, as well as the family background, that rendered them fully capable of making a positive contribution:

[A] group of intelligent, moral, highly-cultivated women, whose ancestors for generations have fought the battles of liberty and have made this country all it is to-day. These come from the schools and colleges as teachers and professors; from the press and pulpit as writers and preachers; from the courts and hospitals as lawyers and physicians; and from happy and respectable homes as honored mothers, wives and sisters. Knowing the needs of humanity subjectively in all the higher walks of life, and objectively in the world of work, in the charities, in the asylums and prisons, in the sanitary condition of our streets and public buildings, they are peculiarly fitted to write, speak and vote intelligently on all these questions of such vital, far-reaching consequence to the welfare of society.[45]

Describing how those women were forced to withdraw in humiliation as officials jeered and policemen drove them away from the ballot box, Cady Stanton lamented that never before had "so large a class of such a character [been] subordinated politically to the ignorant masses."[46] Aileen Kraditor asserted that those comments marked Cady Stanton's repudiation of the liberal natural rights argument for suffrage. Instead of arguing that everyone had the right to participate in governing, she suggested that women deserved the vote because of their superior qualities. While the cultivated ladies were morally and intellectually qualified to vote, clearly the degraded, ignorant men were not. In addition, her remarks implied that educated women were capable of voting for both groups because they knew what was in the interest of the men much better than the men themselves did.[47] The ascriptivist quality of Cady Stanton's claims for woman suffrage stands in clear contrast to liberal egalitarian claims. Still, as we have seen, even in the 1840s her arguments contained strains of illiberal inegalitarianism. Consequently, it is most accurate to view the developments of Cady Stanton's arguments as a nuanced shift in emphasis among the multiple traditions, rather than as a repudiation of one approach in favor of another.

As noted previously, although Cady Stanton did not agree with proposals to institute a literacy requirement for immigration, she enthusiastically advocated a literacy test and a requirement that voters be able to read and write English. She claimed that she did not have a problem with newcomers arriving and living in the United States but objected to "their speedy appearance at the ballot-box and there becoming an impoverished and ignorant balance of power in the hands of wily politicians."[48] There was also a strategic element to her advocacy of educated suffrage—foreign-born men generally did not support woman suffrage and, as Cady Stanton observed, the "ignorant vote is solid against woman's emancipation," a "hostile force playing football with the most sacred rights of one-half of the people."[49] Thus, eliminating the influence of male immigrants would increase the chances for women to obtain the vote. In addition, with an educational requirement for suffrage, opponents of woman suffrage could no longer claim that the enfranchisement of women would double the ignorant vote. Indeed, she reasoned that if voting were limited to educated men and women, the net effect would be a decrease in the number of uneducated voters.[50] That there was a racial element to proposals for literacy qualifications for suffrage is well known. Although Cady Stanton's concern seemed to be primarily with the impact of the foreign vote, she was also aware of the appeal of her proposal to white Southerners. She wrote in her diary in January 1895 that the speech she was preparing for the NAWSA convention to be held in Atlanta, Georgia, would be "devoted largely to the question of immigration, and I air my present belief in an educated suffrage open to men and women alike. My view ought to be well received in a southern city."[51]

In addition, Cady Stanton's support for a literacy requirement might be interpreted as an expression of the republican principle that the privilege of citizenship properly belongs to those who are sufficiently enlightened to make a contribution to the community. She argued that the requirement would promote civic virtue by inspiring "our people with a new sense of their sacred duties as citizens of a republic"[52] She also made the claim in 1894 that a literacy test would make Americans more homogeneous and that by the time foreigners fulfilled the requirement, they would know something about American institutions and their national origin would become irrelevant.[53] There are weaknesses in the republican interpretation, however. As Aileen Kraditor, pointed out, Cady Stanton indicated her desire to eliminate the "foreign vote" as the most important benefit of an educational qualification. Moreover, the connection that she made between the English language and democratic institutions reflected her assumption that Anglo-Saxons had a special capacity for self-government—a standard principle of the popular Anglo-Saxonism. In short, her enthusiasm for educated suffrage may well have been grounded not so much in an interest in promoting literacy as in an ascriptivist sentiment toward immigrants.[54]

In spite of the way her arguments reflected the Anglo-Saxonist prejudice against foreigners, Cady Stanton reserved most of her aversion to foreigners who were also males. Indeed, she frequently expressed support for women of different nationalities, cultures, and religions. In her address to the International Council of Women in 1888, she stated that women of all nationalities have a universal sense of injustice that creates a common bond between them:

> Whether our feet are compressed in iron shoes, our faces hidden with veils and masks, whether yoked with cows to draw the plow through its furrows, or classed with idiots, lunatics, and criminals in the laws and constitutions of the state, the principle is the same, for the humiliations of spirit are as real as the visible badges of servitude. A difference in government, religion, laws, and social customs makes but little change in the relative status of woman to the self-constituted governing classes, so long as subordination in all nations is the rule of her being. . . . There is a language of universal significance, more subtle than that used in the busy marts of trade, that should be called the mother-tongue, by which with a sigh or a tear, a gesture, a glance of the eye, we know the experiences of each other in the varied forms of slavery.[55]

She also alluded to the bond among all women in her frequent comments castigating all religions for oppressing women. For example, she declared in 1885 that "You may go over the world and you will find that every form of religion which has breathed upon this earth has degraded woman. There is not one which has not made her subject to man."[56]

Major themes of social Darwinism are also reflected in Cady Stanton's later work. It is important to keep in mind, however, that while those themes grew more pronounced in the 1880s and were frequently connected to the works of Darwin and Spencer, ideas about heredity and the inevitability of human progress were present in her earlier speeches and writings. In fact, a general hereditarian theory was at the core of Cady Stanton's claim that "The right idea of marriage is at the foundation of all reforms."[57] Her commitment to reform in the laws and customs of marriage, dating back to 1848 and never abandoned, was inextricably intertwined with her conviction that parents passed characteristics to their children. Heredity was crucial, as she made clear in a letter to Anthony in 1853:

> [L]et [law makers] fine a woman fifty dollars for every child she conceive by a Drunkard. Women have no right to saddle the state with idiots to be supported by the public. Only look at the statistics of the idiot asylums, nearly all the offspring of Drunkards. Woman must be

made to feel that the transmitting of immortal life is a most solemn responsible act and never should be allowed, except when the parents are in the highest condition of mind and body.[58]

By 1870 she had made public her argument that the state should take steps to prevent the marriage of the morally, physically, and mentally unfit.[59] The same theme was clear in a letter she wrote in 1879 advising a friend about the proposed marriage of her daughter. Cady Stanton confided to her friend that one of her concerns would be "whether his ancestors were strong and vigorous in mind and body. . . . If I were a mother about to marry a daughter, the distinction of good, honest, healthy blood is the nobility I would most prize in my future son-in-law."[60]

The type of reform in both marriage and divorce that Cady Stanton long advocated and her concept of self-sovereignty, which would give women the ability to control their own sexual lives and, thereby, their reproductive lives, was clearly linked to Darwinian ideas concerning strategies for improving society. She argued that the reforms she embraced would contribute to the progress of the human race insofar as they would encourage the birth of more healthy, intelligent children. In a speech that she frequently delivered on the Lyceum circuit in the 1870s, she underlined that theme:

When marriage results from a true union of intellect and spirit and when Mothers and Fathers give to their holy offices even that preparation of soul and body that the artist gives to the conception of his poem, statue or landscape, then will marriage, maternity and paternity acquire a new sacredness and dignity and a nobler type of manhood and womanhood will glorify the race!![61]

By the 1880s, Cady Stanton's work reflected even more clearly the ideas of social Darwinism as she utilized the evolutionary framework explicitly to link the progress of civilization to the rise of women. In 1882, for example, in a letter to the NWSA convention, she quoted from a passage in Francis Galton's *Hereditary Genius* in which he lamented the lack of abilities in people in all stations of life to cope with modern civilization. She proclaimed, "If the average ability were raised a grade or two, a new class of statesmen would conduct our complex affairs at home and abroad, as easily as our best business men now do their own private trades and professions. The needs of centralization, communication and culture call for more brains and mental stamina than the average of our race possesses."[62] She made clear that women, with political, legal, social, and economic rights, could make that possible. Again, in 1898, her letter to the NAWSA convention reiterated the connection between women's rights and the progress of society:

> Let this generation pay its debt to the past by continuing this great work until the last vestige of woman's subjection shall be erased from our creeds and codes and constitutions. Then the united thought of man and woman will inaugurate a pure religion, a just government, a happy home and a civilization in which ignorance, poverty and crime will exist no more. They who watch behold already the dawn of a new day.[63]

She made her hereditarian ideas most explicit in an article published in 1901 in which she related principles of Darwin and Galton, declaring that "heredity is the law," and reiterated her conviction that it was essential to improve the abilities of future generations: "The needs of centralization, communication and culture, call for more brains and mental stamina than the average of our race possess."[64] She lamented policies that had the effect of discouraging the most able individuals from having children while leaving the weak to continue to reproduce at a higher rate:

> [the] effect would be such as to cause the race of the prudent to fall after a few centuries into an almost incredible inferiority of numbers to that of the imprudent, and it is therefore calculated to bring utter ruin upon the breed of any country where the doctrine prevailed. I protest against the able being encouraged to withdraw in this way from the struggle for existence. It may seem monstrous that the weak should be crowded out by the strong, but it is still monstrous that the races best fitted to play their part on the stage of life should be crowded out by the incompetent, the ailing and the desponding.[65]

The Solitude of Self

In addition to adopting the evolutionary framework of Darwininism, Cady Stanton's work in her final years began to reflect the version of individualism that ran through Spencer's and Sumner's thought. That individualism differed, both in degree and in kind, from the liberal vision of the individual who exercises natural rights in pursuit of his or her own personally defined happiness. The "new" individualism, shaped by the idea of the survival of the fittest, implied the isolation of each person in the competitive struggle to succeed. Moreover, as Sumner emphasized in *What Social Classes Owe to Each Other,* strong individuals acting in vigorous competition with one another would increase the prospects for the survival of the human race against the harsh forces of nature. In such a view, unencumbered competition among individuals was crucial to the progress of civilization. That version of individualism ran through one of Cady Stanton's most important speeches, "The Solitude of Self," which she delivered to the NAWSA convention in 1892.[66]

She began by evoking an image of woman with rights that belong to her as an individual, "in a world of her own, the arbiter of her own destiny, an imaginary Robinson Crusoe, with her woman, Friday, on a solitary island. Her rights under such circumstances are to use all her faculties for her own safety and happiness."[67] As citizens, women must have the same rights as others, and, as "an equal factor in civilization, her rights and duties are still the same—individual happiness and development."[68] She then explained that the "strongest reason" for giving women equality in all realms of life was "the solitude and personal responsibility of her own individual life" and "because, as an individual, she must rely on herself." Although women might choose to be protected,

> they must make the voyage of life alone, and for safety in an emergency, they must know something of the laws of navigation. To guide our own craft, we must be captain, pilot, engineer; with chart and compass to stand at the wheel; to watch the winds and waves, and know when to take in the sail, and to read the signs. . . .
>
> It matters not whether the solitary voyager is man or woman; nature, having endowed them equally, leaves them to their own skill and judgment in the hour of danger, and, if not equal to the occasion, alike they perish.[69]

As its title suggests, "The Solitude of Self" is permeated by the theme that each individual is alone in life and must be equipped with the necessary tools to compete in the struggle for survival. Again and again,

Cady Stanton warned her audience that the individual is unceasingly alone in the struggle of life and, therefore, must be prepared: "So it ever must be in the conflicting scenes of life, in the long weary march, each one walks alone. We may have many friends, love, kindness, sympathy and charity, to smooth our pathway in everyday life, but in the tragedies and triumphs of human experience, each mortal stands alone."[70]

Cady Stanton made an easy link between the Darwinian—or Spencerian—never-ending struggle for existence and women's rights by underscoring how, in a world where each soul must depend wholly on itself, so long as women were denied equal rights, they would remain unfit to join the competition and therefore would be destined to lose. If they remained hampered by such disabilities, women would hold back the progress of society. Thus, Cady Stanton demonstrated that it was essential for women to be recognized as individuals on an equal footing with men and to be given equal rights: "Seeing then, that life must ever be a march and a battle, that each soldier must be equipped for his own protection, it is the height of cruelty to rob the individual of a single natural right."[71] The following passage also underlines the interrelationship of women's rights, the struggle for survival, and the progress of civilization, as well as the inevitable solitude of the individual:

> But when all artificial trammels are removed, and women are recognized as individuals, responsible for their own environments, thoroughly educated for all positions in life they may be called to fill; with all the resources in themselves that liberal thought and broad culture can give; guided by their own conscience and judgment, trained to self-protection, by a healthy development of the muscular system, and skill in the use of weapons and defense; and stimulated to self-support by a knowledge of the business world and the pleasure that pecuniary independence must ever give; when women are trained in this way, they will in a measure be fitted for those hours of solitude that come alike to all, . . . As in our extremity we must depend on ourselves, the dictates of wisdom point to complete individual development.[72]

While Cady Stanton's revision of her earlier liberal individualism was consistent with social Darwinism, it was not in itself ascriptive. Indeed, in her hands it was an argument for women's equality based not on natural rights so much as on the importance of equality for the survival of the individual and progress for society. Nevertheless, her analysis must be considered in conjunction with her antiforeign, Anglo-Saxonist perspective and her ascriptivist assertions that women's special qualities would enable them to improve public life.

Cady Stanton drew on Darwinian ideas to develop her own theory to explain the development of women's subordinate position from an evolutionary perspective. In the "Matriarchate," an essay she wrote for the meeting of the National Council of Women in 1891, she appealed to anthropology to support her arguments for women's equality. Taking her theory of the Matriarchate, or Mother-Age, from Lewis Henry Morgan's *Ancient Society,* she argued that "savage" woman had been free and independent and the originator of civilization and that woman's caring for her children had led to the development of love, altruism, and domesticity. She rejected the argument, however, that women had been held back in the evolutionary process as a result of men's domination and argued instead that woman's present inferiority was not an evolutionary but a cultural inheritance—one that could be corrected by "truer education and by educational devices such as the ballot."[73]

Evolutionary thinking is also echoed in some of her most sweeping statements about the past and the future—in relation to religion, for example: "People seem to think we have reached the very end of theology; but let me say that the future is to be as much purer than the past as our immediate past has been better than the dark ages."[74] Finally, she envisioned a future in which women had gained their rightful place in the world: "The true woman is as yet a dream of the future. A just government, a humane religion, a pure social life await her coming. Then, and not till then, will the golden age of peace and prosperity be ours."[75] Cady Stanton would have known that the "golden age" would not be a reality during her lifetime. Still, she could contemplate a much improved future populated by humans who had developed to the point where they could transcend the injustices and inequalities of the nineteenth century.

Conclusion

This chapter has examined the impact of prevailing intellectual currents on Cady Stanton's work during the last two decades of her life. The ubiquitous social Darwinism and the overlapping ideology of Anglo-Saxonism played an important role in pushing her ideas in a more ascriptive direction. Her own predilections, as well, made Anglo-Saxonism an attractive vehicle for airing her anti-immigrant sentiments. Popular nativist views reinforced her own inclinations and provided her with material with which she could articulate her views. Similarly, Cady Stanton had earlier expressed some of the ideas that were identified with the social Darwinism that became popular in the 1880s. Social Darwinism was used by a variety of thinkers of various persuasions to prescribe progressive reforms, as well as the laissez-faire policies espoused by Spencer and Sumner. Thus, the stark, rather pessimistic, individualism that Cady Stanton articulated in "The Solitude of Self" was not determined simply by the fact that she was influenced by social Darwinism but rather was a result of the interaction of her own normative preferences with popular intellectual forces. In short, she made creative use of the prevailing intellectual forces, utilizing them in a way that was consistent with her analysis of the problem of women's subordination that she had been developing during the previous forty years.

10

Multiple Feminisms and Multiple Traditions
Elizabeth Cady Stanton in American Political Thought

When Cady Stanton died, on October 26, 1902, she was nearly eighty-seven years old and had been working for women's rights for fifty-five years. Women's lives had changed a great deal during that half century: the states had changed their laws so that married women had property rights, and in cases of divorce women could gain custody of their children, although judges tended to interpret the laws narrowly out of deference to common-law rules that established the husband as head of the household.[1] Women frequently attended and graduated from colleges and universities, and a few women had managed to enter the professions and the clergy. Two of the reforms that were most important to Cady Stanton, however, had not been achieved. Suffrage was still eighteen years in the future.[2] In addition, a husband still had the right to demand sex from his wife. In short, the equal union between two autonomous individuals that Cady Stanton envisioned remained out of reach for the overwhelming majority of Americans. Moreover, the doctrine of separate spheres persisted, albeit in a less rigid form, and religious institutions continued to perpetuate women's subordination.

At the end of Cady Stanton's life, the term "feminism" was not yet in use, and it would be more than ten years before women's rights advocates began to divide consciously over the ideas, strategies, and goals that would eventually create the wide variety of feminisms that are so familiar in the early twenty-first century. As we have seen, Cady Stanton's work included many arguments that twenty-first century feminists would consider contradictory, even incoherent. She frequently formulated her arguments in terms that are associated with liberal feminism as she argued that women were essentially the same as men and demanded equal rights and political and legal reform to end women's exclusion from public life. She also relied on the argument, apparently with no idea that she was switching course, that women were different from and morally superior to men—an argument that difference feminists, radical feminists, and dominance feminists would later embrace.

She often worked within the framework of liberal feminism, using a conception of women as individuals who had the right to pursue any interest or enterprise that was available to men. Yet her work also reveals a conception of woman as a sex class—a group that needed to overcome its false consciousness and that had an obligation to organize for change. In that part of her work, her ideas are less akin to liberal feminism and more in line with radical and socialist feminisms. Indeed, that she transcended liberal feminism is evidenced by her statement that "Our religions, laws, customs are all founded on the belief that woman was made for man."[3] Cady Stanton's ideas departed from liberal feminism in the way she constructed her criticisms of religion, marriage, and the doctrine of the separate spheres so as to go far beyond an emphasis on legal change as the solution to inequality. Indeed, her conviction that fundamental cultural and social change would be necessary before women's subordination could end runs though her work.

Instead of attempting to identify Cady Stanton with any one variety of twenty-first-century feminism, we will do well to simply emphasize that she devoted most of her life to reforming the laws and the culture of the United States in order to end women's oppression. Or, perhaps paralleling the terms of the multiple traditions, we can say that Cady Stanton's work encompassed the multiple feminisms.

The overarching goal of this study of Cady Stanton's work has been to demonstrate how her ideas reflect the same tensions that run through the dynamic of the multiple traditions. The three traditions of liberalism, republicanism, and ascriptive Americanisms combined to form her political thought. The multiple traditions of American political culture, what Rogers M. Smith characterized as "a complex pattern of apparently inconsistent combinations of the traditions,"[4] are clearly reflected in Cady Stanton's long campaign to end women's subordination. Moreover, her thought reflects a fourth category of ideas, as well. Her radicalism emerges in her critique of religion, which began early and culminated in *The Woman's Bible,* her views on marriage and divorce, her association with radical movements and radical people such as free-love advocates and Victoria Woodhull, her attempts to form alliances with other reform movements, including temperance and labor, and her conception of women as a group—what later came to be known as a sex class. More generally, the radical elements of Cady Stanton's thought are revealed by the breadth of her reform vision and by her conviction that legal and political reform would not be sufficient to end the subordination of women. Instead, a major transformation in American culture and society was necessary if women were to gain their rightful place.

We have seen that over time the emphasis shifted in the way Cady Stanton combined the multiple traditions. In the antebellum years, beginning with the first Woman's Rights Convention, in 1848, she relied primarily on liberal claims of natural rights and equality, for example, modeling the Declaration of Sentiments on the Declaration of Independence. Likewise, in her campaign for women's property rights in New York, she drew heavily on liberal arguments to convince the legislature of the need for legal reform. In those early years, the ideas of the abolitionists played an important role in shaping her ideas. Nevertheless, interspersed with her liberal claims were republican and ascriptive (in regard to both race and sex) themes, emphasizing the need for redressing the imbalance of power created by the male monopoly and pointing out the advantages that women's participation would bring to political life.

In the years following the Civil War, when the politics of Reconstruction severed the link between women's rights and abolitionism and Positivism began to influence her work, Cady Stanton's arguments began to reflect a stronger ascriptivist emphasis. Finally, in the last twenty years of her life, the illiberal, inegalitarian strains of her thought became even more prominent as she drew from popular intellectual currents that were informed by Darwinian theory.

During the course of Cady Stanton's long career, a variety of ideological, intellectual, and political trends influenced her work, including the ideas of the American Revolution, abolitionism, the cult of domesticity, transcendentalism, free love and sexual radicalism, the politics of Reconstruction, with its emphasis on securing the vote for black males, developments in the religious establishment, social Darwinism, and Anglo-Saxonism. In combination, these currents of thought also encompass the conflicting strands of the multiple traditions.

Liberal claims of natural rights and equality declined in prominence but never entirely disappeared from Cady Stanton's arguments even as she turned increasingly to ascriptive claims. Thus, the tension remained;

liberalism never prevailed over the illiberal, inegalitarian components of her thought. Likewise, ascriptivism never entirely supplanted Cady Stanton's commitment to liberal principles of natural rights and equality. Finally, her radicalism, although she never developed it fully, led to major disagreements with her colleagues in the woman's rights movement and led to her isolation and marginalization and, finally, to her complete separation from the organized movement.

This study of the dynamics of Cady Stanton's thought has emphasized that from the 1840s until the end of her life, the underlying themes in her work exhibit a definite continuity. Thus, for example, she modified the liberal individualism that dominated her thought in the early years with her acceptance of Positivism in the 1870s. Subsequently, her individualism was reawakened in the 1880s under the influence of the extreme individualism of social Darwinism. Moreover, from the beginning of her career, Cady Stanton argued that the vote would not be sufficient to remove all obstacles to women's freedom and equality. She maintained that position for the rest of her life, focusing in her later years on the ways in which organized religion was a major source of women's oppression. Finally, the hereditarian bent that is discernible in Cady Stanton's arguments as early as 1850 when, advocating divorce reform in New York, she declared that drunkards should not be allowed to marry[5] and that a woman who bears a child with a drunkard should be punished by the state, became increasingly pronounced as the years passed until it became a major theme in her work that was consistent with social Darwinism and the early eugenics movement.

One of the objectives of this study, in addition to demonstrating the presence of the different traditions in Cady Stanton's ideas, has been to make a convincing claim that the presence of inconsistencies in an individual's political thought should not be taken as an indication of a weakness in her or his work. Inconsistencies in Cady Stanton's ideas should not by any means detract from her position as a major figure in the history of American political thought. As I noted in chapter 1, ideas are invariably connected to the circumstances in which they are formulated. They cannot be severed from the prevailing intellectual forces and the historical context. Ideas are also inevitably intertwined with goals and strategies. As we have seen, there were major strategic elements in Cady Stanton's arguments throughout her career. She was not only a political thinker but also a political actor. As such, she was attentive to whether her arguments were effective; she considered the impact that they had on her audience—both supporters and opponents—and attempted to appeal to men in positions of power, large numbers of women, and other reform movements. Consequently, her arguments shifted as she gauged the responses and modified her tactics accordingly, trying different approaches that might prove to be more effective in her quest to overcome the massive obstacles to reform.

This study was motivated by my conviction that following a historical institutional approach and using the Multiple-Traditions Thesis as a framework to examine Cady Stanton's political thought would contribute to an understanding of a major figure in the history of American political ideas. This approach facilitated the focus on the interplay between the development of her ideas and a variety of contextual factors, including the changing political conditions and the shifting climate of ideas in the nineteenth century. It also encouraged an exploration of the connections between the strategic components of her arguments and her normative commitments.

My study of Cady Stanton's thought has sought to fill a gap in the literature in American political thought, as well as the history of women's rights. Women have been fully included in only the most recent histories of American political thought.[6] Moreover, Cady Stanton was badly neglected in analyses of the history of women's rights in part as a result of the relationship she had with the NAWSA during the last ten years of her life. Her radicalism also had much to do with that neglect. Her decisive stand against the religious establishment and her continuing commitment to the idea that suffrage alone could not bring an end to women's subordination and that fundamental social and cultural change would be essential resulted in general disregard for her among the younger suffrage leaders, who were by then in control of the NAWSA.[7] Biographies of Susan B. Anthony appeared within a few years of her death, but there was no full-length biography of Cady Stanton until 1940. Although the work of historians and social scientists has gone far to bring Cady Stanton the attention her work deserves, she still suffers from the legacy of a hundred years during which her contributions were ignored or undervalued. It is my hope that this study will help to give Cady Stanton the prominent place that she deserves in the history of women's rights.

My analysis of Cady Stanton's work suggests that her ideas mattered to nineteenth-century American political thought and that she should be recognized as a major figure in the history of American ideas. Why?

What was her contribution? She combined liberalism, republicanism, ascriptivism, and radicalism, as did many others. In that, the study of her ideas serves to support the Multiple-Traditions Thesis. There is more, however. As we have seen, Cady Stanton used ascriptivist themes in a variety of ways. When she relied on liberal arguments she refuted ascriptive notions of women's nature, but she also employed ascriptivism in a subversive way to challenge women's subordination by arguing that women were morally superior to men. Moreover, especially after the Civil War, she frequently used ascriptive ideas about black men and foreigners in a way that reinforced inequalities. Indeed, when she argued that black men were not worthy of suffrage but white women were, she challenged the enfranchisement of black males and gave her support to arguments that would lead to black disenfranchisement before the end of the nineteenth century. She virtually ignored black women throughout her campaign for woman suffrage and when she spoke of refined, educated women who deserved the franchise, she was clearly speaking of white women. There were undoubtedly strategic concerns in her arguments. She needed the support of white Southerners if women were to get the vote. But such arguments put her on the side of white racists against the rights of black people—both men and women.

Cady Stanton was defending victims of gender ascriptivism, arguing against a firmly entrenched tradition that posited women's natural inferiority. One would not expect her to use the same kind of arguments that she was rejecting and especially not to reinforce racial and nationality ascriptivism. Yet she did so. Did she believe in equality for all of humanity or only for certain people who deserved it (white women)? Is her thought more akin to that of John C. Calhoun and George Fitzhugh —who believed that inequality was natural—or to the ideas of someone like Thomas Jefferson, who professed a belief in equality but pulled back when it came to blacks? In spite of her long association with the Garrisonians, she seems not to have shared William Lloyd Garrison's belief in the natural right to liberty of all human beings. In any case, the unpleasant reality—the nasty secret—of American political culture is ascriptivism, and, as we have seen, Cady Stanton, just like other nineteenth-century thinkers, relied on it and often used it strategically to further her own goals. She adapted theories to fit her purposes and formulated arguments that would be useful, that is, arguments that seemed most likely to succeed. Her pragmatism is part of what places her work squarely in the American political tradition.

Still, there is more. Was she a racist? Yes. But racism was a thoroughly entrenched, long-standing tradition in the nineteenth century. As a result, she was able to make use of racism to further the goals of woman's rights. That by no means excuses her racism. But the fact of the matter is that she shared the racial views of the overwhelming majority of thinkers and activists in the nineteenth century. Her racial ascriptivism simply reaffirms that in the history of American political thought no single tradition has been strong enough to overcome the others. In sum, Elizabeth Cady Stanton's racism, like her liberalism, her republicanism, and her radicalism, is what makes her an important American political thinker.

Notes

NOTES TO CHAPTER I

1. I refer to Elizabeth Cady Stanton as "Cady Stanton" rather than as "Stanton" throughout this book. Rather than give up her family name upon marriage, she chose to combine it with her husband's name. A letter she wrote in 1847 suggests that she understood the importance of a woman's right to use her own name:

I have very serious objections . . . to being called Henry. There is a great deal in a name. It often signifies much, and may involve a great principle. Ask our colored brethren if there is nothing in a name. Why are the slaves nameless unless they take that of their master? Simply because they have no independent existence. They are mere chattels, with no civil or social rights. Even so with women. The custom of calling women Mrs. John This and Mrs. Tom That and colored men Sambo and Zip Coon is founded on the principle that white men are the lords of all. I cannot acknowledge this principle as just; therefore I cannot bear the name of another.

Cady Stanton to Rebecca Eyster, May 1, 1847, in Theodore Stanton and Harriot Stanton Blatch, eds., *Elizabeth Cady Stanton As Revealed in Her Letters Diary and Reminiscences* (New York: Harper & Brothers, 1922), 15–16.

2. Lois Banner, *Elizabeth Cady Stanton: A Radical for Woman's Rights* (Boston: Little, Brown, 1980); Elisabeth Griffith, *In Her Own Right: The Life of Elizabeth Cady Stanton* (New York: Oxford University Press, 1985; Alma Lutz, *Created Equal: A Biography of Elizabeth Cady Stanton, 1815–1902* (New York: The John Day Company, 1940); Mary Ann B. Oakley, *Elizabeth Cady Stanton* (Old Westbury, NY: Feminist Press, 1972). There are also a number of books about Cady Stanton for young readers.

3. See, for example, Aileen S. Kraditor, *The Ideas of the Woman Suffrage Movement, 1890–1920* (New York: Norton, 1981); Ellen Carol DuBois, *Feminism and Suffrage: The Emergence of an Independent Women's Movement in America 1848–1869* (Ithaca, NY: Cornell University Press, 1978); Ellen Carol DuBois, *Woman Suffrage and Women's Rights* (New York: New York University Press, 1998); Suzanne M. Marilley, *Woman Suffrage and the Origins of*

Liberal Feminism in the United States, 1820–1909 (Cambridge, MA: Harvard University Press, 1996); Marjorie Spruill Wheeler, ed., *Votes for Women! The Woman Suffrage Movement in Tennessee, the South, and the Nation* (Knoxville: University of Tennessee Press, 1995); Marjorie Spruill Wheeler, *New Women of the New South: The Leaders of the Woman Suffrage Movement in the Southern States* (New York: Oxford University Press, 1993); Jean V. Matthews, *Women's Struggle for Equality: The First Phase, 1828–1876* (Chicago: Ivan R. Dee, 1997); Sara Hunter Graham, *Woman Suffrage and the New Democracy* (New Haven, CT: Yale University Press, 1996). All of the works cited here have built on yet go beyond the classic, Eleanor Flexner, *Century of Struggle: The Woman's Rights Movement in the United States* (Cambridge, MA: Harvard University Press, 1959).

4. Thomas Jefferson, *Notes on the State of Virginia*. From *The Writings of Thomas Jefferson*, Vol. 2, Electronic Text Center, University of Virginia Library. Available at http://etext.lib.virginia.edu/etcbin/toccer-new2?id=JefBv021.sgm& images=images/modeng&data=/texts/english/modeng/parsed&tag=public&part= 14&division=div2.

5. Carole Pateman, *The Sexual Contract* (Stanford, CA: Stanford University Press, 1988).

6. Rogers M. Smith, "Beyond Tocqueville, Myrdal, and Hartz: The Multiple Traditions in America," *American Political Science Review* 87 (1993): 549–566; Rogers M. Smith, *Civic Ideals: Conflicting Visions of Citizenship in U.S. History* (New Haven, CT: Yale University Press, 1997).

7. Elizabeth Cady Stanton, *Eighty Years and More: Reminiscences 1815–1897* (Boston: Northeastern University Press, 1993; orig., 1898), 31.

8. Ibid., 32.

9. Banner, *Elizabeth Cady Stanton*, 8–9.

10. In *Mrs. Stanton's Bible* (Ithaca, NY: Cornell University Press, 2001), Kathi Kern notes that Cady Stanton subverted a narrative convention of women's autobiographies by relating her conversion experience (47–48). Cady Stanton's conversion was not to religion, however, but away from it to science and religion.

11. For example, Lutz, *Created Equal*, 6: "Yet even in her happiest moments, the threat of hell-fire hung like a cloud over her. Everything connected with religion filled her with gloom." Banner noted that she had nightmares about funerals, with bodies in black, mourners in crepe, and ministers ranting over the misdeeds of the living and the dead. "At one point she imagined that she was a secret child of the devil, who was bent on claiming her. Under the spell of this dread, for many nights she shivered in secret on the stairs." *Elizabeth Cady Stanton*, 3.

12. Keith J. Hardman, *Charles Grandison Finney, 1792–1875: Revivalist and Reformer* (Syracuse, NY: Syracuse University Press, 1987); Allen C. Guelzo,

"An Heir or a Rebel? Charles Grandison Finney and the New England Theology," *Journal of the Early Republic* 17 (Spring 1997): 61–94.

13. Cady Stanton, *Eighty Years and More*, 41–43.

14. Ibid., 44.

15. Richard Hofstadter, *The American Political Tradition* (New York: Knopf, 1973; orig., 1948), xxix–xxx.

16. Louis Hartz, *The Liberal Tradition in America: An Interpretation of American Political Thought Since the Revolution* (New York: Harcourt, Brace, and Jovanovich, 1955). Alexis de Tocqueville's *Democracy in America,* ed. J. P. Mayer (New York: Harper and Row, 1969; orig., 1840) also provided major support for the Hartz thesis.

17. Hartz, *The Liberal Tradition in America*, 8.

18. J. David Greenstone, *The Lincoln Persuasion: Remaking American Liberalism* (Princeton, NJ: Princeton University Press, 1993), 6.

19. Ibid., 113. Emphasis in original.

20. Ibid., 114.

21. Ibid.

22. Ibid.

23. Smith, *Civic Ideals,* 548, note 1.

24. James P. Young, *Reconsidering American Liberalism: The Troubled Odyssey of the Liberal Idea* (Boulder, CO: Westview Press, 1996), 6.

25. Ibid., 11.

26. Ibid., 113, 125.

27. Ibid., 327–328.

28. Some notable examples are Bernard Bailyn, *The Ideological Origins of the American Revolution* (Cambridge, MA: Belknap Press, 1967); Gordon W. Wood, *The Creation of the American Republic, 1776–1787* (Chapel Hill: University of North Carolina Press, 1969); J. G. A. Pocock, *The Machiavellian Moment: Florentine Political Thought and the Atlantic Republican Tradition* (Princeton, NJ: Princeton University Press, 1975). Most notably, for present purposes, the received wisdom has been refuted by Rogers M. Smith.

29. Eric Foner, *The Story of American Freedom* (New York: Norton, 1998), in many ways parallels Smith's analysis, although Foner focuses on the concept of freedom rather than on the liberal tradition per se. Foner noted, for example, that at a number of points in history, civil liberties have been seriously curtailed and that "The growth of civil liberties in this country is not a story of linear progress or simply a series of Supreme Court decisions, but a highly uneven and bitterly contested part of the story of American freedom" (xvii). Foner also noted that "It is hardly original to point out that the United States, founded on the premise that liberty is an entitlement of all humanity, blatantly deprived many of its own people of freedom. Less immediately apparent is how the study of freedom calls into question the universalities of what Gunnar Myrdal called

'the American Creed'—a belief in the essential dignity of all human beings and their inalienable right to democracy, liberty, and equal opportunity" (xix). Foner, like Smith, readily acknowledges that inequality was central to the American tradition.

30. Smith, "Beyond Tocqueville, Myrdal, and Hartz," 549.

31. Smith, *Civic Ideals*, 3.

32. Smith, "Beyond Tocqueville, Myrdal, and Hartz," 558.

33. Rogers M. Smith, "The 'American Creed' and American Identity: The Limits of Liberal Citizenship in the United States," *Western Political Quarterly* 41 (1988): 225–251, 233 (citations omitted).

34. Rogers M. Smith, " 'One United People': Second-Class Female Citizenship and the American Quest for Community," *Yale Journal of Law and the Humanities* 1 (1989): 229–293, 237.

35. Ibid., 238.

36. Ibid., 289.

37. Linda Kerber, *Women of the Republic: Intellect and Ideology in Revolutionary America* (New York: Norton, 1986), 33–68; Paula Baker, "The Domestication of Politics: Women and American Political Society, 1780–1920," *American Historical Review* 89 (1984): 620–647, 624.

38. In Carole Pateman's interpretation of liberalism, men's domination over women is presumed. See Pateman, *The Sexual Contract*. Pateman's interpretation of liberalism as a major source of women's subordination is a point on which she and Rogers Smith disagreed, as he argued that liberalism's emphasis on natural rights and equality could be and often was used to challenge traditional ideas of natural inequalities. See also Zillah R. Eisenstein, *The Radical Future of Liberal Feminism* (Boston: Northeastern University Press, 1986; orig., 1981). Women used liberal arguments in the late eighteenth and early nineteenth centuries: Judith Sargent Murray, *The Gleaner* (Schenectady, NY: Union College Press, 1992, orig., 1792); Mary Wollstonecraft, *A Vindication of the Rights of Women* (New York: Norton, 1975; orig., 1792); Frances Wright, "Education," and "Of Free Inquiry," in Alice S. Rossi, ed., *The Feminist Papers: From Adams to de Beauvoir* (New York: Bantam Books, 1973), 100–117.

39. Pateman, *The Sexual Contract*, 48–49.

40. Linda K. Kerber, *No Constitutional Right to Be Ladies: Women and the Obligations of Citizenship* (New York: Hill and Wang, 1998), 9.

41. Ibid., 11.

42. See also Joan Wallach Scott's analysis of the history of French feminism, *Only Paradoxes to Offer: French Feminist and the Rights of Man* (Cambridge, MA: Harvard University Press, 1996). Scott notes that liberal political theory equated individuality with masculinity and thereby excluded women: "The political individual was then taken to be both universal and male; the female was not an individual, both because she was nonidentical with the human prototype

and because she was the other who confirmed the (male) individual's individuality" (8).

43. For a discussion of republican motherhood, see Kerber, *Women of the Republic*; Mary Beth Norton, *Liberty's Daughters: The Revolutionary Experience of American Women, 1750–1800* (Boston: Little, Brown, 1980).

44. See, for example, Barbara Welter, "The Cult of True Womanhood: 1820–1860," *American Quarterly* 18 (1966): 151–174; Nancy F. Cott, *The Bonds of Womanhood: "Woman's Sphere" in New England, 1780–1835*, 2nd ed. (New Haven, CT: Yale University Press, 1997, orig., 1977); Gerda Lerner, "The Lady and the Mill Girl: Changes in the Status of Women in the Age of Jackson," in Gerda Lerner, ed., *The Majority Finds Its Past: Placing Women in History* (New York: Oxford University Press, 1979), 15–30; Daniel Scott Smith, "Family Limitation, Sexual Control, and Domestic Feminism in Victorian America," in Mary Hartman and Lois W. Banner, eds., *Clio's Consciousness Raised: New Perspectives on the History of Women* (New York: Harper Torchbooks, 1974), 119–136; Carroll Smith-Rosenberg, "Beauty, the Beast, and the Militant Woman: A Case Study in Sex Roles and Social Stress in Jacksonian America," in Carroll Smith-Rosenberg, ed., *Disorderly Conduct: Visions of Gender in Victorian America* (New York: Oxford University Press, 1985), 109–128; Barbara J. Berg, *The Remembered Gate: Origins of American Feminism: The Woman and the City: 1800–1860* (New York: Oxford University Press, 1978); Joan Hoff Wilson, "The Illusion of Change: Women and the American Revolution," in Jean E. Friedman, William G. Shade, and Mary Jane Capozzoli, eds., *Our American Sisters: Women in Life and Thought*, 4th ed. (Lexington, MA: D. C. Heath, 1987), 76–95; Mary P. Ryan, *Womanhood in America: From Colonial Times to the Present*, 3rd ed. (New York: Franklin Watts, 1983); Carl N. Degler, *At Odds: Women and the Family in America from the Revolution to the Present* (New York: Oxford University Press, 1980).

45. Historians disagree about whether women's lives improved or deteriorated in the nineteenth century. The standard of living rose, and infant mortality declined, but women were more isolated in the home, and opportunities outside the home declined with the advent of increased licensing requirements in the professions that excluded women. Compare Lerner, "The Lady and Mill Girl," and Daniel Scott Smith, "Family Limitation." Nancy F. Cott noted that women gained new recognition within the home and that the cult of domesticity changed the older view that assumed men's superiority in all spheres of life. Cott, *The Bonds of Womanhood*, 200–201.

46. It has also been called the cult of true womanhood; see Welter, "The Cult of True Womanhood."

47. Lerner, "The Lady and the Mill Girl," 28–29

48. Sarah Josepha Hale, as quoted in Nancy Woloch, *Women and the American Experience* (New York: Knopf, 1984), 102.

49. Sarah Josepha Hall, as quoted in Degler, *At Odds,* 27.

50. As quoted in Woloch, *Women and the American Experience,* 103.

51. Mary Beth Norton, "The Evolution of White Women's Experience in Early America, *American Historical Review* 89 (1984): 593–619, 617.

52. Ann M. Boylan, "Woman and Politics in the Era Before Seneca Falls," *Journal of the Early Republic* 10 (1990): 363–382.

53. Smith noted that women's rights reformers in the antebellum period worked out principles of liberal individualism more consistently than anyone had previously. The liberal language of equal rights, he observed, "however limited the scope of those rights and however qualified by implicit commitments to existing social forms, [was] nonetheless a natural vehicle for their protests." *Civic Ideals,* 231.

54. Alma Phelps, Address to Students at Troy Female Seminary, quoted in Wolloch, *Women and the American Experience,* 127.

55. On the importance of women's culture see Smith-Rosenberg, "Beauty, the Beast, and the Militant Woman"; and Smith-Rosenberg's reply to DuBois in "Politics and Culture in Women's History: A Symposium," *Feminist Studies* 6 (1980): 55–64.

56. For an analysis of the shift in the focus of the movement from natural rights to women's special qualities see Kraditor, *Ideas of the Woman Suffrage Movement.*

57. Address by Cady Stanton on Woman's Rights, in Ann D. Gordon, *The Selected Papers of Elizabeth Cady Stanton and Susan B. Anthony,* Vol. 1, *In the School of Anti-Slavery 1840–1866* (New Brunswick, NJ: Rutgers University Press, 1997), 95–123, 104.

58. For a discussion of Cady Stanton and women as a sex class, see Eisenstein, *The Radical Future of Liberal Feminism,* 156.

59. See Kern, *Mrs. Stanton's Bible,* 52–53.

60. Smith, *Civic Ideals,* 349.

61. For example, Kraditor, *Ideas of the Woman Suffrage Movement*; Judith N. Shklar, *American Citizenship: The Quest for Inclusion* (Cambridge, MA: Harvard University Press, 1991).

62. See Carl N. Degler, *In Search of Human Nature: The Decline and Revival of Darwinism in American Social Thought* (New York: Oxford University Press, 1991), and Cynthia Eagle Russett, *Sexual Science: The Victorian Construction of Womanhood* (Cambridge, MA: Harvard University Press, 1989). Both of these works examine challenges from feminists who worked within the evolutionary framework, such as Charlotte Perkins Gilman, Eliza Burt Gamble, and Lydia Commander.

63. Kraditor, *Ideas of the Woman Suffrage Movement,* 133. See Elizabeth Cady Stanton to Matilda Joslyn Gage and the National Woman Suffrage Asso-

ciation, 1877, in Ann D. Gordon, ed., *The Selected Papers of Elizabeth Cady Stanton and Susan B. Anthony,* Vol. 3, *National Protection for National Citizens, 1873–1880* (New Brunswick, NJ: Rutgers University Press, 2003), 309–312, 311.

64. Kraditor, *Ideas of the Woman Suffrage Movement.*

65. See Rogers M. Smith, "If Politics Matters: Implications for a 'New Institutionalism,'" *Studies in American Political Development* 6 (1992): 1–36.

66. DuBois, *Feminism and Suffrage,* 96.

67. DuBois identifies these issues in "The Limitations of Sisterhood: Elizabeth Cady Stanton and Division in the American Suffrage Movement, 1875–1902," in Barbara J. Harris and JoAnn K. McNamara, eds., *Women and the Structure of Society: Selected Research from the Fifth Berkshire Conference on the History of Women* (Durham, NC: Duke Press Policy Studies, 1984), 161.

68. Nancy F. Cott, *The Grounding of Modern Feminism* (New Haven, CT: Yale University Press, 1987), 3, 13.

69. Ibid., 3.

70. Ibid., 3–5. See also Nancy Cott, "Feminist Theory and Feminist Movements: The Past Before Us," in Juliet Mitchell and Ann Oakley, eds., *What Is Feminism?* (New York: Pantheon Books, 1986), 49–62.

71. See, for example, Joan C. Williams, "Deconstructing Gender," *Michigan Law Review* 87 (1989): 797–845; Katha Pollitt, "Are Women Morally Superior to Men?" *The Nation,* December 28, 1992, 799–805.

72. See, for example, Alison M. Jaggar, *Feminist Politics and Human Nature* (Totowa, NJ: Rowman and Allanheld, 1983); Pateman, *The Sexual Contract.*

73. See, for example, Jean Bethke Elshtain, "The Liberal Captivity of Feminism: A Critical Appraisal of (Some) Feminist Answers," in Philip Abbott and Michael B. Levy, eds., *The Liberal Future in America: Essays in Renewal* (Westport, CT: Greenwood Press, 1985), 63–84.

74. See, for example, Catharine A. MacKinnon, *Feminism Unmodified: Discourses on Life and Law* (Cambridge, MA: Harvard University Press, 1987).

75. The postegalitarians' argument is that "legal theory needs to recognize the reality of existing systemic and persistent inequality and move beyond the simplistic equality paradigm, establishing an affirmative feminist theory of difference." Martha Albertson Fineman, *The Neutered Mother, the Sexual Family, and Other Twentieth Century Tragedies* (New York: Routledge, 1995), 41.

76. Karen Offen, "Defining Feminism: A Comparative Historical Approach," in Gisela Bock and Susan James, eds., *Beyond Equality and Difference: Citizenship, Feminist Politics and Female Subjectivity* (New York: Routledge, 1992), 69–88, 74. See also Joan W. Scott, "Deconstructing Equality-Versus-Difference: Or, the Uses of Poststructuralist Theory for Feminism," *Feminist Studies* 14 (1) (1988): 33–50. Scott asserted that "it is a mistake for feminist historians to

write this [the equality-difference] debate uncritically into history for it reifies an 'antithesis' that may not actually have existed. We need instead to 'deconstruct' feminist arguments and read them in their discursive contexts, all as explorations of 'the difference dilemma' " (50, note 8).

77. Williams, "Deconstructing Gender," 798, note 2, quoting a letter written to her by Suzanne Lebsock.

78. Cott, *The Grounding of Modern Feminism,* 50.

79. Carole Pateman, "Equality, Difference, Subordination: The Politics of Motherhood and Women's Citizenship," in Gisela Bock and Susan James, eds., *Beyond Equality and Difference: Citizenship, Feminist Politics and Female Subjectivity* (New York: Routledge, 1992),17–31,18.

80. Offen, "Defining Feminism," 76. Offen's categories of relational and individual feminisms are not the same as the identity-difference dichotomy, which she does not find useful. Relational feminist arguments proposed a gender-based but egalitarian vision of social organization, emphasized the primacy of a companionate, nonhierarchical, male-female couple as the basic unit of society, and stressed women's rights as women in relation to men. There are many others. For example, William Leach, in *True Love and Perfect Union: The Feminist Reform of Sex and Society,* 2nd ed. (Middletown, CT: Wesleyan University Press, 1989), contended that advocates of women's rights often grounded their arguments simultaneously on natural rights and on woman's moral superiority beginning in the 1850s. Several other studies have also pointed out that women's rights advocates blended disparate arguments. See, for example, Steven M. Buechler, *The Transformation of the Woman Suffrage Movement: The Case of Illinois, 1850–1920* (New Brunswick, NJ: Rutgers University Press, 1986); Carole Nichols, "Votes and More for Women: Suffrage and After in Connecticut," *Women and History* 5 (Spring 1983): 29–30; Eisenstein, *The Radical Future of Liberal Feminism.*

81. Banner, *Elizabeth Cady Stanton,* 77, 78.

82. Valerie Bryson, *Feminist Political Theory: An Introduction* (New York: Paragon House, 1992), 48 (emphasis in original).

83. Josephine Donovan, *Feminist Theory: The Intellectual Traditions of American Feminism* (New York: Continuum, 1985), 18, 39.

84. Eisenstein, *The Radical Future of Liberal Feminism,* 4–6, 145–173.

85. Offen, "Defining Feminism." Offen defined relational feminism as follows:

arguments in the relational feminist tradition proposed a gender-based but egalitarian vision of social organization. They featured the primacy of a companionate, non-hierarchical, male-female couple as the basic unit of society, whereas individualist arguments posited the individual, irrespective of sex or gender, as the basic unit. Relational feminism emphasized women's rights *as women* (defined principally by their child-bearing, and/or nurturing capacities) in relation to men. It insisted on *women's* distinctive contribution in these roles to the broader society and made claims on the commonwealth on the basis of these contributions.

In Bock and James, *Beyond Equality and Difference*, 76 (emphasis in original). It is important to Offen's argument that the distinction between relational and individualist feminism is not the same as the identity-difference dualism While the latter does not provide a useful way of examining nineteenth-century arguments for woman's rights, the former does.

86. Ellen Carol DuBois, "Comment on Karen Offen's 'Defining Feminism: A Comparative Historical Approach,'" *Signs* 15 (Autumn 1989): 195–197.

87. Karen Offen, "Reply to DuBois," *Signs* 15 (1989): 198–202, 198.

88. Rosalyn Terborg-Penn, *African American Women in the Struggle for the Vote, 1850–1920* (Bloomington: Indiana University Press, 1998).

NOTES TO CHAPTER 2

1. Elizabeth Cady Stanton, *Eighty Years and More: Reminiscences 1815–1897* (Boston: Northeastern University Press, 1993, orig., 1898), 152–153. The Seneca Falls Conversation Club, which Cady Stanton began in late 1848, was modeled on Margaret Fuller's Boston "conversations." A group of men and women met every Saturday evening to discuss public issues.

2. Cady Stanton began contributing to the *Lily* in 1849 and continued to do so until 1853. From 1853 until 1856, she wrote monthly essays for the *Una*. From 1856 on, she sent articles to newspapers, including Horace Greeley's *New York Tribune*.

3. Cady Stanton to Elizabeth J. Neall, Friday, February 3, 1843, in Ann D. Gordon, ed., *The Selected Papers of Elizabeth Cady Stanton and Susan B. Anthony*, Vol. 1, *In the School of Anti-Slavery, 1840 to 1866* (New Brunswick, NJ: Rutgers University Press, 1997), 40–41.

4. Phyllis Cole, "Stanton, Fuller, and the Grammar of Romanticism," *The New England Quarterly* 73 (2000): 553–559.

5. On her interest in Henry Stanton's political activities see, for example, Cady Stanton to Elizabeth Smith Miller, June 4, 1851, in Theodore Stanton and Harriot Stanton Blatch, eds., *Elizabeth Cady Stanton, As Revealed in Her Letters, Diary, and Reminiscences*, Vol. 2 (New York: Harper and Brothers, 1922), 28–31. On his political ambitions and failures, see Vivian Gornick, *The Solitude of Self: Thinking About Elizabeth Cady Stanton* (New York: Farrar, Straus and Giroux, 2005), 31–33.

6. Elizabeth Cady Stanton, Susan B. Anthony, and Matilda Joslyn Gage, eds., *History of Woman Suffrage*, Vol. 1 (New York: Fowler and Wells, 1881),

459. As quoted in Alice S. Rossi, "A Feminist Friendship: Elizabeth Cady Stanton and Susan B. Anthony," in Rossi, ed., *The Feminist Papers From Adams to de Beauvoir* (New York: Bantam Books, 1974), 378–396, 379.

7. For example, Aileen S. Kraditor, *The Ideas of the Woman Suffrage Movement* (New York: Norton, 1981); Ellen Carol DuBois, *Woman Suffrage and Women's Rights* (New York: New York University Press, 1998); Ellen Carol DuBois, *Feminism and Suffrage: The Emergence of an Independent Women's Movement in America 1848–1869* (Ithaca, NY: Cornell University Press, 1978); Lois W. Banner, *Elizabeth Cady Stanton: A Radical for Woman's Rights* (New York: HarperCollins, 1980); Sylvia D. Hoffert, *When Hens Crow: The Woman's Rights Movement in Antebellum America* (Bloomington: Indiana University Press, 1995); Suzanne M. Marilley, *Woman Suffrage and the Origins of Liberal Feminism in the United States,* 1820–1920 (Cambridge, MA: Harvard University Press, 1996). Marilley asserted that a liberal feminism of equal rights emerged during the Jacksonian era and prevailed until the mid-1870s.

8. See, for example, Blanche Glassman Hersh, *The Slavery of Sex: Feminist-Abolitionists in America* (Urbana: University of Illinois Press, 1978); Keith E. Melder, *Beginnings of Sisterhood: The American Woman's Rights Movement, 1800–1850* (New York: Schocken Books, 1977).

9. As quoted in Marilley, *Woman Suffrage*, 21.

10. For a discussion of the "woman question" in abolitionism see Melder, *Beginnings of Sisterhood*, 77–112; Aileen S. Kraditor, *Means and Ends in American Abolitionism: Garrison and His Critics on Strategy and Tactics, 1834–1850* (New York: Vintage Books, 1967), 39–77.

11. Dubois pointed out that, in the 1820s and 1830s, women "evidenced a critical awareness of the importance of their femaleness in determining their experiences, began to think of themselves united by the fact of their sex, and, most important, exhibited considerable discontent with their womanly lot" (*Woman Suffrage and Women's Rights,* 54–55, 57). See also DuBois, *Feminism and Suffrage,* 32.

12. Elisabeth Griffith, *In Her Own Right: The Life of Elizabeth Cady Stanton* (New York: Oxford University Press, 1984), 24.

13. See, for example, Hersh, *The Slavery of Sex*, 93–104; DuBois, *Feminism and Suffrage;* Catherine Clinton, *The Other Civil War: American Women in the Nineteenth Century* (New York: Hill and Wang, 1984), 70.

14. Griffith, *In Her Own Right,* 45.

15. Alma Lutz, *Created Equal: A Biography of Elizabeth Cady Stanton* (New York: The John Day Company, 1940), 38.

16. Elizabeth Cady Stanton to Elizabeth J. Neall, November 26, 1841, in Gordon, ed., *The Selected Papers,* 1: 25. Lori D. Ginzberg noted that women took a less prominent role in the benevolent associations and charitable organizations as those groups began to turn to electoral politics in the 1850s. Ginz-

berg, *Women and the Work of Benevolence: Morality, Politics, and Class in the Nineteenth-Century United States* (New Haven, CT: Yale University Press, 1990), 99.

17. Gordon, ed., *The Selected Papers,* 1: 25.

18. As quoted in Hersh, *The Slavery of Sex,* 97.

19. Shortly before the couple sailed for England, Henry Stanton introduced his new wife to Sarah Grimké and her sister, Angelina Grimké Weld. Cady Stanton corresponded with the sisters, and in 1852 the Stantons enrolled two of their sons in the Welds' boarding school.

20. Elizabeth Cady Stanton to Elizabeth J. Neall, January 25, 1841, in Gordon, ed., *The Selected Papers,* 1: 18.

21. DuBois identified the three theoretical aspects of Garrisonian abolitionism. See *Feminism and Suffrage,* 32.

22. Ibid., 36–37.

23. Cady Stanton to Elizabeth Pease, February 12, 1842, in Gordon, ed., *The Selected Papers,* 1: 29.

24. For a discussion of the use of the parallel by other woman's rights and antislavery activists see Hersh, *The Slavery of Sex,* 196–201. See also Allison M. Parker, "The Case for Reform Antecedents for the Woman's Rights Movement," in Jean H. Baker, ed., *Votes for Women: The Struggle for Suffrage Revisited* (New York: Oxford University Press, 2000), 21–41.

25. Cady Stanton to Mary Ann White Johnson and the Ohio Women's Convention, April 7, 1850, in Gordon, ed., *The Selected Papers,* 1: 165.

26. Cady Stanton et al., *History of Woman Suffrage,* 1: 860.

27. DuBois, *Feminism and Suffrage,* 38–39.

28. Cady Stanton to Elizabeth J. Neall, November 26, 1841, in Gordon, ed., *The Selected Papers,* 1: 25–26.

29. Cady Stanton to Elizabeth Pease, February 12, 1842, ibid., 30.

30. Cady Stanton, *Eighty Years and More,* 145.

31. Marilley, *Woman Suffrage,* 21.

32. On the shift in moral reform to a focus on electoral politics and institutional reform rather than moral suasion see Ginzburg, *Women and the Work of Benevolence,* 98–132.

33. Cady Stanton to Susan B. Anthony, April 2, 1852, in Stanton and Stanton Blatch, eds., *Elizabeth Cady Stanton As Revealed in Her Letters Diary and Reminiscences,* 2: 38–42, 39. She also referred to the Fugitive Slave Law, the gag rule in the House of Representatives, and the assault on Senator Charles Sumner on the floor of the Senate in 1858 in her Address to the American Anti-Slavery Society in 1860: slavery had "laid violent hands on Northern freemen at their own firesides; it has gagged our statesmen, and stricken our Northern Senators dumb in their seats." Gordon, ed., *The Selected Papers,* 1: 410.

34. Cady Stanton to Susan B. Anthony, November 4, 1855, in Gordon, ed.,

The Selected Papers, 1: 62–63. The correspondence between Cady Stanton and Henry indicates her interest in his political activities in the New York legislature as a New Soil Democrat. He played a major role in organizing that antislavery faction in the Democratic Party in the late 1840s. See, for example, Henry B. Stanton to Elizabeth Cady Stanton, March 6, 1851; Cady Stanton to Henry B. Stanton, September 2, 1851, in Patricia G. Holland and Ann D. Gordon, eds., *The Papers of Elizabeth Cady Stanton and Susan B. Anthony* (Wilmington, DE: Scholarly Resources, 1992), Microfilm, Series 3, Roll 7.

35. See, for example, Cady Stanton to Elizabeth Smith Miller, June 4, 1854, regarding Gerrit Smith's speech in Congress on the Kansas-Nebraska Act, in Stanton and Stanton Blatch, eds., *Elizabeth Cady Stanton As Revealed in Her Letters Diary and Reminiscences,* 2: 57–58.

36. Cady Stanton to Elizabeth Smith Miller, November 15, 1856, in Stanton and Stanton Blatch, eds., *Elizabeth Cady Stanton As Revealed in Her Letters Diary and Reminiscences,* 2: 68–69, 69; Cady Stanton to Susan B. Anthony, December 1857, in ibid., 71–72, asking her opinion on the Lecompton government.

37. Cady Stanton to Susan B. Anthony, December 23, 1859, in ibid., 74–75.

38. Cady Stanton to Susan B. Anthony, April 24, 1860, in ibid., 76–77, 77.

39. In her Autobiography, Cady Stanton recalled that she and Mott had conceived the plan while walking in London after the humiliating experience of the World's Anti-Slavery Convention. Cady Stanton, *Eighty Years and More,* 82–83. But in a letter that she wrote to Cady Stanton in 1855, Mott recalled that the Cady Stanton made the suggestion when they were walking in Boston together in 1841. Lucretia Mott to Cady Stanton, in Holland and Gordon, eds., *The Papers of Elizabeth Cady Stanton and Susan B. Anthony,* Microfilm, Series 3, Roll 8.

40. Martha Coffin Wright (who was Lucretia Mott's sister), Mary Ann Mc-Clintock, and Jane Hunt were the other three. All were Garrisonian abolitionists.

41. Cady Stanton et al., *History of Woman Suffrage,* 1: 68. See also Linda K. Kerber's summary of the Declaration of Sentiments, "From the Declaration of Independence to the Declaration of Sentiments: The Legal Status of Women in the Early Republic, 1776–1848," *Human Rights* 6 (1977): 115–125.

42. "Declaration of Sentiments and Resolutions," *The Elizabeth Cady Stanton & Susan B. Anthony Papers Project.* All of the quotations from the Declaration of Sentiments are available at http://ecssba.rutgers.edu/docs/seneca.html as well as in Gordon, ed., *The Selected Papers,* 1: 75–88.

43. As quoted in. Nancy Woloch, *Women and the American Experience* (New York: Knopf, 1984), 129.

44. See especially Carroll Smith-Rosenberg, "Beauty, the Beast, and the Militant Woman: A Case Study in Sex Roles and Social Stress in Jacksonian Amer-

ica," in Carroll Smith Rosenberg, ed., *Disorderly Conduct: Visions of Gender in Victorian America* (New York: Oxford University Press, 1985), 109–128.

45. Nancy F. Cott, *The Bonds of Womanhood: "Woman's Sphere" in New England, 1780–1835*, 2nd ed. (New Haven, CT: Yale University Press, 1997, orig., 1977), 201. See also Ellen DuBois, Mari Jo Buhle, Temma Kaplan, Gerda Lerner, and Carroll Smith-Rosenberg, "Politics and Culture in Women's History: A Symposium," *Feminist Studies* 6 (1980): 26–63. See also Jean V. Matthews, "Consciousness of Self and Consciousness of Sex in Antebellum Feminism," *Journal of Women's History* 5 (1993): 61–78, 69, arguing that the women who made the transition from moral reform to woman's rights reform drew strength from the community of women but had an ambiguous relationship to women's culture—"they were more likely to find women's culture a prison house of the self rather than its foundation."

46. Oberlin College was the only exception at that time.

47. Henry Stanton, who also opposed including the suffrage resolution, claimed it would turn the convention into a farce. He refused to attend the meeting and left town. Griffith, *In Her Own Right*, 55.

48. DuBois, *Feminism and Suffrage*, 46.

49. Lucretia Mott told Cady Stanton that Sarah Grimké's *Letters on the Equality of the Sexes* was the best work after Wollstonecraft's. Letter from Lucretia Mott to Cady Stanton, March 16, 1855, in Holland and Gordon, eds., *The Papers of Elizabeth Cady Stanton and Susan B. Anthony*, Microfilm, Series 3, Reel 8.

50. Mary Wollstonecraft, *A Vindication of the Rights of Woman* (New York: Norton, 1975, orig., 1792), 147

51. Woloch, *Women and the American Experience*, 164.

52. Margaret Fuller, *Woman in the Nineteenth Century*, in Mason Wade, ed., *The Writings of Margaret Fuller* (New York: Viking Press, 1941), 124.

53. On the influence of Fuller on Cady Stanton, see, Phyllis Cole, "Stanton, Fuller, and the Grammar of Romanticism," *The New England Quarterly* 73 (2000): 553–559.

54. This speech has been identified as the address Cady Stanton delivered to the conventions in Seneca Falls and Rochester. Gordon noted that it is more likely that Cady Stanton delivered the address for the first time at Waterloo in September 1848. Gordon, ed., *The Selected Papers*, 1: 94.

55. Ibid., 98.

56. Ibid., 102.

57. Ibid.

58. Ibid., 100.

59. Ibid., 101.

60. Ibid., 102–103.

61. Ibid., 104.

62. Ibid., 114–115.

63. Ibid., 104.

64. Thomas Jefferson to John Adams, October 28, 1813, in Merrill D. Peterson, ed., *The Portable Thomas Jefferson* (New York: Penguin Books, 1977), 533–539, 535.

65. Gordon, ed., *The Selected Papers,* 1: 105.

66. Address to the Legislature of New York, February 14, 1854, in ibid., 242.

67. The meetings were held in various locations including Worcester, Massachusetts (1850 and 1851); Syracuse, New York (1852); Cleveland (1853); Philadelphia (1854); Cincinnati (1855); and New York (1856, 1858, 1859, and 1860). Jean V. Matthews, *Women's Struggle for Equality: The First Phase, 1828–1876* (Chicago: Ivan R. Dee, 1997), 67.

68. Woloch, *Women and the American Experience,* 193.

69. For a summary of the organizational characteristics of the early movement see Eleanor Flexner, *Century of Struggle: The Woman's Rights Movement in the United States* (Cambridge, MA: Harvard University Press, 1959), 83–91; Matthews, *Women's Struggle for Equality,* 60–69.

70. DuBois, *Feminism and Suffrage,* 51.

71. Stanton et al., *History of Woman Suffrage,* 1: 540.

72. Ibid., 541.

73. Antoinette Brown became Antoinette Brown Blackwell in 1856.

74. Hoffert, *When Hens Crow,* 15. Hoffert's list includes Susan B. Anthony, Antoinette Brown Blackwell, Paulina Wright Davis, Abby Kelley Foster, Frances Dana Gage, Harriot Kezia Hunt, Lydia Ann Jenkins, Jan Elizabeth Hitchcock Jones, Lucretia Mott, Clarina Howard Nichols, Abby Price, Ernestine Potowski Rose, Elizabeth Cady Stanton, and Lucy Stone. The men were Charles Burleigh, William H. Channing, Frederick Douglass, William Lloyd Garrison, Horace Greeley, Thomas Wentworth Higginson, Samuel J. May, Wendell Phillips, and Gerrit Smith.

75. Frederick Douglass was the only African American. Ernestine Rose, a native of Poland, was the only leader who was not born in the United States.

76. Gerder Lerner, "The Lady and the Mill Girl," in *The Majority Finds Its Past: Placing Women in History* (New York: Oxford University Press, 1979), 15–30, 27. For biographical background see Miriam Gurko, *The Ladies of Seneca Falls: The Birth of the Woman's Rights Movement* (New York: Schocken, 1976), 30–81, 108–140.

77. Flexner, *Century of Struggle,* 83.

78. Stanton et al., *History of Woman Suffrage,* 1: 634.

79. Cady Stanton to Susan B. Anthony, June 10, 1856, in Gordon, ed., *The Selected Papers,* 1: 325.

80. Cady Stanton to Mary Ann White Johnson and the Ohio Women's Convention, April 7, 1850, in ibid., 164.

81. Ibid.

82. Ibid.,165.

83. Ibid., 165–166. She articulated the same argument in subsequent statements. See, for example, Appeal to the Women of the State of New York, December 11, 1854, in ibid., 285–288.

84. Ibid., 166.

85. Ibid.

86. Ibid. Emphasis in original.

87. Woman's Convention, Akron, Ohio, May 25, 1851, in Stanton et al., *History of Woman Suffrage*, 1: 815.

88. Ibid.

89. Ibid.

90. Ibid., 816. Margaret Fuller urged women not to imitate men—not to be taught and led by men—but to discover themselves. Fuller, *Woman in the Nineteenth Century*, 124. The passage also evokes Ralph Waldo Emerson's essay "Self-Reliance," which was part of his first series of essays, published in 1841. Ralph Waldo Emerson, *Essays and Lectures* (New York: The Library of America, 1983), 257–282.

91. September 6, 1852, letter to the Third National Woman's Rights Convention, in Stanton et al., *History of Woman Suffrage*, 1: 849.

92. Ibid.

93. Ibid., 851.

94. Ibid.

95. Ibid., 825.

96. See ibid., 707.

97. See, for example, William H. Channing, September 1853, Charles C. Burleigh, Lucy Stone, in Stanton et al., *History of Woman Suffrage* 1: 552, 558–560, 565–566.

98. Cady Stanton to Susan B. Anthony, June 14, 1860, in Stanton and Stanton Blatch, eds., *Elizabeth Cady Stanton As Revealed in Her Letters Diary and Reminiscences*, 2: 82–83, 82.

NOTES TO CHAPTER 3

1. Elizabeth Cady Stanton, Susan B. Anthony, and Matilda Joslyn Gage, eds., *History of Woman Suffrage*, Vol. 1 (New York: Fowler and Wells, 1881), 634.

2. Ibid., 70–71.

3. As quoted in Kathleen Barry, *Susan B. Anthony: A Biography of a Singular Feminist* (New York: New York University Press, 1988), 13.

4. Norma Basch, *In the Eyes of the Law: Women, Marriage, and Property in Nineteenth-Century New York* (Ithaca, NY: Cornell University Press, 1982), 26.

5. Linda Kerber, *Women of the Republic: Intellect and Ideology in Revolutionary America* (New York: Norton, 1986), 150–151. Some states enacted statutes in the early nineteenth century that allowed abandoned wives to become sole traders without a special petition. Basch, *In the Eyes of the Law*, 25–26.

6. Basch, *In the Eyes of the Law*, 27.

7. The territorial legislature of Arkansas in 1835 enacted a statute that protected a wife's property from debts incurred by her husband prior to the marriage. Elizabeth Bowles Warbasse, *The Changing Legal Rights of Married Women: 1800–1861* (New York: Garland, 1987), 159; Richard H. Chused, "Married Women's Property Law: 1800–1850," in Kermit L. Hall, ed., *Women, the Law, and the Constitution* (New York: Garland, 1987), 203. Mississippi, Maryland, Maine, Massachusetts, Iowa, Michigan, Ohio, Indiana, Vermont, and Rhode Island passed such legislation. Bills were introduced in New York from the late 1830s through the 1840s.

8. See Lucy Stone's address to the National Woman's Rights Convention in New York, November 1856, in Cady Stanton et al., *History of Woman Suffrage*, 1: 631–633.

9. Basch, *In the Eyes of the Law*, 28.

10. Ibid., 113–135. For an overview of the codification movement in relation to marital property reform see Warbasse, *The Changing Legal Rights of Married Women*, 57–87.

11. Jean V. Matthews, *Women's Struggle for Equality: The First Phase, 1828–1876* (Chicago: Ivan R. Dee, 1997), 44.

12. Basch, *In the Eyes of the Law*, 38. See also Chused, "Married Women's Property Law," 163–229, 205–206.

13. Basch, *In the Eyes of the Law*, 164.

14. Ellen Carol DuBois, *Feminism and Suffrage: The Emergence of an Independent Women's Movement in America, 1848–1869* (Ithaca, NY: Cornell University Press, 1978), 41.

15. Basch, *In the Eyes of the Law*, 138.

16. Cady Stanton et al., *History of Woman Suffrage*, 1: 63.

17. Basch, *In the Eyes of the Law*, 113–135.

18. Letter to Elizabeth Smith, February 15, 1843, in Theodore Stanton and Harriot Stanton Blatch, eds., *Elizabeth Cady Stanton, As Revealed in Her Letters, Diary, and Reminiscences* Vol. 2 (New York: Harper and Brothers, 1922), 8–9. See also Cady Stanton et al., *History of Woman Suffrage*, 1: 38–39.

19. "Petition of Forty-four Ladies of Genesee and Wyoming, Praying for the Repeal of Certain Laws to the Legislature of the State of New York," *New York Assembly Documents*, March 15, 1848, Vol. 5, no. 129, as quoted in Basch, *In*

the Eyes of the Law, 156. Emphasis in original. Women who later joined the woman's rights movement worked for property rights reform in other states. In Vermont and Kansas, Clarina Howard Nichols, editor of the *Windham County Democrat,* published editorials in 1847 that encouraged action in the legislature. Jane Gray Swisshelm published editorials in her newspaper in Pittsburgh, and legislation was enacted in 1847 with the help of Lucretia Mott, who organized petition campaigns. Matthews, *Women's Struggle for Equality,* 43–44.

20. Laws of New York, 1848, chap. 200, as quoted in Basch, *In the Eyes of the Law,* 158–159.

21. Laws of New York, 1849, chap. 375, secs. 3 and 4, as quoted in ibid., 159.

22. Cady Stanton to Susan B. Anthony, March 1,1853, in Stanton and Stanton Blatch, eds., 2: 48–49, 48.

23. Barry, *Susan B. Anthony,* 78.

24. Cady Stanton et al., *History of Woman Suffrage,* 1: 581.

25. Ibid., 583.

26. Nearly all the accounts of Cady Stanton's address relate that she addressed the legislature. Gordon, however, points out that she did not speak to the legislature in 1854. Ann D. Gordon, ed., *The Selected Papers of Elizabeth Cady Stanton and Susan B. Anthony,* Vol. 1, *In the School of Anti-Slavery, 1840–1866* (New Brunswick, NJ: Rutgers University Press, 2003), 240.

27. For example, "But what is property without the right to protect that property by law? It is mockery to say a certain estate is mine, if, without my consent, you have the right to tax me when and how you please, while I have no voice in making the tax-gatherer, the legislator of the law." Address to the Legislature of New York, February 1854, in Gordon, ed., *The Selected Papers,* 1: 240–260, 248.

28. Ibid., 241.

29. Elisha Powell Hurlbut, *Essays on Human Rights, and Their Political Guaranties* (Edinburgh: Maclachlan, Stewart & Co., 1847), 2. See Gordon, ed., *The Selected Papers,* 1: 86, note, 13; 256, note 3. Hurlbut was elected to the Supreme Court in 1847, the same year as Judge Cady, and Cady Stanton met him in Albany in the 1840s.

30. Hurlbut, *Essays,* 52–53.

31. Gordon, ed., *The Selected Papers,* 1: 240–260, 248. She made the same point in a letter to Gerrit Smith in 1856: "It needs but little forethought to perceive that in due time these property holders must be represented in the government." January 3, 1856, in Stanton and Stanton Blatch, eds., *Elizabeth Cady Stanton As Revealed in Her Letters Diary and Reminiscences,* 2: 63–64.

32. Gordon, ed., *The Selected Papers,* 1: 254.

33. Ibid., 247–248.

34. Ibid., 251–252.

35. Ibid., 252.
36. Cady Stanton et al., *History of Woman Suffrage,* 1: 617–618.
37. Cady Stanton, "To the Women of the Empire State," July 12, 1859, in Gordon, ed., *The Selected Papers,* 1: 389.
38. Basch, *In the Eyes of the Law,* 194.
39. Address to the New York Legislature, February 18, 1860, in Cady Stanton et al., *History of Woman Suffrage,* 1: 679.
40. Ibid., 680.
41. Ibid.
42. Ibid., 684.
43. Ibid., 681.
44. Ibid.
45. The law provided that a married woman's property,

which comes to her by descent, devise, bequest, gift or grant; that which she acquires by her trade, business, labor or services, . . . that which a woman married in this tate owns at the time of her marriage, and the rents, issues and proceeds of all such property, shall, notwithstanding her marriage be and remain her sole and separate property, and may be used, collected and invested by her in her own name, and shall not be subject to the interference or control of her husband, or liable for his debts.

Laws of New York, 1860 Chapter 90, as quoted in Basch, *In the Eyes of the Law,* 234.
46. Appeal to the Women of New York, November 1860, in Cady Stanton et al., *History of Woman Suffrage,* 1: 743.
47. Ibid., 744.
48. Letter to the Mary Ann White Johnson and the Ohio Women's Convention, April 7, 1850, in Gordon, ed., *The Selected Papers,* 1: 164.
49. Cady Stanton et al., *History of Woman Suffrage,* 1: 70–71.
50. Annulments were sometimes granted, as were bed and board divorces that provided alimony and child support but prohibited the parties from remarrying. Glenda Riley, *Divorce: An American Tradition* (New York: Oxford University Press, 1991), 69.
51. Indiana raised the residency requirement to one year in 1859 but continued to grant divorces to out-of-state petitioners, inviting the branding of the state as a divorce mill. Ibid., 65–69.
52. Ibid., 59.
53. See John C. Spurlock, *Free Love: Marriage and Middle-Class Radicalism in America, 1825–1860* (New York: New York University Press, 1988).
54. See Elizabeth Clark, "Matrimonial Bonds: Slavery and Divorce in Nineteenth Century America," *Law and History Review* 8 (1990): 25–54. Clark argued that Cady Stanton and others based their arguments for divorce reform on

the equal rights argument and that this translated well into the legal concept of a contract.

55. Address to the Womans Rights Convention, May 11, 1860, in Gordon, ed., *The Selected Papers,* 1: 422.

56. Ibid., 425.

57. "Divorce," *The Lily,* April 1850, in ibid.,162.

58. Ibid. Emphasis in original.

59. Ibid.

60. In another article of that same issue of the *Lily,* Cady Stanton provided figures that had been reported by the governor of Massachusetts at a recent temperance meeting: of the 1,200 to 1,300 idiots in the state, between 1,100 and 1,200 were the children of drunken parents. Ibid., 163, note 3.

61. Cady Stanton et al., *History of Woman Suffrage,* 1: 482–483.

62. Cady Stanton to Susan B. Anthony, March 1, 1852, in Gordon, ed., *The Selected Papers,* 1: 194.

63. Clark, "Matrimonial Bonds."

64. Gordon, ed., *The Selected Papers,* 1: 860.

65. Robert Dale Owen was the son of Robert Owen, the founder of the experimental community New Harmony, in Indiana, in 1825. The younger Owen worked with his father in the short-lived community, edited the *New Harmony Gazette,* and collaborated with Frances Wright, who modeled her Nashoba on New Harmony. With Wright, Robert Dale Owen helped organize an early labor movement in New York. Although Robert Dale Owen moved away from communitarian reform in the late 1820s, he advocated liberal divorce laws on the grounds that the availability of divorce would improve the institution of marriage—it would help marriage to be a union of two freely consenting individuals and guarantee the affections of husband and wife. As a state legislator in Indiana, he worked for divorce reform, as well as for protection of married women's property. See Spurlock, *Free Love,* 23–72.

66. *New York Daily Tribune,* March 1, 5, 6, 12, 17, 28, April 7, 21, May 1, 1860.

67. At the 1860 convention, Ernestine Rose introduced a series of more general resolutions that included suffrage. See Cady Stanton et al., *History of Woman Suffrage*1: 707–708.

68. Gordon, ed., *The Selected Papers,* 1: 418–419.

69. Ibid., 426.

70. Ibid.

71. Ibid., 420.

72. Antoinette Brown and Clarina Nichols both argued at the 1853 temperance convention that marriage was a sacred institution that legal divorce could never terminate. In addition, Lucy Stone, knowing that Cady Stanton planned

to make divorce the subject of her speech, declined the invitation to join her on the platform at the 1860 convention.

73. Cady Stanton et al., *History of Woman Suffrage,* 1: 725.

74. Ibid., 727.

75. Ibid., 733.

76. Ibid., 735.

77. The bill provided divorce after desertion for a period of three years, when there were continuous and repeated instances of cruel and inhuman treatment for a period of one year by either party that impaired health or were life-threatening, It also provided that women should have the same right as men to divorce on grounds of adultery. Ibid., 745.

78. Norma Basch, *Framing American Divorce: From the Revolutionary Generation to the Victorians* (Berkeley: University of California Press, 1999), 77.

79. Temperance actually dates to the late eighteenth century, when ministers and physicians began to speak out against drinking. By the turn of the century, temperance societies had been established in a number of New England towns, most often through the work of local ministers. Then, in 1826, representatives of several Protestant churches formed the American Temperance Society. Studies show that alcohol consumption in the United States reached its peak around 1830, and some scholars have argued that the temperance movement was a product of the tensions caused by developing capitalism. See, for example, W. J. Rorabaugh, *The Alcoholic Republic: An American Tradition* (New York: Oxford University Press, 1979); Ian R. Tyrrell, *Sobering Up: From Temperance to Prohibition in Antebellum America, 1800–1860* (Westport, CT: Greenwood Press, 1979), 6: "The organized temperance movement which emerged in the 1820s, . . . had its roots in the process of industrialization and the commercialization of agriculture; more important, the men and women who fashioned the temperance crusade sought to hasten the processes of social and economic change."

80. See Barbara Leslie Epstein, *The Politics of Domesticity: Women, Evangelism and Temperance in Nineteenth-Century America* (Middletown, CT: Wesleyan University Press, 1981).

81. "ECS to Women's Temperance Meeting, Albany," January 28, 1852, in Gordon, ed., *The Selected Papers,* 1: 191–193, 191.

82. Ibid., 191–192.

83. Ibid., 192.

84. Elizabeth Cady Stanton, "A Startling Fact," *The Lily,* April 1850.

85. Elizabeth Cady Stanton, "Henry Neil and His Mother," *The Lily,* February 1850. Emphasis in original.

86. Aileen S. Kraditor, *The Ideas of the Woman Suffrage Movement, 1890–1920* (New York: Norton, 1981), 58; Ruth Bordin, *Woman and Temperance:*

The Quest for Power and Liberty, 1873–1900 (New Brunswick, NJ: Rutgers University Press, 1990), 118–119.

87. Epstein, *The Politics of Domesticity,* 109.

88. Cady Stanton et al., *History of Woman Suffrage,* 1: 481–483, 482.

89. Ibid.

90. Ibid., 484.

91. Elizabeth Cady Stanton, "Temperance—Woman's Rights," July 1, 1852, in Gordon, ed., *The Selected Papers,* 1: 201–205, 201–202.

92. Ibid., 485.

93. Elizabeth Cady Stanton, "Appeal for the Maine Law," in Ellen Carol DuBois, ed., *The Elizabeth Cady Stanton–Susan B. Anthony Reader: Correspondence, Writings, Speeches,* rev. ed. (Boston: Northeastern University Press, 1992), 40–43, 42.

94. Ibid., 43.

95. Ibid.

96. Cady Stanton et al., *History of Woman Suffrage,* 1: 487.

97. Ibid., 495.

98. As quoted in Elisabeth Griffith, *In Her Own Right: The Life of Elizabeth Cady Stanton* (New York: Oxford University Press, 1984), 77.

99. Lori D. Ginzberg, *Women and the Work of Benevolence: Morality, Politics, and Class in the Nineteenth-Century United States* (New Haven, CT: Yale University Press, 1990), 111.

100. Elizabeth Cady Stanton to Gerrit Smith, December 21, 1855, in Gordon, ed., *The Selected Papers,* 1: 305–311, 307.

101. Elizabeth Cady Stanton, "To the Women of the Empire State," in ibid., 389–391, 390.

102. Cady Stanton to Susan B. Anthony, June 14, 1860, in Stanton and Stanton Blatch, eds., *Elizabeth Cady Stanton As Revealed in Her Letters Diary and Reminiscences,* 2: 82–83, 82.

NOTES TO CHAPTER 4

1. Elizabeth Cady Stanton, Susan B. Anthony, and Matilda Joslyn Gage, eds., *History of Woman Suffrage,* Vol. 1 (New York: Fowler and Wells, 1881), 560.

2. Ibid.

3. Ibid.

4. *New York Herald,* September 7, 1853, in ibid., 1: 556.

5. Ibid.

6. *New York Daily Herald,* November 27, 1856, p. 4. As quoted in Sylvia D. Hoffert, *When Hens Crow: The Woman's Rights Movement in Antebellum America* (Bloomington: Indiana University Press, 1995), 98.

7. *New York Daily Herald,* November 27, 1856, p. 4; September 14, 1852, p. 4; August 8, 1855, p. 2; September 6, 1853, p. 4. As quoted in ibid., 102.

8. Ibid., 102.

9. Jean V. Matthews, *Women's Struggle for Equality: The First Phase, 1828–1876* (Chicago: Ivan R. Dee, 1997), 72.

10. *New York Daily Tribune,* May 15, 1858, p. 4. As quoted in ibid., 105.

11. The dress reform movement that emerged in 1849 was linked to a variety of other antebellum reforms including utopianism, perfectionism, and health and hygiene. See William Leach, *True Love and Perfect Union: The Feminist Reform of Sex and Society,* 2nd ed. (Middletown, CT: Wesleyan University Press, 1980), ch. 9.

12. Matthews, *Women's Struggle for Equality,* 74.

13. *Albany Evening Journal,* February 20, 1854, as quoted in Norma Basch, *In the Eyes of the Law: Women, Marriage, and Property in Nineteenth-Century New York* (Ithaca, NY: Cornell University Press, 1982), 192.

14. As quoted in ibid., 193.

15. As quoted in ibid., 194.

16. Ibid. 195.

17. "Female Emancipation," *New York Times,* February 10, 1860, as quoted in ibid., 196.

18. Lori D. Ginzburg, *Women and the Work of Benevolence: Morality, Politics, and Class in the Nineteenth-Century United States* (New Haven, CT: Yale University Press, 1990).

19. See, for example, Kathryn Kish Sklar, *Catharine Beecher: A Study in American Domesticity* (New York: Norton, 1976).

20. "Address by ECS on Woman's Rights," in Ann D. Gordon, ed., *The Selected Papers of Elizabeth Cady Stanton and Susan B. Anthony,* Vol. 1, *In the School of Anti-Slavery, 1840–1866* (New Brunswick, NJ: Rutgers University Press, 2006), 94–123, 98.

21. Elizabeth Cady Stanton to Susan B. Anthony, April 2, 1852, in Patricia G. Holland and Ann D. Gordon, eds., *The Papers of Elizabeth Cady Stanton and Susan B. Anthony* (Wilmington, DE: Scholarly Resources, 1992), Microfilm, Series 3, Reel 7, 189.

22. Cady Stanton et al., *History of Woman Suffrage,* 1: 80.

23. "ECS and Elizabeth W. McClintock to the Editors, *Seneca County Courier,*" in Gordon, ed., *The Selected Papers,* 1:88–94, 89.

24. Ibid.

25. Holland and Gordon, eds., *The Papers of Elizabeth Cady Stanton and Susan B. Anthony,* Microfilm, Series 3, Reel 7, 10–13, 13.

26. Ibid.

27. Ibid., 100.

28. Ibid., 114.

29. Ibid., 103.

30. Ibid., 104.

31. Ibid., 110, 111.

32. Ibid., 111.

33. Holland and Gordon, eds., *The Papers of Elizabeth Cady Stanton and Susan B. Anthony*, Microfilm, Series 3, Reel 7, 3–5.

34. Published in the *National Reformer*, September, 1848. See Cady Stanton et al., *History of Woman Suffrage*, 1: 806.

35. Ibid., 106.

36. Ibid., 105.

37. Ibid.

38. Cady Stanton had adopted the costume in 1851 and wore it for two years but was one of the first to give it up. Other activists followed, and by the middle of the 1850s, the bloomer had virtually disappeared. Eleanor Flexner, *Century of Struggle: The Women's Rights Movement in the United States* (Cambridge, MA: Harvard University Press, 1959), 84. Griffith notes that Elizabeth Smith Miller word an ankle-length version of the dress for seven years and that Amelia Bloomer wore hers for eight years. Elisabeth Griffith, *In Her Own Right: The Life of Elizabeth Cady Stanton* (New York: Oxford University Press, 1984), 72.

39. Holland and Gordon, eds., *The Papers of Elizabeth Cady Stanton and Susan B. Anthony*, Microfilm, Series 3, Reel 7, 88.

40. Elizabeth Cady Stanton to Lucretia Mott, October 1852, in Gordon, ed., *The Selected Papers*, 1: 212.

41. As quoted in Griffith, *In Her Own Right*, 72.

42. Gerrit Smith to Elizabeth Cady Stanton, December 1, 1855, in Cady Stanton et al., *History of Woman Suffrage*, 1: 836–839, 837.

43. Elizabeth Cady Stanton to Gerrit Smith, December 21, 1855, in ibid., 839–842, 841.

44. Ibid.

45. Address by Elizabeth Cady Stanton on Woman's Rights, in Gordon, ed., *The Selected Papers* 1: 94–123, 96.

46. Ibid., 106.

47. Cady Stanton et al., *History of Woman Suffrage*, 1: 858–859.

48. "I Have All the Rights I Want," *Una*, March 1855, in Holland and Gordon, eds., *The Papers of Elizabeth Cady Stanton and Susan B. Anthony*, Microfilm, Series 3, Reel 8, 206.

49. "Letter from Mrs. Stanton," to the Seventh National Woman's Rights Convention, November 24, 1856, in Holland and Gordon, eds., *The Papers of Elizabeth Cady Stanton and Susan B. Anthony*, Microfilm, Series 3, Reel 8, 807–808, 807.

50. "I Have All the Rights I Want," in Holland and Gordon, eds., *The*

Papers of Elizabeth Cady Stanton and Susan B. Anthony, Microfilm, Series 3, Reel 9, 501–504.

51. Ibid.

52. Tract by Elizabeth Cady Stanton, "I Have All the Rights I Want," in Gordon, ed., *Selected Papers,* 1: 402–405, 405.

53. Elizabeth Cady Stanton to Susan B. Anthony, August 1857, in ibid., 351.

NOTES TO CHAPTER 5

1. *Dred Scott v. Sandford,* 19 How. 393 (1857).

2. Kathleen Barry, *Susan B. Anthony: A Biography* (New York: New York University Press, 1988), 111–112, 147.

3. The disagreement over divorce is discussed at length in chapter 3. Disagreement between Cady Stanton and Anthony on the one hand and Phillips and Garrison on the other also arose over a Massachusetts woman, Phoebe Harris Phelps, who sought Anthony's help. Phelps was hiding from her husband, who had beaten her, taken her property, had her confined to a mental institution, and refused to allow her to see her three children. She had taken her thirteen-year-old daughter and run away to New York. Anthony found a place for her to stay and refused to reveal her whereabouts. Phillips and Garrison argued that Anthony was violating the laws of Massachusetts that gave guardianship of children to fathers.

4. "Address by ECS to the American Anti-Slavery Society," May 8, 1860, in Ann D. Gordon, ed., *The Selected Papers of Elizabeth Cady Stanton and Susan B. Anthony,* Vol. 1, *In the School of Anti-Slavery, 1840–1866* (New Brunswick, NJ: Rutgers University Press, 1997), 409–418, 411.

5. In the years preceding the Civil War, the Garrisonians advocated disunionism; since the 1840s, they had argued that the free states should separate from the slaveholding Union. Secession, they reasoned, would help to bring an end to the slavery that the federal government and the Constitution protected. Without the protection of the U.S. military forces, the South would be vulnerable to slave insurrections; without enforcement of the federal Fugitive Slave Law, more slaves would be able to escape to the North; and, in general, the South would be isolated and susceptible to moral condemnation. Thus, disunion would allay the North's responsibility for slavery. The Garrisonians thus welcomed the secession of most of the slave states and opposed any concessions to try to keep them in the Union. Many Garrisonians, including William Lloyd Garrison himself, were pacifists and thus opposed to war. Most of them revised their views after the firing on Fort Sumter, however, and rallied to the Union cause. Garrison endorsed the war, proclaiming "Better civil war, . . . than for us to crouch in the dust, and allow ourselves to be driven to the wall by a miser-

able and merciless slave oligarchy! This war has come because of the increasing love of liberty here at the North" ("Garrison Endorses the War (1862)," in George M. Fredrickson, ed., *William Lloyd Garrison* [Englewood Cliffs, NJ: Prentice-Hall, 1968], 63–66, 65). Although the Garrisonians viewed the war as a crusade to liberate the slaves and a form of atonement for participating in the sin of slavery, they also had to recognize that emancipation was not an official war aim. Moreover, Garrisonian abolitionists earlier had hesitated to support the Republican Party and a presidential candidate who expressed moral opposition to slavery but who also made it clear that he was not in favor of immediate and complete abolition. Still, as the election approached in 1860, most Garrisonians began to view the prospect of Abraham Lincoln's election as a step in the right direction. The abolitionists were firmly convinced that emancipation of the slaves would cripple the Confederacy and bring a speedy end to the war. The Union army's defeat at the battle of Bull Run in July 1861 reinforced that conviction among Northerners in general, and Congress passed the first Confiscation Act in August 1861, authorizing the Union to sieze slaves who were directly involved in the Confederate military effort. At the end of August, John C. Frémont, the commander of the Union troops in Missouri, declared martial law and freed all the slaves of rebel sympathizers in the state. Lincoln ordered Frémont to revise the order to make it consistent with the First Confiscation Act. Appalled by Lincoln's actions, the Garrisonians increased their efforts to pressure the administration to adopt an emancipation policy. A major part of their endeavor was to convince Northerners that slavery was a central issue of the war, that emancipation would bring an end to the war, and that the federal government had the constitutional authority under the war powers to free the slaves. President Lincoln's first specific recommendation regarding slavery was a message to Congress in 1862 in which he recommended passage of a joint resolution offering federal compensation to any state that adopted a gradual emancipation policy. The measure failed when a majority of border-state legislators refused to consider it. In the spring of that year, the president took actions that deeply disappointed abolitionists. He revoked General David Hunter's edict declaring all slaves in South Carolina, Georgia, and Florida free and continued to enforce the Fugitive Slave Act in the District of Columbia. In addition, the House of Representatives defeated a bill that would have emancipated all the slaves who were held by rebels. When Congress passed the Second Confiscation Act, declaring all slaves of rebels free as soon as they came within Union lines, abolitionists considered it inadequate, particularly in light of Lincoln's apparent lack of interest in enforcing it. In September, the president issued a preliminary Emancipation Proclamation, providing that on January 1, 1863, all slaves in rebellious states would be free. Lincoln also promised to present Congress with a plan for gradual, compensated abolition in loyal slave states. In his annual message to Congress, in December, he asked for a constitutional amendment that would grant compensation to any state that undertook to abolish slavery by 1900. Only slaves freed "by the chances of the war" would be free; all others would remain in slavery until their states or individual owners emancipated them. Abolitionists could not help but notice that the Emancipation Proclamation applied only to the Confederate states and that it exempted "for the present" Tennessee and parts of Louisiana and Virginia. Still, most abolitionists considered the Proclamation to be another step in the right direction. James M. McPherson, *The Struggle for Equality: Abolitionists and the Negro in the Civil War and Reconstruction* (Princeton, NJ: Princeton University Press, 1964).

6. Woman's Rights Convention in Worcester Massachusetts, October 20, 1850, in Patricia G. Holland and Ann D. Gordon, eds., *The Papers of Elizabeth Cady Stanton and Susan B. Anthony* (Wilmington DE: Scholarly Resources, 1991), Microfilm, Series 3, Reel 7.

7. "SBA to Wendell Phillips," April 29, 1861, in Gordon, ed., *The Selected Papers* 1: 454–465.

8. "To the Secretary of State," September 19, 1861, in Theodore Stanton and Harriot Stanton Blatch, eds., *Elizabeth Cady Stanton As Revealed in Her Letters Diary and Reminiscences*, Vol. 2 (New York: Harper & Brothers, 1922), 88–89, 89.

9. Elizabeth Cady Stanton to Elizabeth Smith Miller, November 15, 1856, in ibid., 2: 68–69, 69.

10. Holland and Gordon, eds., *The Papers of Elizabeth Cady Stanton and Susan B. Anthony*, Microfilm, Series 3, Reel 8.

11. Elizabeth Cady Stanton to Susan B. Anthony, November 4, 1855, in Ellen Carol DuBois, ed., *The Elizabeth Cady Stanton–Susan B. Anthony Reader: Correspondence, Writings, Speeches*, rev. ed. (Boston: Northeastern University Press, 1992), 59.

12. "ECS to Gerrit Smith," December 16, 1861, in Gordon, ed., *The Selected Papers*, 1: 470–471, 470.

13. Elizabeth Cady Stanton to Susan B. Anthony, December 1857, in Stanton and Stanton Blatch, eds., *Elizabeth Cady Stanton As Revealed in Her Letters Diary and Reminiscences*, 71–72, 71.

14. "Appeal to the Women of the Republic," in Elizabeth Cady Stanton, Susan B. Anthony, and Matilda Joslyn Gage, eds., *History of Woman Suffrage*, Vol. 1 (New York: Fowler and Wells, 1881–1922), 51–53, 52.

15. "ECS to Gerrit Smith," December 16, 1861, in Gordon, ed., *The Selected Papers*, 1: 470–471.

16. "To Elizabeth Smith Miller," September 11, 1862, in Stanton and Stanton Blatch, eds., *Elizabeth Cady Stanton As Revealed in Her Letters Diary and Reminiscences*, 90–91.

17. Elisabeth Griffith, *In Her Own Right: The Life of Elizabeth Cady Stanton* (New York: Oxford University Press, 1984), 106.

18. "To Mrs. Gerrit Smith," July 20, 1863, in Stanton and Stanton Blatch, eds., *Elizabeth Cady Stanton As Revealed in Her Letters Diary and Reminiscences,* 2: 94–95, 95.

19. Ibid., 94.

20. "SBA to Wendell Phillips," April 29, 1861, in Gordon, ed., *The Selected Papers,* 1: 464–465.

21. "SBA to Martha Coffin Wright," May 28, 1861, in ibid., 46–48.

22. "SBA to Lydia Mott," After April 10, 1862, in ibid., 475–476, 475.

23. Elizabeth Cady Stanton, *Eighty Years and More: Reminiscences, 1815–1897* (Boston: Northeastern University Press, 1993, orig., 1898), 254.

24. Faye Dudden noted that in New York City during the war, Cady Stanton's close connections with major opinion leaders probably meant that she had some influence on national political issues. She saw Wendell Phillips often, dined with Horace Greeley, and got the latest political news from her brother-in-law Samuel Wilkeson, who was chief correspondent for the *Tribune.* Dudden, "New York Strategy: The New York Woman's Movement and the Civil War," in Jean H. Baker, ed., *Votes for Women: The Struggle for Suffrage Revisited* (New York: Oxford University Press, 2000), 56–76, 63.

25. "Address by ECS to the American Anti-Slavery Society," May 8, 1860, in Gordon, ed., *The Selected Papers,* 1: 409–418, 410.

26. "Free Speech," February 4, 1861, in Holland and Gordon, eds., *The Papers of Elizabeth Cady Stanton and Susan B. Anthony,* Microfilm, Series 3, Reel 9, 1085–1087.

27. Gordon, ed., *The Selected Papers,* 1: 412.

28. Ibid., 415.

29. Elizabeth Cady Stanton, "The Slave's Appeal" 1860, in Holland and Gordon, eds., *The Papers of Elizabeth Cady Stanton and Susan B. Anthony,* Microfilm, Series 3, Reel 9, 936–940.

30. Ibid.

31. "The Loyal Women of the Country to Abraham Lincoln, President of the United States," in Cady Stanton et al., *History of Woman Suffrage,* 2: 67–69, 68.

32. "No Compromise with Slavery Tour," January 3–4, 1861, in Holland and Gordon, eds., *The Papers of Elizabeth Cady Stanton and Susan B. Anthony,* Microfilm, Series 3, Reel 9, 993.

33. Ibid., 1000.

34. Ibid., 1004.

35. "Free Speech," February 4, 1861, in ibid., Series 3, Reel 9, 1085–1087.

36. Dudden, "New York Strategy," 66.

37. Ibid., 66.

38. Cady Stanton et al., *History of Woman Suffrage,* 2: 57.

39. Wendy Hamand Venet, *Neither Ballots nor Bullets: Women Abolition-*

ists and the Civil War (Charlottesville: University Press of Virginia, 1991), 103. See also Mary P. Ryan, *Women in Public: Between Banners and Ballots, 1825–1880* (New Haven, CT: Yale University Press, 1990), 152: "Cady Stanton used the league as a means through which to inject a feminist perspective into the central political debates of the Civil War."

40. "Appeal to the Women of the Republic," Cady Stanton et al., *History of Woman Suffrage*, 2: 51–53.

41. "The Call for a Meeting of the Loyal Women of the Nation," in ibid., 53.

42. "Speech of Mrs. E. Cady Stanton," Proceedings of the Meeting of the Loyal Women of the Republic, May 14, 1863, in Holland and Gordon, eds., *The Papers of Elizabeth Cady Stanton and Susan B. Anthony*, Microfilm, Series 3, Reel 10, 436–439, 438.

43. Ibid.

44. Ibid., 439–440.

45. McPherson, *The Struggle for Equality*, 241. With regard to the former slaves, Lincoln's plan allowed any policy that would "recognize and declare their permanent freedom, provide for their education, and which may yet be consistent, as a temporary arrangement, with their present condition as a laboring, landless, and homeless class."

46. About four hundred supporters of Fremont gathered in Cleveland on May 31 to nominate their candidate for president on the Radical Democratic Party ticket. The party's platform included demands for a constitutional amendment freeing the slaves in all the states, a congressional reconstruction program to protect the rights of the newly freed slaves, confiscation and redistribution of rebel lands, and a one-term presidency.

47. Stanton and Stanton Blatch, eds., *Elizabeth Cady Stanton As Revealed in Her Letters Diary and Reminiscences*, 2: 97–99, 99.

48. The struggle was more conservative Weed-Seward group and the more radical group of which Henry Stanton and Gerrit Smith were members. Dudden, "New York Strategy," 65–69.

49. Letter from Mrs. C. H. Dall, May 2, 1864, in Holland and Gordon, eds., *The Papers of Elizabeth Cady Stanton and Susan B. Anthony*, Microfilm, Series 3, Reel 10, 775–777.

50. Ibid.

51. Mrs. E. Cady Stanton to Mrs. Dall, May 7, 1864, in ibid., Microfilm, Series 3, Reel 10, 795–796.

52. Dudden, "New York Strategy," 70.

53. Women's Loyal National League, First Annual Convention and Business Meeting, May 12, 1864, in Holland and Gordon, eds., *The Papers of Elizabeth Cady Stanton and Susan B. Anthony*, Series 3, Reel 10, 801–802.

54. Elizabeth Cady Stanton to Susan B. Anthony, September 26, 1864, in ibid., Microfilm, Series 3, Reel 10, 889.

55. Elizabeth Cady Stanton to Susan B. Anthony, December 19, 1864, in ibid., Microfilm, Series 3, Reel 10, 918.

NOTES TO CHAPTER 6

1. Aileen S. Kraditor, *The Ideas of the Woman Suffrage Movement, 1890–1920* (New York: Norton, 1981); Ellen Carol DuBois, *Feminism and Suffrage: The Emergence of an Independent Women's Movement in America, 1848–1869* (Ithaca, NY: Cornell University Press, 1978); Ellen Carol DuBois, *Woman Suffrage and Women's Rights* (New York: New York University Press, 1998), 11.

2. Several scholars have examined the impact that the betrayal by abolitionists after the Civil War had on the woman's rights movement. See especially DuBois, *Feminism and Suffrage*, 53–104, 162–202; Suzanne M. Marilley, *Woman Suffrage and the Origins of Liberal Feminism in the United States, 1820–1920* (Cambridge, MA: Harvard University Press, 1996), 66–99; Eleanor Flexner, *Century of Struggle: The Woman's Rights Movement in the United States*, rev. ed. (Cambridge, MA: Harvard University Press, 1975; orig., 1959), 145–158.

3. See, especially, Louise Michelle Newman, *White Women's Rights: The Racial Origins of Feminism in the United States* (New York: Oxford University Press, 1999).

4. Fay Dudden, "New York Strategy: The New York Woman's Movement and the Civil War," in Jean H. Baker, ed., *Votes for Women: The Struggle for Suffrage Revisited* (New York: Oxford University Press, 2002), 56–76.

5. DuBois, *Feminism and Suffrage*, 54–55.

6. "American Anti-Slavery Anniversary," *Standard*, May 13, 1865, 2, as quoted in DuBois, *Feminism and Suffrage*, 59.

7. DuBois, *Feminism and Suffrage*, 55.

8. Elizabeth Cady Stanton to Susan B. Anthony, August 1, 1865, in Theodore Stanton and Harriot Stanton Blatch, eds., *Elizabeth Cady Stanton As Revealed in Her Letters Diary and Reminiscences*, Vol. 2 (New York: Harper and Brothers, 1922), 105.

9. Daniel A. Farber and Suzanna Sherry, *A History of the American Constitution* (St. Paul, MN: West, 1990), 305.

10. Elizabeth Cady Stanton, Susan B. Anthony, and Matilda Joslyn Gage, eds., *History of Woman Suffrage*, Vol. 2 (New York: Fowler and Wells, 1881), 170.

11. Earlier, at the antislavery meeting in Boston in January 1866, Susan B. Anthony and Lucy Stone proposed that the American Anti-Slavery Society join

the women's rights movement to form a single organization for equal rights and universal suffrage. Phillips prevented the proposal from coming to a vote.

12. Cady Stanton et al., *History of Woman Suffrage,* 2: 172. Emphasis in original.

13. Ibid., 178.

14. Ibid., 181. In the first election in which a woman ran for Congress, the Democratic candidate won and Cady Stanton received twenty-four votes.

15. Ibid., 271–281.

16. Ibid., 275.

17. Ibid., 275–276.

18. Ibid., 276.

19. DuBois, *Feminism and Suffrage,* 79.

20. For a discussion of the Kansas Republicans' campaign to defeat the woman suffrage referendum, see DuBois, *Feminism and Suffrage,* 81–92.

21. As quoted in Jean V. Matthews, *Women's Struggle for Equality: The First Phase, 1828–1876* (Chicago: Ivan R. Dee, 1997), 129.

22. Cady Stanton et al., *History of Woman Suffrage,* 2: 264.

23. Stanton and Stanton Blatch, eds., *Elizabeth Cady Stanton As Revealed in Her Letters Diary and Reminiscences,* 2: 117, 119.

24. Elizabeth Cady Stanton, *Eighty Years and More: Reminiscences, 1815–1897* (Boston: Northeastern University Press), 254.

25. Ibid.

26. Elizabeth Cady Stanton, "To Our Radical Friends," *Revolution,* May 14, 1868, 296; "What Is a Democrat?" *Revolution,* September 30, 1868, 138.

27. Elizabeth Cady Stanton, "Kansas," *Revolution,* January 8, 1868.

28. "We wondered then at the general indifference to that first opportunity of realizing what all those gentlemen had advocated so long; and, in looking back over the many intervening years, we still wonder at the stolid incapacity of all men to understand that woman feels the invidious distinctions of sex exactly as the black man does those of color, or the white man the more transient distinctions of wealth, family, position, place, and power; that she feels as keenly as man the injustice of disfranchisement." Cady Stanton et al., *History of Woman Suffrage,* 2: 265. DuBois argued that the men's incapacity to understand how women feel did not provide a complete explanation of the abolitionists' behavior and that it is important to take into account the "shifting political situation which brought the two movements together before the Civil War and drove them apart in 1867." DuBois, *Feminism and Suffrage,* 102.

29. DuBois, *Feminism and Suffrage,* 103.

30. In May 1870, the *Revolution* was in financial trouble, and Cady Stanton and Anthony were forced to hand it over to Laura Curtis Bullard, who was an heiress to a patent medicine fortune and who had the resources to keep the journal going.

31. DuBois, *Feminism and Suffrage,* 102–103.

32. The Fifteenth Amendment reads: "The right of citizens of the United States to vote shall not be denied or abridged by the United States or by any State on account of race, color, or previous condition of servitude." It also gives Congress the power to enforce the Amendment, "by appropriate legislation." The Fifteenth Amendment was ratified in 1870.

33. Cady Stanton et al., *History of Woman Suffrage,* 2: 381.

34. Ibid.

35. Ibid., 383.

36. Ibid., 391.

37. Cady Stanton et al., *History of Woman Suffrage,* 2: 397.

38. Marilley, *Woman Suffrage,* 77.

39. DuBois, *Feminism and Suffrage,* 190.

40. DuBois noted that "Once Reconstruction issues, particularly black suffrage, were settled, the tense partisanship and political polarization they [the Republicans] had generated would disappear, and with them any strategic possibilities for the enactment of woman suffrage." Ibid., 171–172.

41. Ann D. Gordon, ed., *The Selected Papers of Elizabeth Cady Stanton and Susan B. Anthony,* Vol. 2, *Against and Aristocracy of Sex, 1866–1873* (New Brunswick, NJ: Rutgers University Press, 1997), 196.

42. DuBois, *Feminism and Suffrage,* 181.

43. Marilley, *Woman Suffrage,* 66.

44. Elisabeth Griffith, *In Her Own Right: The Life of Elizabeth Cady Stanton* (New York: Oxford University Press, 1984), 162.

45. DuBois, *Woman Suffrage & Women's Rights* (New York: New York University Press, 1998), 94–98; Michele Louise Newman, *White Women's Rights: The Racial Origins of Feminism in the United States* (New York: Oxford University Press, 1999).

46. Newman, *White Women's Rights,* 57.

47. "Universal Suffrage," July 29, 1865, in Gordon, ed., *The Selected Papers,* 550–552, 550.

48. Ibid., 551.

49. Elizabeth Cady Stanton to Martha C. Wright, December 20, 1865, in Stanton and Stanton Blatch, eds., *Elizabeth Cady Stanton As Revealed in Her Letters Diary and Reminiscences,* 2: 108–109.

50. Letter to the Editor, December 26, 1865, in Gordon, ed., *The Selected Papers,* 1: 564–565, 564.

51. Ibid.

52. Ibid., 565.

53. Cady Stanton et al., *History of Woman Suffrage,* 2: 174.

54. Ibid., 2: 173.

55. Ibid., 91.

56. Ibid.

57. Ibid.,181.

58. Ibid.

59. Ibid., 185–186.

60. Ibid., 188.

61. Elizabeth Cady Stanton, "Gerrit Smith on Petitions," in Ellen Carol DuBois, ed., *The Elizabeth Cady Stanton–Susan B. Anthony Reader: Correspondence, Writings, Speeches,* rev. ed. (Boston, MA: Northeastern University Press, 1992), 119–124, 120.

62. Ibid.

63. Ibid., 121.

64. Ibid., 123.

65. Ibid., 123–124.

66. Gordon, ed., *The Selected Papers,* 2: 194–199, 198, note 1.

67. Ibid., 194.

68. Ibid.

69. Ibid., 195.

70. Ibid., 196.

71. Ibid.

72. Ibid.

73. Vivian Gornick, *The Solitude of Self: Thinking About Elizabeth Cady Stanton* (New York: Farrar, Straus and Giroux, 2005), 87, 90.

74. Cady Stanton et al., *History of Woman Suffrage,* 3: 45–48.

75. Elizabeth Cady Stanton to Matilda Joslyn Gage and the National Woman Suffrage Association, in Gordon, ed., *The Selected Papers,* 3: 309–311, 309.

76. Comte accomplished his goal in his two major works, *Cours de philosophie positive,* 6 vols. (Paris: Bachiel, 1830–1842) and *Système de politique positive,* 4 vols. (Paris: Mathias, Carilian-Goury et Delmont, 1851–1854).

77. Mike Hawkins, *Social Darwinism in European and American Thought, 1860–1945* (Cambridge: Cambridge University Press, 1997), 54.

78. Lewis A. Coser, *Masters of Sociological Thought: Ideas in Historical and Social Context* (New York: Harcourt Brace Jovanovich, 1971), 12.

79. Gordon, ed., *The Selected Papers,* 2: 197.

80. As quoted in William Leach, *True Love and Perfect Union: The Feminist Reform of Sex and Society,* 2nd ed. (Middletown, CT: Wesleyan University Press, 1980), 152.

81. Elizabeth Cady Stanton, "Home Life," in DuBois, *The Elizabeth Cady Stanton–Susan B. Anthony Reader,* 131–138, 137.

82. Ibid., 151, "Maternity," *Revolution,* February 10, 1870.

83. Letter to the 1882 NWSA Convention, September 1, 1882, in Cady Stanton et al., *History of Woman Suffrage,* 3: 181. As quoted in Leach, *True Love and Perfect Union,* 151.

84. Leach, *True Love and Perfect Union,* 154.

85. Gertrude Lenzer, ed., *Auguste Comte and Positivism: The Essential Writings* (New York: Harper, 1975), 383.

86. Stanton and Stanton Blatch, eds., *Elizabeth Cady Stanton As Revealed in Her Letters Diary and Reminiscences,* 2: 198.

87. Newman, *White Women's* Rights, 57.

88. "Reverend Henry Edgar," *Revolution,* June 10, 1869, as quoted in Leach, *True Love and Perfect Union,* 388, note 73.

89. Dickinson Papers, Library of Congress, as quoted in ibid., 388, note 72.

90. *Revolution,* August 13, November 26, December 17, 1868, and May 13, 1869, as quoted in ibid., 148.

91. Elizabeth Cady Stanton, "Why We Need Women as Physicians," Commencement Address to New York Medical College for Women, *Phrenological Journal and Life Illustrated* 52 (May 1871): 347–349, 347.

92. "The True Republic," *Woodhull and Claflin's Weekly,* May 18, 1872, as quoted in Leach, *True Love and Perfect Union,* 148–149.

93. Several others have commented on the influence of Positivism on Cady Stanton. See Leach, who argued that the influence on Cady Stanton was so extensive that she moved "in ideological consciousness from a strong emphasis on individualism in the antebellum period to an attempt after the Civil War to combine individualism with structure, organization, and centralization. In the same breath in which she heralded an age in which both men and women would be 'absolutely free,' she sought to control this freedom and harmonize it with the demands of social order and community" (*True Love and Perfect Union,* 143). Kathi Kern, in *Mrs. Stanton's Bible* (Ithaca, NY: Cornell University Press, 2001), focused on the way Cady Stanton used Positivism in her later work, including *The Woman's Bible* (53–60). See also Lois Banner, *Elizabeth Cady Stanton: A Radical for Women's Rights* (Boston: Little Brown, 1980), 86.

94. Marilley, *Woman* Suffrage, 68; also, Rogers M. Smith, *Civic Ideals: Conflicting Visions of Citizenship in U.S. History* (New Haven, CT: Yale University Press, 1997): "The quarrels over Kansas and the Fifteenth Amendment prompted Stanton, and to a lesser degree Anthony, to set their claims for educated, native-born white women like themselves in opposition to those of immigrants, as well as newly freed blacks and other ethnic outsiders" (315).

95. Stanton and Stanton Blatch, eds., *Elizabeth Cady Stanton As Revealed in Her Letters Diary and Reminiscences,* 131.

NOTES TO CHAPTER 7

1. Ellen Carol DuBois, *Feminism and Suffrage: The Emergence of an Independent Women's Movement in America 1848–1869* (Ithaca, NY: Cornell University Press, 1978), 99.

2. The Fourteenth Amendment provides in relevant part: "All persons born or naturalized in the United States, and subject to the jurisdiction thereof, are citizens of the United States and of the State wherein they reside. No State shall make or enforce any law which shall abridge the privileges or immunities of citizens of the United States."

3. As quoted in Ellen Carol DuBois, *Woman Suffrage and Women's Rights* (New York: New York University Press, 1998), 100.

4. *Minor v. Happersett*, 21 Wall 162 (1875).

5. "National Protection for National Citizens," Speech by Elizabeth Cady Stanton to the Senate Committee on Privileges and Elections, in Ann D. Gordon, ed., *The Selected Papers of Elizabeth Cady Stanton and Susan B. Anthony*, Vol. 3, *National Protection for National Citizens, 1873–1888* (New Brunswick, NJ: Rutgers University Press, 2003), 345–373, 346.

6. Ibid.

7. Ibid., 347.

8. Ibid.

9. Ibid., 348. Article IV, Section 2, reads: "The citizens of each State shall be entitled to all the privileges of citizens in the several states."

10. Ibid., 349. Article VI provides, in relevant part: "This Constitution, and the Laws of the United States, which shall be made in pursuance thereof; . . . shall be the supreme Law of the Land; and the Judges in every state shall be bound thereby, any Thing in the Constitution or Laws of any State to the Contrary notwithstanding."

11. Ibid., 353.

12. See speeches of Elizabeth Harbert and Mrs. Stewart in Elizabeth Cady Stanton, Susan B. Anthony, and Matilda Joslyn Gage, eds., *History of Woman Suffrage*, Vol. 2 (New York: Fowler and Wells, 1881), 73–80, 95–96.

13. Gerald N. Grob, "Reform Unionism: The National Labor Union," *Journal of Economic History* 14 (1954): 126–142.

14. Ellen Carol DuBois, "Of Labor and Free Love: Two Unpublished Speeches of Elizabeth Cady Stanton." *Signs* 1 (1975): 257–268, 259; DuBois, *Feminism and Suffrage*.

15. DuBois, "Of Labor and Free Love," 260, 261.

16. Ibid.

17. Ibid., 262.

18. As quoted in DuBois, *Feminism and Suffrage*, 143.

19. DuBois explained that typesetters were skilled women in a male-dominated trade from which the men initially tried to exclude them and then agreed to support their efforts to organize. Their situation was very different from that of the sewing machine operators, the next group that Anthony tried to organize, who were underpaid and subject to deplorable conditions in a female-only trade. Thus, efforts to organize sewing machine workers and others failed, and

the Working Women's Association was unable to organize any more groups of working women. Ibid., 144.

20. Alma Lutz, *Created Equal: A Biography of Elizabeth Cady Stanton* (New York: The John Day Company, 1940), 162.

21. Cady Stanton, *Revolution*, November 1868, in Ann D. Gordon, ed., *The Selected Papers of Elizabeth Cady Stanton and Susan B. Anthony*, Vol. 2, *Against an Aristocracy of Sex 1866 to 1873* (New Brunswick, NJ: Rutgers University Press, 2000), 191–193,191–192.

22. Ibid., 193, n. 2.

23. Karl Marx and Friedrich Engels, *The Communist Manifesto* (New York: Penguin Classics, 2002; orig., 1848).

24. Elizabeth Cady Stanton, "Proposal to Form a New Party," May 1872, in Ellen Carol DuBois, *The Elizabeth Cady Stanton–Susan B. Anthony Reader: Correspondence, Writings, Speeches* (Boston: Northeastern University Press, 1981), 166–169.

25. As quoted in John C. Spurlock, *Free Love: Marriage and Middle Class Radicalism in America, 1825–1860* (New York: New York University Press, 1988), 121. Andrews explained his views in the New York Tribune in 1852, and when Horace Greeley refused to continue to publish his articles, he published his views in *Love, Marriage, and Divorce and the Sovereignty of the Individual,* in 1853.

26. As quoted in Spurlock, *Free Love,* 126.

27. Ibid. See also Linda Gordon, *Woman's Body, Woman's Right: A Social History of Birth Control in America* (New York: Penguin Books, 1974), 95–115, for a comparison of free-love groups and the woman suffrage movement.

28. Emma Goldman, "Marriage and Love," in *Anarchism and Other Essays* (Mineola, NY: Dover Publications, 1969; orig., 1917), 227–240.

29. Barbara Goldsmith, *Other Powers: The Age of Suffrage, Spiritualism, and the Scandalous Victoria Woodhull* (New York: Knopf, 1998), 207.

30. Ibid., 206.

31. Ibid., 183.

32. Ellen DuBois, "Of Labor and Free Love." The speech was titled "On Marriage and Divorce." DuBois argued that free love provided a source for her ideas during the Reconstruction period, when she was looking for a new theoretical basis for her arguments, and that she privately embraced the philosophy of free love but remained circumspect in public in order to gain more support for women's rights.

33. Elizabeth Cady Stanton, "On Marriage and Divorce" in ibid., 266.

34. Ibid.

35. Ibid., 267.

36. Spurlock, *Free Love,* 210–211. At least Woodhull's arguments resembled the writings of Andrews, as well as those of Benjamin Butler and of her

second husband, Colonel James Blood. Woodhull claimed that Colonel Blood took down her words as she spoke in a trance state two or three evenings a week. See Goldsmith, *Other Powers,* 213–214.

37. As quoted in Spurlock, *Free Love,* 211.

38. As quoted in ibid., 212. Emphasis in original.

39. In 1871, details of Woodhull's unconventional domestic arrangements became public. She was divorced from Colonel Blood but continued to live with him as well as her previous husband, Canning Woodhull. Additional scandals continued to surface. Goldsmith, *Other Powers,* 275–286.

40. Cady Stanton et al., *History of Woman Suffrage,* 2: 516–517, 516.

41. Elizabeth Cady Stanton, "Marriages and Mistresses," *Revolution,* October 15, 1868, 233–234.

42. Elizabeth Cady Stanton, "Does the *Revolution* Believe in Marriage?" *Revolution,* April 8, 1869, 212.

43. Elizabeth Cady Stanton, "Man Marriage," *Revolution,* April 8, 1869, 217–218, 218.

44. Elizabeth Cady Stanton to Elizabeth Smith Miller, August 11, 1875, as quoted in Elisabeth Griffith, *In Her Own Right: The Life of Elizabeth Cady Stanton* (New York: Oxford University Press, 1984), 157.

45. DuBois, *The Elizabeth Cady Stanton–Susan B. Anthony Reader,* 127.

46. Ibid., 56.

47. For background on the Lyceum and an analysis of a lecture, "Our Boys," that Cady Stanton delivered that contained radical arguments, see Lisa S. Hogan and J. Michael Hogan, "Feminine Virtue and Practical Wisdom," *Rhetoric and Public Affairs* 6 (2003): 415–435.

48. September 6, 1883, in Theodore Stanton and Harriot Stanton Blatch, eds., *Elizabeth Cady Stanton As Revealed in Her Letters Diary and Reminiscences,* Vol. 2 (New York: Harper & Brothers, 1922). 210.

49. As quoted in Linda Gordon, 109.

50. "Marriage and Maternity," *Woodhull and Claflin's Weekly,* January 16, 1875, in Patricia G. Holland and Ann Gordon, eds., *The Papers of Elizabeth Cady Stanton and Susan B. Anthony* (Wilmington DE: Scholarly Resources, 1991), Microfilm, Series 3, Roll 18. Emphasis in original.

51. For a detailed, informative, and entertaining discussion of both scandals see Goldsmith, *Other Powers.*

52. As quoted in ibid., 216.

53. Ibid., 217. At the meeting in May 1870, in an attempt to unite the NWSA and the AWSA, Tilton suggested the creation of a Union Society that would absorb all the branches of the old American Equal Rights Association. The effort failed. The NWSA abandoned its woman-only policy when it elected Tilton president.

54. Ibid., 224.

55. Tilton's employer was Henry Bowen, whose wife had confessed on her deathbed that Henry Ward Beecher had seduced her. Bowen, using Tilton to accomplish his own political and personal ends, convinced him to write a letter to Beecher demanding his resignation from the ministry of Plymouth Church. When Bowen realized that his attempt to remove Beecher had failed, he negotiated a financially beneficial agreement with Beecher that included Tilton's dismissal. Ibid., 73, 236–239.

56. Beecher to Frank Moulton, as quoted in ibid., 245. Emphasis in original.

57. Woodhull also tried to blackmail a number of members of the woman suffrage movement. She compiled a set of "slips" detailing their sexual behavior and sent them to the women, demanding an end to the accusations against her and payment to support her presidential campaign. Ibid., 317.

58. Ibid., 290.

59. Ibid., 354.

60. Ibid., 397.

61. Elizabeth Cady Stanton to Susan B. Anthony, July 30, 1874, in Stanton and Stanton Blatch, eds., *Elizabeth Cady Stanton As Revealed in Her Letters Diary and Reminiscences*, 2: 145–146.

62. Goldsmith, *Other Powers*, 403.

63. "Letter from Mrs. Elizabeth Cady Stanton," *Chicago Daily Tribune,* October 1, 1874, in Holland and Gordon, eds., *The Papers of Elizabeth Cady Stanton and Susan B. Anthony,* Microfilm, Series 3, Roll 18. Emphasis in original.

64. Ibid.

65. Goldsmith, *Other Powers*, 412, 416.

66. Ibid.

67. "A Talk with Mrs. Stanton," *Sun,* July 17, 1875, in Holland and Gordon, eds., *The Papers of Elizabeth Cady Stanton and Susan B. Anthony,* Microfilm, Series 3, Roll 18.

68. Ibid.

69. *Newark Sunday Call,* January 2, 1876, in ibid., Microfilm, Series 3, Roll 18.

NOTES TO CHAPTER 8

1. Kathi Kern, *Mrs. Stanton's Bible* (Ithaca, NY: Cornell University Press, 2001), 84.

2. Ibid., 4.

3. Elisabeth Griffith, *In Her Own Right: The Life of Elizabeth Cady Stanton* (New York: Oxford University Press, 1984), 217.

4. Ellen Carol DuBois, ed., *The Elizabeth Cady Stanton–Susan B. Anthony Reader: Correspondence, Writings, Speeches,* rev. ed. (Boston: Northeastern University Press, 1992), 172, 175.

5. International Council of Women, *Women in a Changing World: The Dynamic Story of the International Council of Women Since 1888* (London: Routledge and Kegan Paul, 1966), 11, as quoted in ibid., 177.

6. Elizabeth Cady Stanton, "Address of Welcome to the International Council of Women," March 25, 1888, in DuBois, *The Elizabeth Cady Stanton–Susan B. Anthony Reader,* 210.

7. Ibid., 214.

8. Ibid.

9. Ibid., 212.

10. As quoted in ibid., 177.

11. Ibid., 179.

12. Ibid., 182.

13. Theodore Stanton and Harriot Stanton Blatch, eds., *Elizabeth Cady Stanton as Revealed in Her Letters, Diary and Reminiscences,* Vol. 2 (New York: Harper and Brothers, 1922), 307, as quoted in ibid., 197, note 38.

14. Elizabeth Cady Stanton, "Address to the Founding Convention of the National American Woman Suffrage Association," February 1890, in DuBois, *The Elizabeth Cady Stanton–Susan B. Anthony Reader,* 226.

15. As quoted in Alma Lutz, *Created Equal: A Biography of Elizabeth Cady Stanton, 1815–1902* (New York: The John Day Company, 1940), 316.

16. The women in the NAWSA who supported Cady Stanton included Matilda Joslyn Gage, Clara Colby, and Olympia Brown.

17. Elizabeth Cady Stanton to Lillie Devereux Blake, June 12, 1899, Blake Manuscript, Missouri Historical Society, as quoted in Griffith, *In Her Own Right,* 260.

18. Elizabeth Cady Stanton to Elizabeth Boynton Harbert, June 7, 1900, Elizabeth Boynton Harbert Papers, Huntington Library, as quoted in DuBois, ed., *The Elizabeth Cady Stanton–Susan B. Anthony Reader,* 191.

19. Kern, *Mrs. Stanton's Bible,* 3.

20. Kern provides an extensive and insightful analysis of the way both religion and secularism affected Cady Stanton's thought and the woman's movement at the end of the nineteenth century.

21. Elizabeth Cady Stanton, *Eighty Years and More: Reminiscences, 1815–1897* (Boston: Northeastern University Press, 1993), 44.

22. Ida Husted Harper, *The Life and Work of Susan B. Anthony,* Vol. 2 (Indianapolis: Hollenbeck Press, 1898, 1908), 857, as quoted in Aileen S. Kraditor, *The Ideas of the Woman Suffrage Movement: 1890–1920* (New York: Norton, 1981), 79, note 5.

23. Kern, *Mrs. Stanton's Bible,* 52.

24. Ibid., 70.

25. Ibid., 76.

26. Elizabeth Cady Stanton, "Has Christianity Benefited Woman?" *North American Review* 342 (May 1885): 389–399, 389. She made the same point at the NWSA convention in 1885:

> There is not one which has not made her subject to man. Men may rejoice in them because they make man the head of the woman. I have been traveling over the old world during the last few years and have found new food for thought. What power is it that makes the Hindoo woman burn herself on the funeral pyre of her husband? Her religion. What holds the Turkish woman in the harem? Her religion. By what power do the Mormons perpetuate their system of polygamy? By their religion. Man, of himself, could not do this; but when he declares, "Thus saith the Lord," of course he can do it.

Elizabeth Cady Stanton, Susan B. Anthony, and Matilda Joslyn Gage, eds., *History of Woman Suffrage*, Vol. 4 (New York: Fowler and Wells, 1881), 60.

27. Cady Stanton, "Has Christianity Benefited Woman?" 389.

28. Ibid., 396. She made the same point earlier in a speech she delivered in 1881. Address of Elizabeth Cady Stanton to the Free Religious Association, Boston, in Ann G. Gordon, ed., *The Selected Papers of Elizabeth Cady Stanton and Susan B. Anthony*, Vol. 4, *When Clowns Make Laws for Queens, 1880–1887* (New Brunswick, NJ: Rutgers University Press, 2006), 72–89.

29. Cady Stanton, "Has Christianity Benefited Woman?" 397.

30. Ibid.

31. Ibid., 399.

32. Ibid., 396.

33. Ibid.

34. Address of Elizabeth Cady Stanton to the Free Religious Association, Boston, in Gordon, ed., *The Selected Papers*, 4: 75. Emphasis in original.

35. Elizabeth Cady Stanton, *The Woman's Bible* (Boston: Northeastern University Press, 1993), Part II, 8.

36. Cady Stanton, *Eighty Years and More*, 396.

37. Kraditor, *Ideas of the Woman Suffrage* Movement, 86.

38. Cady Stanton, *The Woman's Bible*, Part II, 8.

39. Ibid.

40. Kraditor, *Ideas of the Woman Suffrage* Movement, 82.

41. Cady Stanton, *The Woman's Bible*, Part I, 20.

42. Ibid., Part I, 20, 21.

43. Ibid., Part I, 20.

44. Ibid., Part I, 34.

45. Ibid., Part I, 66.

46. As quoted in ibid., Part II, 159.

47. Ibid. The suffragist Ida Porter-Boyer, in 1914, disposed of Paul's injunction more decisively when she said, "Paul never possessed the democratic spirit of Christ." "The Scriptural Authority for Woman's Equality," *Woman's Journal,* April 18, 1914, s quoted in Kraditor, *Ideas of the Woman Suffrage* Movement, 90.

48. Cady Stanton, *The Woman's Bible,* Part I, 21.

49. Ibid., Part I, 63.

50. Ibid., Part I, 63–64.

51. Ibid., Part I, 74.

52. Ibid., Part I, 10.

53. Ibid., Part I, 60.

54. Ibid., Part I, 71.

55. Ibid., Part I, 73.

56. Griffith, *In Her Own Right,* 212.

57. Ibid.

58. Cady Stanton, "Has Christianity Benefited Woman?" 396.

59. Cady Stanton, *The Woman's Bible,* Part I, 126.

NOTES TO CHAPTER 9

1. See also Louise Michele Newman, *White Women's Rights: The Racial Origins of Feminism in the United States* (New York: Oxford University Press, 1999).

2. Mike Hawkins, *Social Darwinism in European and American Thought, 1860–1945: Nature as Model and Nature as Threat* (Cambridge: Cambridge University Press, 1997), 53.

3. Cady Stanton's diary entry for November 25, 1882, reads, in part:, "I have dipped into Darwin's *Descent of Man* and Spencer's *First Principles,* which have cleared up many of my ideas on theology and left me more than ever reconciled to rest with many debatable ideas relegated to the unknown." Theodore Stanton and Harriot Stanton Blatch, eds., *Elizabeth Cady Stanton as Revealed in Her Letters, Diary and Reminiscences,* Vol. 2 (New York: Harper and Brothers, 1922), 198.

4. Stanton and Stanton Blatch, eds., *Elizabeth Cady Stanton as Revealed in Her Letters, Diary and Reminiscences,* 2: 113.

5. Rogers M. Smith, *Civic Ideals: Conflicting Visions of Citizenship in U.S. History* (New Haven, CT: Yale University Press, 1997), 349.

6. The first American edition was published in 1860. Richard Hofstadter, *Social Darwinism in American Thought,* rev. ed. (Boston.: Beacon Press, 1955), 34.

7. Ibid., 36.

8. See ibid., 37–38.

9. Spencer's earliest work was not published in the United States until the 1860s. Hofstadter, *Social Darwinism,* 34.

10. As quoted in Robert C. Bannister, *Social Darwinism: Science and Myth in Anglo-American Social Thought* (Philadelphia: Temple University Press, 1979), 42.

11. As quoted in Carl N. Degler, *In Search of Human Nature: The Decline and Revival of Darwinism in American Social Thought* (New York: Oxford University Press, 1991), 11.

12. As quoted in Bannister, *Social Darwinism,* 54.

13. Hofstadter, *Social Darwinism,* 6.

14. William Graham Sumner, *What Social Classes Owe to Each Other* (Caldwell, ID: Caxton Printers, 1986), 98.

15. Ibid., 111.

16. Ibid., 145.

17. Ibid.

18. William Graham Sumner, *The Challenge of Facts and Other Essays,* as quoted in Mason Drukman, *Community and Purpose in America: An Analysis of American Political Theory* (New York: McGraw-Hill, 1971), 202.

19. Sumner, *What Social Classes Owe to Each Other,* 57.

20. Who qualified as members of this elite group? Clearly, those who were descended from northern Europeans and the British were included. Beyond that, it was never clear. As Eric Goldman explained, the definition of "Anglo-Saxon" was always conveniently vague: "Usually it meant an American from Western Europe or from anywhere long enough ago unless it was Africa." Goldman, *Rendevous with Destiny: A History of Modern American Reform* (Chicago: Ivan R. Dee, 2001; orig., 1953), 69. The category was also readily adaptable to a changing political climate. In New England, in the 1870s, native-born Americans blamed the Irish, French Canadians, Germans, and Scandinavians for what they perceived as the deterioration of American society and politics. By the 1890s, however, those groups were said to be closely associated with Anglo-Saxons, while newer immigrants from eastern and southern Europe were identified as posing the gravest threat to American civilization.

21. *Congressional Record,* 54th Cong. 1st Session (1896), 2817–2820, 2819.

22. Ibid., 2820. Although both houses of Congress approved the literacy bill, President Grover Cleveland vetoed it in 1897.

23. Charles Darwin, *The Descent of Man, and Selection in Relation to Sex,* Vol. 1 (Princeton, NJ: Princeton University Press, 1981; orig. 1871), 168 .

24. Victoria C. Woodhull, *The Origin, Tendencies and Principles of Government* (New York: Woodhull, Claflin, 1871), 48. As quoted in Hawkins, *Social Darwinism,* 105.

25. Victoria C. Woodhull, *Humanitarian Government* (London: no pub., 1890), 49, as quoted in ibid., 243.

26. Stanton and Stanton Blatch, eds., *Elizabeth Cady Stanton as Revealed in Her Letters, Diary and Reminiscences,* 2: 200.

27. As quoted in Degler, *In Search of Human Nature,* 107.

28. As quoted in ibid., 27.

29. Susan E. Marshall, *Splintered Sisterhood: Gender and Class in the Campaign Against Women Suffrage* (Madison: University of Wisconsin Press, 1997), 88.

30. Charlotte Perkins Gilman, *Women and Economics,* in *The Yellow Wallpaper and Other Writings by Charlotte Perkins Gilman* (New York: Bantam Books, 1989), 159.

31. A number of scholars have recognized that the growth of ascriptive ideas in the United States influenced the arguments that the suffragists in general used to advance their cause. For example, Aileen S. Kraditor, *The Ideas of the Woman Suffrage Movement: 1890–1920* (New York: Norton, 1981); Suzanne M. Marilley, *Woman Suffrage and the Origins of Liberal Feminism in the United States, 1820–1920* (Cambridge, MA: Harvard University Press, 1996); Judith N. Shklar, *American Citizenship: The Quest for Inclusion* (Cambridge, MA: Harvard University Press, 1991).

32. Ellen Carol DuBois, ed., *The Elizabeth Cady Stanton–Susan B. Anthony Reader: Correspondence, Writings, Speeches,* rev. ed. (Boston: Northeastern University Press, 1992), 222.

33. Manuscript letter, Susan B. Anthony Papers, University of Rochester, as quoted in ibid., 197–198, note 38.

34. Lois W. Banner, *Elizabeth Cady Stanton: A Radical for Woman's Rights* (New York: Harper Collins, 1980), 167–168.

35. DuBois, *The Elizabeth Cady Stanton–Susan B. Anthony Reader,* 226.

36. Ibid., 227.

37. Marilley, *Woman Suffrage,* 187.

38. Elizabeth Cady Stanton, "Self-Government the Best Means of Self-Development," in Elizabeth Cady Stanton, Susan B. Anthony, and Matilda Joslyn Gage, eds., *History of Woman Suffrage,* Vol. 4 (New York: Fowler and Wells, 1881), 41.

39. Ibid.

40. Ibid., 41.

41. Ibid., 42.

42. Ibid., 138.

43. Elizabeth Cady Stanton, "The Degradation of Disfranchisement," in ibid., 177.

44. Ibid., 269.

45. Ibid.

46. Ibid.

47. Kraditor, *The Ideas of the Woman Suffrage Movement,* 130.

48. Cady Stanton et al., *History of Woman Suffrage,* 4: 316.

49. Ibid., 317.

50. Ibid.

51. Stanton and Stanton Blatch, eds., *Elizabeth Cady Stanton As Revealed in Her Letters Diary and Reminiscences,* 2: 310.

52. Cady Stanton et al., *History of Woman Suffrage,* 4: 317.

53. Kraditor, *The Ideas of the Woman Suffrage Movement,* 133.

54. Ibid., 133–134.

55. DuBois, *The Elizabeth Cady Stanton–Susan B. Anthony Reader,* 210.

56. Cady Stanton et al., *History of Woman Suffrage,* 4: 61.

57. DuBois, *The Elizabeth Cady Stanton–Susan B. Anthony Reader,* 55.

58. Ibid., 55–56.

59. Elizabeth Cady Stanton, "Maternity," *Revolution,* February 10, 1870.

60. Stanton and Stanton Blatch, eds., *Elizabeth Cady Stanton As Revealed in Her Letters Diary and Reminiscences,* 2: 156.

61. DuBois, *The Elizabeth Cady Stanton–Susan B. Anthony Reader,* 138.

62. Cady Stanton et al., *History of Woman Suffrage,* 3: 245.

63. Ibid., 4: 292.

64. Elizabeth Cady Stanton, "Heredity," *Free Thought Magazine* 19 (September 1901), 495–510, 501.

65. Ibid., 504.

66. It was to be her last appearance before the organization. Her speech was also delivered in written form to the House Committee on the Judiciary and to the Senate Committee on Woman Suffrage.

67. DuBois, *The Elizabeth Cady Stanton–Susan B. Anthony Reader,* 247.

68. Ibid.

69. Ibid., 247–248.

70. Ibid., 251–252.

71. Ibid., 249.

72. Ibid., 252.

73. Kraditor, *The Ideas of the Woman Suffrage Movement,* 101.

74. Cady Stanton et al., *History of Woman Suffrage,* 4: 61.

75. DuBois, *The Elizabeth Cady Stanton–Susan B. Anthony Reader,* 212.

NOTES TO CHAPTER 10

1. Hendrik Hartog, *Man and Wife in America: A History* (Cambridge, MA: Harvard University Press, 2000), 212–217, 290–291.

2. The Nineteenth Amendment, which prohibited denial of the vote on the basis of sex, was ratified in 1920.

3. Cady Stanton to Susan B. Anthony, June 14, 1860, in Theodore Stanton and Harriot Stanton Blatch, eds., *Elizabeth Cady Stanton, As Revealed in Her*

Letters, Diary, and Reminiscences, Vol. 2 (New York: Harper and Brothers, 1922), 82–83, 82.

4. Rogers M. Smith, "Beyond Tocqueville, Myrdal, and Hartz: The Multiple Traditions in America," *American Political Science Review* 87 (1993): 549–566, 558.

5. "Divorce," *The Lily,* April 1850, in Ann D. Gordon, ed., *The Selected Papers of Elizabeth Cady Stanton and Susan B. Anthony,* Vol. 1: *In the School of Anti-Slavery, 1840–1866* (New Brunswick, NJ: Rutgers University Press, 1997), 162.

6. See, for example, Sue Davis, *American Political Thought: Four Hundred Years of Ideas and Ideologies* (Englewood Cliffs, NJ: Prentice-Hall, 1996); Robert Isaak, *American Political Thinking: Readings from the Origins to the 21st Century* (Fort Worth, TX: Harcourt Brace, 1994).

7. Ellen Carol DuBois, *Woman Suffrage and Women's Rights* (New York: New York University Press, 1998), 171.

Bibliography

SECONDARY SOURCES

Bailyn, Bernard. *The Ideological Origins of the American Revolution.* Cambridge, MA: Belknap Press, 1967.

Baker, Paula. "The Domestication of Politics: Women and American Political Society, 1780–1920." *American Historical Review* 89 (1984): 620–647.

Banner, Lois W. *Elizabeth Cady Stanton: A Radical for Woman's Rights.* Boston: Little, Brown, 1980. Reissued by Addison-Wesley, 1998.

Bannister, Robert C. *Social Darwinism: Science and Myth in Anglo-American Social Thought.* Philadelphia: Temple University Press, 1979.

Barry, Kathleen. *Susan B. Anthony: A Biography of a Singular Feminism.* New York: New York University Press, 1988.

Bartlett, Elizabeth Ann. *Liberty, Equality and Sorority: The Origins and Interpretation of American Feminist Thought: Frances Wright, Sarah Grimké, and Margaret Fuller.* Brooklyn, NY: Carlson, 1994.

Basch, Norma. *Framing American Divorce: From the Revolutionary Generation to the Victorians.* Berkeley: University of California Press, 1999.

Basch, Norma. *In the Eyes of the Law: Women, Marriage, and Property in Nineteenth-Century New York.* Ithaca, NY: Cornell University Press, 1982.

Berg, Barbara J. *The Remembered Gate: Origins of American Feminism: The Woman and the City, 1800–1860.* New York: Oxford University Press, 1978.

Boller, Paul F. Jr., *American Thought in Transition: The Impact of Evolutionary Naturalism, 1865–1900.* Chicago: Rand McNally, 1969.

Bordin, Ruth. *Woman and Temperance: The Quest for Power and Liberty, 1873–1900.* New Brunswick, NJ: Rutgers University Press, 1990.

Boylan, Ann M. "Woman and Politics in the Era Before Seneca Falls." *Journal of the Early Republic* 10 (1990): 363–382.

Bryson, Valerie. *Feminist Political Theory: An Introduction.* New York: Paragon House, 1992,

Buechler, Steven M. *The Transformation of the Woman Suffrage Movement: The Case of Illinois, 1850–1920.* New Brunswick, NJ: Rutgers University Press, 1986.

Buhle, Mari Jo. "Politics and Culture in Women's History: A Symposium." *Feminist Studies* 6 (Spring 1980): 37–42.

Chused, Richard H. "Married Women's Property Law: 1800–1850." In Kermit L Hall, ed., *Women, the Law, and the Constitution*. New York: Garland, 1987.

Clark, Elizabeth. "Matrimonial Bonds: Slavery and Divorce in Nineteenth Century America." *Law and History Review* 8 (1990): 25–54.

Clinton, Catherine. *The Other Civil War: American Women in the Nineteenth Century*. New York: Hill and Wang, 1984.

Cole, Phyllis. "Stanton, Fuller, and the Grammar of Romanticism." *The New England Quarterly* 73 (2000): 553–559.

Cott, Nancy F. "Feminist Theory and Feminist Movements: The Past Before Us." In Juliet Mitchell and Ann Oakley, eds., *What Is Feminism?* New York: Pantheon Books, 1986, 49–62.

Cott, Nancy F. *Public Vows: A History of Marriage and the Nation*. Cambridge, MA: Harvard University Press, 2000.

Cott, Nancy F. *The Bonds of Womanhood: "Woman's Sphere" in New England, 1780–1835*, 2nd ed. New Haven, CT: Yale University Press, 1997.

Cott, Nancy F. *The Grounding of Modern Feminism*. New Haven, CT: Yale University Press, 1987.

Davis, Sue. *American Political Thought: Four Hundred Years of Ideas and Ideologies*. Englewood Cliffs, NJ: Prentice-Hall, 1996.

Degler, Carl N. *At Odds: Women and the Family in America from the Revolution to the Present*. New York: Oxford University Press, 1980.

Degler, Carl N. *In Search of Human Nature: The Decline and Revival of Darwinism in American Social Thought*. New York: Oxford University Press, 1991.

Dillon, Merton L. *The Abolitionists: The Growth of a Dissenting Minority*. New York: Norton, 1979.

Donovan, Josephine. *Feminist Theory: The Intellectual Traditions of American Feminism*. New York: Continuum, 1985.

Drukman, Mason. *Community and Purpose in America: An Analysis of American Political Theory*. New York: McGraw-Hill, 1971.

DuBois, Ellen Carol. "Comment on Karen Offen's 'Defining Feminism: A Comparative Historical Approach.'" *Signs* 15 (Autumn 1989): 195–197.

DuBois, Ellen Carol. *Feminism and Suffrage: The Emergence of an Independent Women's Movement in America 1848–1869*. Ithaca, NY: Cornell University Press, 1978.

DuBois, Ellen Carol. "Of Labor and Free Love: Two Unpublished Speeches of Elizabeth Cady Stanton." *Signs* 1 (1975): 257–268.

DuBois, Ellen Carol. "The Limitations of Sisterhood: Elizabeth Cady Stanton and Division in the American Suffrage Movement, 1875–1902," in Barbara

J. Harris and JoAnn K. McNamara, eds., *Women and the Structure of Society: Selected Research from the Fifth Berkshire Conference on the History of Women.* Durham, NC: Duke Press Policy Studies, 1984, 160–169.

DuBois, Ellen Carol. *Woman Suffrage and Women's Rights.* New York: New York University Press, 1998.

DuBois, Ellen Carol, Mari Jo Buhle, Temma Kaplan, Gerda Lerner, and Carroll Smith-Rosenberg, "Politics and Culture in Women's History: A Symposium." *Feminist Studies* 6 (1980): 26–63.

Dudden, Faye. "New York Strategy: The New York Woman's Movement and the Civil War." In Jean H. Baker, ed., *Votes for Women: The Struggle for Suffrage Revisited.* New York: Oxford University Press, 2000, 56–76.

Eisenstein, Zillah R. *The Radical Future of Liberal Feminism.* Boston: Northeastern University Press, 1986.

Elshtain, Jean Bethke. "The Liberal Captivity of Feminism: A Critical Appraisal of (Some) Feminist Answers." In Philip Abbott and Michael B. Levy, eds., *The Liberal Future in America: Essays in Renewal.* Westport, CT: Greenwood Press, 1985, 63–84.

Emerson, Ralph Waldo. *Essays and Lectures.* New York: The Library of America, 1983.

Epstein, Barbara Leslie. *The Politics of Domesticity: Women, Evangelism and Temperance in Nineteenth-Century America.* Middletown, CT: Wesleyan University Press, 1981

Evans, Richard J. *The Feminists: Women's Emancipation Movements in Europe, America and Australasia 1848–1920.* New York: Barnes and Noble, 1977.

Farber, Daniel A., and Suzanna Sherry. *A History of the American Constitution.* St. Paul, MN: West, 1990.

Fineman, Martha Albertson. *The Neutered Mother, The Sexual Family, and Other Twentieth Century Tragedies.* New York: Routledge, 1995.

Fitzgerald, Maureen "The Religious Is Personal Is Political: Foreword to the 1993 Edition of *The Woman's Bible.*" In Elizabeth Cady Stanton, *The Woman's Bible.* Boston: Northeastern University Press, 1993, vii–xxxiv.

Flexner, Eleanor. *Century of Struggle: The Woman's Rights Movement in the United States.* Cambridge, MA: Harvard University Press, 1959.

Foner, Eric. *The Story of American Freedom.* New York: Norton, 1998.

Fredrickson, George M., ed. *William Lloyd Garrison.* Englewood Cliffs, NJ: Prentice-Hall, 1968.

Ginzburg, Lori D. *Women and the Work of Benevolence: Morality, Politics, and Class in the Nineteenth-Century United States.* New Haven, CT: Yale University Press, 1990.

Goldman, Eric F. *Rendezvous with Destiny: A History of Modern American Reform.* Chicago: Ivan R. Dee, 2001; orig., 1953.

Goldsmith, Barbara. *Other Powers: The Age of Suffrage, Spiritualism, and the Scandalous Victoria Woodhull.* New York: Knopf, 1998.

Gordon, Ann D. *African American Women and the Vote, 1837–1965.* Amherst: University of Massachusetts Press, 1997.

Gordon, Linda. *Woman;s Body, Woman's Right: A Social History of Birth Control in America.* New York: Penguin Books, 1974.

Gornick, Vivian. *The Solitude of Self: Thinking about Elizabeth Cady Stanton.* New York: Ferrar, Straus and Giroux, 2005.

Graham, Sara Hunter. *Woman Suffrage and the New Democracy.* New Haven, CT: Yale University Press, 1996.

Greenstone, J. David. *The Lincoln Persuasion: Remaking American Liberalism.* Princeton, NJ: Princeton University Press, 1993,

Griffith, Elisabeth. *In Her Own Right: The Life of Elizabeth Cady Stanton.* New York: Oxford University Press, 1985.

Grob, Gerald N. "Reform Unionism: The National Labor Union." *Journal of Economic History* 14 (1954): 126–142.

Gurko, Miriam. *The Ladies of Seneca Falls: The Birth of the Woman's Rights Movement.* New York: Schocken, 1976.

Haller, John S. *Outcasts from Evolution: Scientific Attitudes of Racial Inferiority, 1859–1900.* Urbana: University of Illinois Press, 1971.

Handy, Robert T. *A Christian America: Protestant Hopes and Historical Realities.* 2nd ed. New York: Oxford University Press, 1984.

Hartog, Hendrik. *Man and Wife in America: A History.* Cambridge, MA: Harvard University Press, 2000.

Hartz, Louis. *The Liberal Tradition in America: An Interpretation of American Political Thought Since the Revolution.* New York: Harcourt, Brace, Jovanovich, 1955.

Hawkins, Mike. *Social Darwinism in European and American Thought, 1860–1945: Nature as Model and Nature as Threat.* Cambridge: Cambridge University Press, 1997.

Haynes, Carolyn A. *Divine Destiny: Gender and Race in Nineteenth-Century Protestantism.* Jackson: University Press of Mississippi, 1998.

Hersh, Blanche Glassman. *The Slavery of Sex: Feminist-Abolitionists in America.* Urbana: University of Illinois Press, 1978.

Himmelfarb, Gertrude. *Darwin and the Darwinian Revolution.* New York: Norton, 1959.

Hoffert, Sylvia D. *When Hens Crow: The Woman's Rights Movement in Antebellum America.* Bloomington: Indiana University Press, 1995.

Hofstadter, Richard. *The American Political Tradition.* New York: Knopf, 1973; orig., 1948.

Hogan, Lisa S., and J. Michael Hogan. "Feminine Virtue and Practical Wisdom." *Rhetoric and Public Affairs* 6 (2003): 415–435.

Hurlbut, Elisha Powell. *Essays on Human Rights, and Their Political Guaranties.* Edinburgh: Maclachlan, Stewart & Co., 1847.

Isaak, Robert. *American Political Thinking: Readings from the Origins to the 21st Century.* Fort Worth, TX: Harcourt, Brace, 1994.

Isenberg, Nancy. *Sex and Citizenship in Antebellum America.* Chapel Hill: University of North Carolina Press, 1998.

Jaggar, Alison M. *Feminist Politics and Human Nature.* Totowa, NJ: Rowman and Allanheld, 1983.

Kerber, Linda K "From the Declaration of Independence to the Declaration of Sentiments: The Legal Status of Women in the Early Republic, 1776–1848." *Human Rights* 6 (1977): 115–125.

Kerber, Linda K. *No Constitutional Right to Be Ladies: Women and the Obligations of Citizenship.* New York: Hill and Wang, 1998.

Kerber, Linda K. *Women of the Republic: Intellect and Ideology in Revolutionary America.* New York: Norton, 1986.

Kern, Kathi. *Mrs. Stanton's Bible.* Ithaca, NY: Cornell University Press, 2001.

Kern, Kathi L. "Rereading Eve: Elizabeth Cady Stanton and the 'Woman's Bible.'" *Women's Studies* 19 (1990): 381–383.

Kraditor, Aileen S. *Means and Ends in American Abolitionism: Garrison and His Critics on Strategy and Tactics, 1834–1850.* New York: Vintage Books, 1967, 39–77.

Kraditor, Aileen S. *The Ideas of the Woman Suffrage Movement, 1890–1920.* New York: Norton, 1981.

Leach, William. *True Love and Perfect Union: The Feminist Reform of Sex and Society.* 2nd ed. Middletown, CT: Wesleyan University Press, 1989.

Lerner, Gerda. "The Lady and the Mill Girl: Changes in the Status of Women in the Age of Jackson." In Gerda Lerner, ed., *The Majority Finds Its Past: Placing Women in History.* New York: Oxford University Press, 1979, 15–30.

Loeffelholz, Mary. "Posing the Woman Citizen: The Contradictions of Stanton's Feminism." *Genders* 7 (1990): 87–97.

Lutz, Alma. *Created Equal: A Biography of Elizabeth Cady Stanton, 1815–1902.* New York: The John Day Company, 1940.

MacKinnon, Catharine A. *Feminism Unmodified: Discourses on Life and Law.* Cambridge, MA: Harvard University Press, 1987.

Marilley, Suzanne M. *Woman Suffrage and the Origins of Liberal Feminism in the United States, 1820–1920.* Cambridge, MA: Harvard University Press, 1996.

Marshall, Susan E. *Splintered Sisterhood: Gender and Class in the Campaign Against Woman Suffrage.* Madison: University of Wisconsin Press, 1997.

Matthews, Jean V. "Consciousness of Self and Consciousness of Sex in Antebellum Feminism." *Journal of Women's History* 5 (1993): 61–78.

Matthews, Jean V. *Women's Struggle for Equality: The First Phase, 1828–1876.* Chicago: Ivan R. Dee, 1997.

McPherson, James M. *The Struggle for Equality: Abolitionists and the Negro in the Civil War and Reconstruction.* Princeton, NJ: Princeton University Press, 1964.

Melder, Keith E. *Beginnings of Sisterhood: The American Woman's Rights Movement, 1800–1850.* New York: Schocken Books, 1977.

Miller, Perry. *The Life of the Mind in America: From the Revolution to the Civil War.* New York: Harcourt, Brace & World, 1965.

Murray, Judith Sargent. *The Gleaner.* Schenectady, NY: Union College Press, 1992; orig., 1792.

Newman, Michele Louise. *White Women's Rights: The Racial Origins of Feminism in the United States.* New York: Oxford University Press, 1999.

Nichols, Carole. "Votes and More for Women: Suffrage and After in Connecticut." *Women and History* 5 (Spring 1983): 29–30.

Norton, Mary Beth. *Liberty's Daughters: The Revolutionary Experience of American Women, 1750–1800.* Boston: Little, Brown, 1980.

Norton, Mary Beth. "The Evolution of White Women's Experience in Early America." *American Historical Review* 89 (1984): 593–619.

Oakley, Mary Ann B. *Elizabeth Cady Stanton.* Old Westbury, NY: Feminist Press, 1972.

Offen, Karen. "Defining Feminism: A Comparative Historical Approach." In Gisela Bock and Susan James, eds., *Beyond Equality and Difference: Citizenship, Feminist Politics and Female Subjectivity.* New York: Routledge, 1992, 69–88,.

Offen, Karen. "Reply to DuBois." *Signs* 15 (1989): 198–202.

Parker, Allison M. "The Case for Reform Antecedents for the Woman's Rights Movement." In Jean H. Baker, ed., *Votes for Women: The Struggle for Suffrage Revisited.* New York: Oxford University Press, 2000, 21–41.

Pateman, Carole, "Equality, Difference, Subordination: The Politics of Motherhood and Women's Citizenship." In Gisela Bock and Susan James, eds., *Beyond Equality and Difference: Citizenship, Feminist Politics and Female Subjectivity.* New York: Routledge, 1992, 17–31.

Pateman, Carole. *The Sexual Contract.* Stanford, CA: Stanford University Press, 1988.

Peterson, Merrill D., ed. *The Portable Thomas Jefferson.* New York: Penguin Books, 1977.

Pocock, J. G. A. *The Machiavellian Moment: Florentine Political Thought and the Atlantic Republican Tradition.* Princeton, NJ: Princeton University Press, 1975.

Pollitt, Katha. "Are Women Morally Superior to Men?" *The Nation,* December 28, 1992, 799–805.

Riley, Glenda. *Divorce: An American Tradition*. New York: Oxford University Press, 1991.

Rorabaugh, W. J. *The Alcoholic Republic: An American Tradition*. New York: Oxford University Press, 1979.

Russett, Cynthia Eagle. *Sexual Science: The Victorian Construction of Womanhood*. Cambridge, MA: Harvard University Press, 1989.

Ryan, Mary P. *Womanhood in America: From Colonial Times to the Present*. 3rd ed. New York: Franklin Watts, 1983.

Ryan, Mary P. *Women in Public: Between Banners and Ballots, 1825–1880*. Baltimore, MD: Johns Hopkins University Press, 1990.

Scott, Joan W. "Deconstructing Equality-Versus-Difference: Or, the Uses of Poststructuralist Theory for Feminism." *Feminist Studies* 14 (1) (1988): 33–50.

Scott, Joan Wallach. *Only Paradoxes to Offer: French Feminist and the Rights of Man*. Camabridge, MA: Harvard University Press, 1996.

Shklar, Judith N. *American Citizenship: The Quest for Inclusion*. Cambridge, MA: Harvard University Press, 1991.

Sklar, Kathryn Kish. *Catharine Beecher: A Study in American Domesticit*. New York: Norton, 1976.

Smith, Daniel Scott. "Family Limitation, Sexual Control, and Domestic Feminism in Victorian America." In Mary Hartman and Lois W. Banner, eds., *Clio's Consciousness Raised: New Perspectives on the History of Women*. New York: Harper Torchbooks, 1974, 119–136.

Smith, Rogers M. "Beyond Tocqueville, Myrdal, and Hartz: The Multiple Traditions in America," *American Political Science Review* 87 (1993), 549–566.

Smith, Rogers M. *Civic Ideals: Conflicting Visions of Citizenship in U.S. History*. New Haven, CT: Yale University Press, 1997.

Smith, Rogers M. "If Politics Matters: Implications for a 'New Institutionalism.'" *Studies in American Political Development* 6 (1992): 1–36.

Smith, Rogers M. "'One United People': Second-Class Female Citizenship and the American Quest for Community." *Yale Journal of Law and the Humanities* 1 (1989): 229–293.

Smith, Rogers M. "The 'American Creed' and American Identity: The Limits of Liberal Citizenship in the United States." *Western Political Quarterly* 41 (1988): 225–251.

Smith-Rosenberg, Carroll. "Beauty, the Beast, and the Militant Woman: A Case Study in Sex Roles and Social Stress in Jacksonian America." In Carroll Smith-Rosenberg, ed., *Disorderly Conduct: Visions of Gender in Victorian America*. New York: Oxford University Press, 1985, 109–128.

Smith-Rosenberg, Carroll. Reply to Ellen Carol DuBois, in "Politics and Culture in Women's History: A Symposium," *Feminist Studies* 6 (1980): 55–64.

Spurlock, John C. *Free Love: Marriage and Middle-Class Radicalism in America, 1825–1860*. New York: New York University Press, 1988.

Terborg-Penn, Rosalyn. *African American Women in the Struggle for the Vote, 1850–1920*. Bloomington: Indiana University Press, 1998.

Tyrrell, Ian R. *Sobering Up: From Temperance to Prohibition in Antebellum America, 1800–1860*. Westport, CT: Greenwood Press, 1979.

Venet, Wendy Hamand. *Neither Ballots nor Bullets: Women Abolitionists and the Civil War*. Charlottesville: University Press of Virginia, 1991.

Warbasse, Elizabeth Bowles. *The Changing Legal Rights of Married Women: 1800–1861*. New York: Garland, 1987.

Welter, Barbara. "The Cult of True Womanhood: 1820–1860." *American Quarterly* 18 (1966): 151–174.

Wheeler, Marjorie Spruill. *New Women of the New South: The Leaders of the Woman Suffrage Movement in the Southern States*. New York: Oxford University Press, 1993.

Wheeler, Marjorie Spruill. *Votes for Women! The Woman Suffrage Movement in Tennessee, the South, and the Nation*. Knoxville: University of Tennessee Press, 1995.

Williams, Joan C. "Deconstructing Gender." *Michigan Law Review* 87 (1989): 797–845.

Wilson, Joan Hoff. "The Illusion of Change: Women and the American Revolution." In Jean E. Friedman, William G. Shade, and Mary Jane Capozzoli, eds., *Our American Sisters: Women in Life and Thought*. 4th ed. Lexington, MA: D. C. Heath, 1987, 76–95.

Woloch, Nancy. *Women and the American Experience*. New York: Knopf, 1984.

Wood, Gordon W. *The Creation of the American Republic, 1776–1787*. Chapel Hill: University of North Carolina Press, 1969.

Wright, Frances. "Education," and "Of Free Inquiry." In Alice S. Rossi, ed., *The Feminist Papers: From Adams to de Beauvoir*. New York: Bantam Books, 1973, 100–117.

Young, James P. *Reconsidering American Liberalism: The Troubled Odyssey of the Liberal Idea*. Boulder, CO: Westview Press, 1996.

PRIMARY SOURCES

Darwin, Charles. *The Descent of Man, and Selection in Relation to Sex*. Princeton, NJ: Princeton University Press, 1981; orig., 1871.

Darwin, Charles. *The Origin of Species*. New York: Signet Classics, 2003; orig., 1859.

de Tocqueville, Alexis. *Democracy in America*, ed. J. P. Mayer. New York: Harper and Row, 1969; orig., 1840.

DuBois, Ellen Carol, ed. *The Elizabeth Cady Stanton-Susan B. Anthony Reader: Correspondence, Writings, Speeches*, rev. ed. Boston: Northeastern University Press, 1992.

Fuller, Margaret. *Woman in the Nineteenth Century.* In Mason Wade, ed., *The Writings of Margaret Fuller.* New York: Viking Press, 1941, 124.

Gilman, Charlotte Perkins. *Women and Economics.* In *The Yellow Wallpaper and Other Writings by Charlotte Perkins Gilman.* New York: Bantam Books, 1989.

Goldman, Emma. *Anarchism and Other Essays.* Mineola, NY: Dover, 1969; orig., 1917.

Gordon, Ann D., ed. *The Selected Papers of Elizabeth Cady Stanton and Susan B. Anthony,* vol. 1: *In the School of Anti-Slavery, 1840–1866.* New Brunswick, NJ: Rutgers University Press, 1997.

Gordon, Ann D., ed. *The Selected Papers of Elizabeth Cady Stanton and Susan B. Anthony,* vol. 2: *Against An Aristocracy of Sex, 1866 to 1873.* New Brunswick, NJ: Rutgers University Press, 2000.

Gordon, Ann D., ed. *The Selected Papers of Elizabeth Cady Stanton and Susan B. Anthony,* vol. 3: *National Protection for National Citizens, 1873–1880.* New Brunswick, NJ: Rutgers University Press, 2003.

Gordon, Ann D, ed. *The Selected Papers of Elizabeth Cady Stanton and Susan B. Anthony,* vol. 4: *When Clown Make Laws for Queens, 1880–1887.* New Brunswick, NJ: Rutgers University Press, 2006.

Holland, Patricia G., and Ann Gordon, eds. *The Papers of Elizabeth Cady Stanton and Susan B. Anthony.* Wilmington DE: Scholarly Resources, 1991.

Jefferson, Thomas. *Notes on the State of Virginia.* From *The Writings of Thomas Jefferson,* vol. 2, Electronic Text Center, University of Virginia Library, available at http://etext.lib.virginia.edu/etcbin/toccer-new2?id=JefBvo21.sgm&images=images/modeng&data=/texts/english/modeng/parsed&tag=public&part=14&division=div2.

Stanton, Elizabeth Cady. *Eighty Years and More: Reminiscences 1815–1897.* Boston: Northeastern University Press, 1993; orig., 1898.

Stanton, Elizabeth Cady. *The Woman's Bible.* Boston: Northeastern University Press, 1993; orig., 1895.

Stanton, Elizabeth Cady, Susan B. Anthony, and Matilda Joslyn Gage, eds. *History of Woman Suffrage.* 6 vols. New York: Fowler and Wells, 1881–1922.

Stanton, Theodore, and Harriot Stanton Blatch, eds. *Elizabeth Cady Stanton As Revealed in Her Letters Diary and Reminiscences.* New York: Harper & Brothers, 1922.

Sumner, William Graham. *What Social Classes Owe to Each Other.* Caldwell, ID: Caxton Printers, 1986.

Wollstonecraft, Mary. *A Vindication of the Rights of Women.* New York: Norton, 1975; orig., 1792.

Index

abolitionism, 41–49, 113–117; Anthony and, 27; antislavery fairs, 41; black male suffrage, 130–131; CS and, 7, 27, 39, 43–49, 107, 119; CS's parents, 42; electoral politics, rejection of, 47–48, 49; Emancipation Proclamation, 250n5; equality, 45; female benevolent associations, 41; Frémont and, 126; Garrisonian abolitionism, 41–49, 113–117, 250n5; Lincoln and, 114, 124, 125–126, 250n5; moral suasion, emphasis on, 47, 49; political abolitionism, 42–43; religion, 45; republican motherhood, 48–49; Republican Party, 130, 250n5; secessionism, 114, 250n5; Smith and, Gerrit, 42–43; Stanton and, Henry Brewster, 7, 43; theory of social change, 47–48; woman suffrage, 126, 127, 130–131, 135, 155; woman's rights movement, 36, 40, 42–43, 44, 99, 113–114, 128, 130–131, 256n28; Women's Loyal National League, 125–126; women's role in, 7, 41–42; World's Anti-Slavery Convention (1840), 7
Adams, John, 9
Address on Women's Rights (CS), 58–61
AERA (American Equal Rights Association), 132–139, 143, 145
Albany, New York, 43, 73, 74, 85
American and Foreign Anti-Slavery Society, 41
American Anti-Slavery Convention (1860), 114
American Anti-Slavery Society: Anthony and, 113–114, 117, 255n11; cancellation of annual meeting, 117; CS and, 43, 114, 117, 118, 237n33; founders, 41; Phillips and, 130; Smith and, Gerrit,

42; Stanton and, Henry Brewster, 7; Stone and, 255n11; women in, 42
"American Creed," 229n29
American Equal Rights Association, 262n53
American Equal Rights Association (AERA), 132–139, 143, 145
American political culture: consensus theory of, 8–11; contrasting traditions in, 11, 22, 24 (*see also* ascriptivism; liberalism; radicalism; republicanism); inconsistencies in, 34, 222–223; Multiple-Traditions Thesis about (*see* Multiple-Traditions Thesis)
The American Political Tradition (Hofstadter), 8
American Revolution, 35, 51, 68, 69
American Temperance Society, 85, 246n79
American Woman Suffrage Association. *See* AWSA
"An Appeal to the Women of the Republic" (CS), 122
anarchists, 182
Ancient Society (Morgan), 217
Andrews, Stephen Pearl, 165–166, 167, 261n36
"Anglo-Saxon" (the term), 267n20
Anglo-Saxonism, 208–212; American exceptionalism, 201–202; Anglo-Saxons' capacity for self-government, 211; antiforeign rhetoric, 208–212; ascriptivism, 26; CS and, 25–26, 37, 196, 202, 208, 218; Darwin on Anglo-Saxons, 198; discrimination, 13; immigration restriction, 201–202; nativism, 197; segregation, 13; slavery, 13; Smith on, Rogers M., 25; social Darwinism, 13

About the Author

Sue Davis is Professor of Political Science at the University of Delaware. She is the author of *American Political Thought: Four Hundred Years of Ideas and Ideologies, Justice Rehnquist and the Constitution,* and *Understanding the Constitutuion,* 17th ed.